7 50

THE
WEEPEEPLE ™

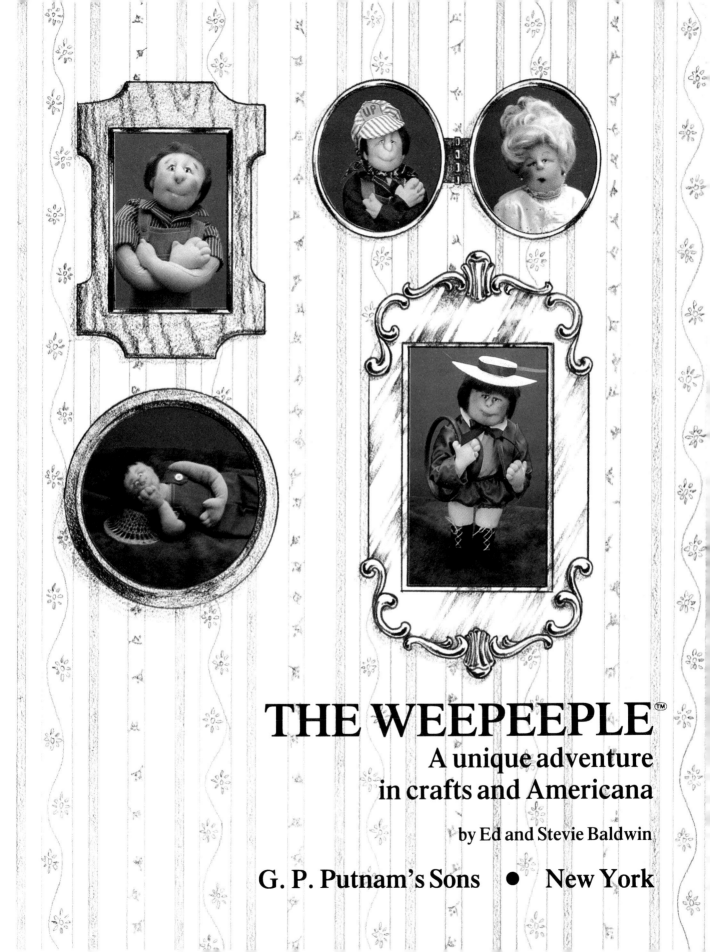

THE WEEPEEPLE™
A unique adventure in crafts and Americana

by Ed and Stevie Baldwin

G. P. Putnam's Sons • New York

Dedicated to Preston, Sander, and Mark

The Weepeeple™
was conceived and created by
The Family Workshop, Inc.
P. O. Box 52000, Tulsa, Oklahoma 74152

Editorial Director: Janet Weberling
Art Director: Dale Crain
Illustration & Production: Roberta Taff, Curtis Hale
                          Jacqueline Nelson,
                          Deborah Howell,
                          Christopher Berg
Project Designs: April Bail & Stevie Baldwin
Photography: Bill Welch

Library of Congress Cataloging in Publication Data

Baldwin, Ed.
    The weepeeple : a unique adventure in crafts and
Americana.

    The weepeeple was conceived, edited, and designed by
The Family Workshop.
    1. Dollmaking.   2. Soft sculpture.   3. United States
—History—1865–   —Miscellanea.   4. Americana.
5. Family recreation.   I. Baldwin, Stevie.   II. Family
Workshop (Firm)   III. Title.
TT175.B34   1983   745.592'21   83-3109
ISBN 0-399-12813-1

Printed in the United States of America

Contents

Facing page—seated (left to right) Maude, Gal, Turnip, Barney, JayJay; standing (left to right) T.J., Birdie holding Baby Gladys, Jane Chicken; hunkered down (on his stomach) Hugger

Above—standing (left to right) Casey, Hugo, Brentwood, Susie; peeking (left to right) Marmalade; seated (left to right) Victoria, Amanda; hunkered down (again) Hugger

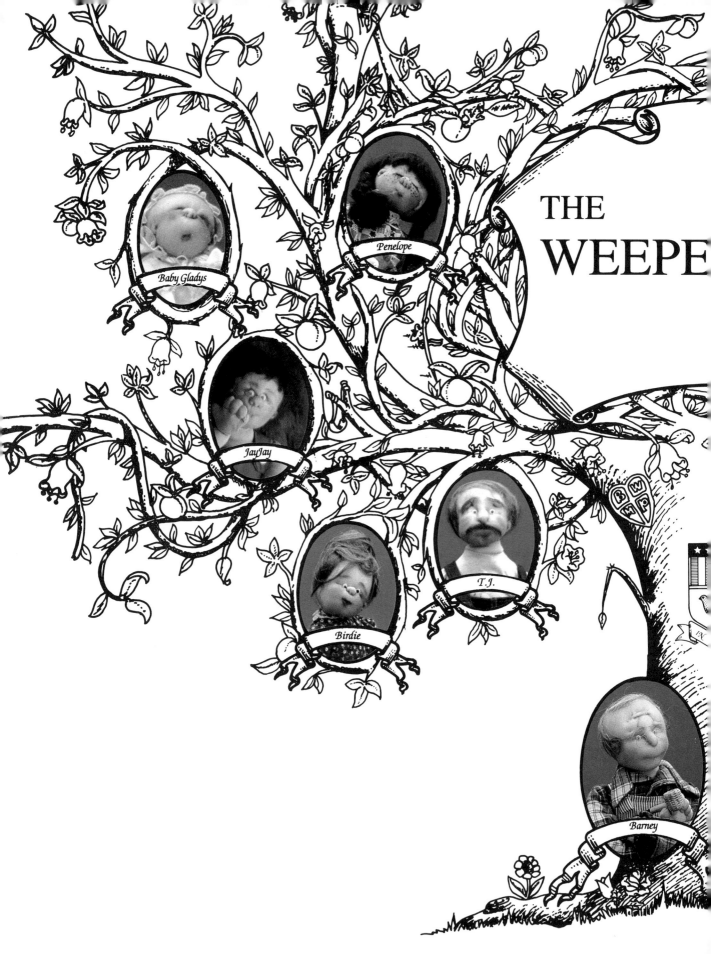

THE

WEEPE

Baby Gladys

Penelope

JayJay

Birdie

T.J.

Barney

PLE
Family Tree

Edward

Brentwood

Amanda

Casey

Victoria

Hugo

Maude

Susie

Engraved by C. Hale, Tulsey Town, Indian Territory, U.S.A

Weepeeple Family History

I first met Maude and Barney Weepeeple in 1934, when Maude (just the day before) won her fortieth consecutive blue ribbon at the Pottawatomie County Fair. Barney and Maude had recently moved into town, since both of them were now in their eighties and had found the hog farm to be a little too much upkeep for them. They now lived in a small white frame house with roses growing around the front porch. In the front yard was a brand new flag pole which Barney had erected himself, and on which he proudly raised and lowered the colors each day. Maude (by then a grandmother several times over) answered the front door when I knocked, and asked me in for a "sit" and a piece of her just-baked apple pie.

Barney, Maude, several of the grandkids, a big old yellow cat named Tom, and I sat around the kitchen table that day and talked about one thing and another; about Barney and Maude's life together, and about "what's important, and what ain't." The story that follows is pieced together from the kitchen-table talk that flowed that warm afternoon in 1934—a sort of Weepeeple family history, being a portion of a semi-true and somewhat accurate account of the life and times of Barney and Maude Weepeeple and their descendants.

1849—The Gold Rush is on, and Barney Weepeeple is born on a small farm just outside Ottumwa, Iowa. It is a premature birth, attended by Bertha Sloane, practicing midwife, who (by her own count) has delivered some six hundred and twenty-four newborns in Wapello County alone. Also in attendance are several members of the church sewing circle who happened to be passing by. Baby Barney weighs only four pounds and eight ounces (as verified by the vegetable scale at Gross & Sons General Store). Bertha pops the scrawny infant into the biscuit oven on the wood stove and instructs Ma Weepeeple to keep him there for two months (when she isn't baking). Bertha also stirs up a lump of growing herbs, ties it in the corner of a handkerchief, and sticks it in wee Barney's mouth.

1850—Barney continues to grow steadily in health and size, and Bertha Sloane is called in for another Weepeeple birth.

1851—Bertha is summoned once more.

1852—Another call for Bertha. This time Ma and Pa Weepeeple arrange for Bertha to come to the farm every year on May 1st and stay until the next baby arrives. Her timing is perfect in 1853 and 1854.

1855—Cousin Bessie's middle son Roy marries a girl from Davenport, Iowa, and Pa and Ma take Barney to the wedding. While in Davenport, they are part of the crowd witnessing the opening of the first bridge across the Mississippi River. Young Barney is intrigued by the huge locomotive that makes the crossing. When the officials board the train, young Barney tries to join them. Pa Weepeeple pulls him back, but realizes that he probably will not always be able to keep Barney away from the railroad and the traveling life.

On the way home, Barney originates the first recorded railroad joke, "Why did the chicken cross the railroad tracks?" Unfortunately, everyone is tired from the long trip, and no one cares why the chicken crossed the tracks, so we will never know the punch line. Pa, Ma and Barney just barely make it back to Ottumwa in time—when they arrive, Bertha is waiting on the front porch to do her stuff.

1856-1859—Bertha makes four more yearly visits.

1860—Bertha makes her last professional visit to the Weepeeple farm and ushers in Barney's youngest brother, Hugo, making it an even dozen.

1861—The Civil War erupts and Barney's father answers President Lincoln's first call for volunteers. He most certainly would have performed many heroic deeds had it not been for Bucephalus, an old and ornery civilian horse commandeered for war service. Just before the Battle of Bull Run, Bucephalus decides that army life is not for him, and heads quickly for home with Private Weepeeple hanging on for dear life. It is unfortunate that his hold was so good, since Bucephalus hailed from a Southern plantation. The Dash of Bucephalus, as it was later called, ends behind enemy lines, and Private Weepeeple spends the remainder of the war years as a Confederate prisoner.

1862-1866—The war rages and Barney helps his mother on the farm. He is a model son, reading aloud the infrequent letters from Pa and happily slopping the hogs. Barney has a special fondness for the porcine members of the family, appreciating their down-to-earth friendliness and

their willingness to listen to a boy's problems as long as the table scraps hold out. Barney also exhibits a fine style of horsemanship and has what the neighbors call "the finest seat in the county."

1866—Pa Weepeeple returns from the war. Barney, now seventeen and no longer responsible for the farm, leaves home to find his fortune with the railroad. He carries with him his family's love, sixteen squares of Ma's cornbread, some beef jerky, and his extra shirt.

1867-1869—Barney earns a brakeman's job with the Union Pacific, and works hard toward an engineer's position. The lead foreman, knowing a born railroader when he sees one, offers Barney the promotion he has dreamed of—Chief Engineer on the run to Promontory, Utah, for the joining of the Transcontinental Railroad, which is scheduled for May of 1869.

But fate deals Barney another card. Just before his promotion becomes official, he meets Maude Perkins in Omaha, where she is visiting her aunt. Maude has just arrived from the Territory of Wyoming where she was working for the passage of the Women's Suffrage Law.

It is love at first sight for both Barney and Maude. But Barney is scheduled out on the very next train, so their courtship is not a traditionally lengthy one. Running to catch his train, Barney proposes marriage. Matching him stride for stride, Maude points out that her responsibility lies with the hog farm in Council Bluffs which she has recently inherited from her father. She also makes it perfectly clear (though necessarily succinct) that she can't possibly marry a man who will always be catching the next train out, goodness knows when!

Poor Barney is left with a big decision as the train gathers speed and Maude disappears from sight. But Maude is quite a girl, so at the next stop Barney sends two telegrams. In one he pledges his undying devotion to Maude. The other is his resignation to the Union Pacific. He catches the next train back to Omaha.

Maude's aunt hastily converts her lace tablecloth into a lovely wedding gown (cleverly placing the small blueberry jam stain on an inner fold where it won't show), and Barney and Maude are married that very same week.

1870—Barney and Maude settle down to a life of marital bliss on the hog farm, sharing both the daily chores and the pride of accomplishment; proving the old adage that "The family that slops together, sticks together." In June, the first son, T.J. (named for T.J. Doyle, the famous Union Pacific engineer) is born. Maude is attended by Lucybelle Sloane, eldest daughter of Bertha, who has recently opened the Pottawattamie County branch of the family midwifery business.

1873-1888—The Weepeeple and the hog farm grow and prosper, producing more children and uncounted hordes of piglets. In addition, Barney's brother Hugo is a frequent visitor. Hugo has always admired his older brother and finds any excuse to convince Ma and Pa Weepeeple that he should "help Barney and Maude out with all them children and hogs."

Hugo and T.J. become inseparable, due mostly to their abiding love for hogs and hog farming. But it is this same love which eventually comes between them. For at a hoedown held in celebration of the 1882 hog harvest, Hugo meets one Suzanne Belinda Biggers who steals his heart away. (It is whispered that his undying devotion is at least in part due to her big blue eyes, which resemble those of his prize sow.) They are married within the year.

T.J. remains on the farm and applies himself diligently

to learning all he can about raising and treating hogs. Some of the townsfolk believe that T.J.'s fondness for hogs is perhaps a bit more than is normal, but admit that he is the best in the county at diagnosing and treating pig problems. Besides his chores on the farm, T.J. rustles up odd jobs in town and makes regular deposits to his account at the Council Bluffs Savings & Loan against the day when he will be able to buy his own hog farm.

Casey, the second son, inherits his father's love for the iron horse and spends his spare time listening to Pa's tales of the early days on the railroad. In the fall of 1888, sixteen-year-old Casey (to no one's surprise) leaves home with his father's blessings and his mother's misgivings, to find his career with the Union Pacific.

1889—T.J. marries Birdie Floyd, his grade school sweetheart. T.J. has always admired Birdie because of her outstanding proficiency in arithmetic, a subject which completely eludes T.J. (He was originally more kind to than enamored of Miss Floyd, because she agreed to do his "cipherin' slate," leaving him free to spend his afternoons with his beloved hogs. Over the years, however, he began to appreciate Birdie for her other fine qualities, and eventually pledged her his trough.)

They build a small house and a large pig sty on the acreage T.J. has purchased with his savings. And T.J. begins his life-long dream of collecting hogs. He christens his new home Hog Heaven. Birdie becomes proficient at raising prize hens and together T.J. and Birdie take their place among the respected farmers of Council Bluffs

1890—Birdie presents T.J. with a daughter, Penelope, known to everyone as Gal. Birdie herself is responsible for the nickname because, as she so aptly puts it, "I so often disremember what proper name I gave that gal." (While Birdie retains her talents at cipherin' and no one can beat her when it comes to handling chickens, in other areas of everyday life she seems to be slightly discombobulated.)

1892—Birdie and T.J. collaborate on another project— this time it's a boy. JayJay is born in the wee hours of a wintry morning while Lucybelle Sloane is attempting to extricate herself from a snowdrift, still a mile or so away from the farm. By the time she arrives, the infant is several hours old and Birdie is celebrating by cooking bacon and eggs for everyone.

1894—Casey marries Victoria Mortimer, a well-bred Kansas City girl. They meet as the result of an extremely unfortunate set of circumstances. It seems that an apprentice engineer, uncoupling two railroad cars in the train yard, fails to give the proper warning signal to his brakeman, thereby putting an immediate and untimely end to his apprenticeship. The funeral services are held at the Mortimer Memorial Chapel, where Victoria is assisting her father by playing the organ, since it is Mrs. Mortimer's day at the beauty salon. Casey is mesmerized by Victoria's beauty, and after asking a few discreet questions determines that she assists her father each Thursday. Thereafter, in hopes of catching a glimpse of her, he attends all Thursday funerals whenever he is in town.

They finally meet when Victoria approaches him to offer her heartfelt condolences on the deaths of so many friends and loved ones. Not one to beat about the bush or let such an opportunity slip away, Casey immediately admits the real reason for his presence. Victoria is swept off her feet by Casey's open and forthright manner, so in contrast with that of Jonathan Morganstern Brightly III, her current beau.

Spurning Mr. Brightly III, Victoria accepts Casey's proposal of marriage. They plan a honeymoon in New York, compliments of Victoria's parents. A sumptuously furnished private railroad car, used for transporting notables, is currently not in use and the railroad kindly offers it to the newlyweds for their trip. While they are in New York, they attend the first public showing of Thomas A. Edison's kinetoscope, the earliest motion picture.

When the happy couple returns to Kansas City, Casey learns that he has been promoted to apprentice engineer, replacing the unfortunate fellow who inadvertantly brought the newlyweds together.

1897—T.J. and Birdie's third child, Baby Gladys, is born. The birth of Baby Gladys is a story all to itself. Baby Gladys simply could not have picked a worse time to come. Lucybelle was out of the county and Birdie was on her own. Not only that, but it was the very last day of harvest, the sky was threatening rain, and Birdie's prizewinning hen was down with the croup. Birdie had little time to deliver the baby and return to check on her hen. Birdie hurriedly wrapped the newborn in a blanket, named the baby Gladys, and headed back to the fields (having doctored the hen on the way). It wasn't until three full days later that Birdie noticed that Baby Gladys was a boy.

1898—The United States battleship *Maine* is sunk in Havana Harbor and the Spanish American War begins. Both T.J. and Casey are bent on enlisting. But Barney, remembering the misadventures of his father, advises his sons to, "Forget the *Maine*" and mind their own business.

1900—Casey and Vistoria visit the Iowa homestead. Their marriage has been blessed in every way except one—they have had no children (even though, within the accepted proprieties of the times, they have exercised every effort toward that end). Victoria loves children and pleads with Birdie to allow Gal to visit Kansas City. Birdie at first refuses, but finally is convinced that Gal will be missing the social and cultural opportunity of a lifetime if she is not allowed to go.

While in the big city, Gal is treated to a professional hairdo, a new custom-made dress, and a performance of Oscar Wilde's somewhat risque play, *Lady Windermere's Fan*, starring Gal's idol, Lily Langtry. When she returns to Iowa and is asked what she learned of a cultural nature, Gal quotes a most memorable line from the play,

"One can always recognize women who trust their husbands. They look so thoroughly unhappy." The consensus in the family is that Gal will get over her citified ideas soon enough. As Maude so aptly puts it, "After all, that Gal's already gone back to wearin' pigtails."

1902—A blessed event finally occurs in the Casey Weepeeple household. It's a boy, and for once the Mortimers and the Weepeeple join in happy celebration. Brentwood has the distinction of being the first Weepeeple (or Mortimer, for that matter) whose birth is attended by a medical doctor. Victoria and her newborn son hold court every afternoon at teatime, and Mrs. Mortimer makes sure that Victoria has a new lacy bed jacket for "the visitations."

Back on the farm, the year heralds another birth in the Weepeeple family—Turnip the pig, the most lovable, precocious piglet ever to grace the Weepeeple sty. As fate would have it, the blessed event coincides with a visit from eighty-three-year-old Bertha Sloane who is making a brief stop on her way to Denver. It is particularly fitting that Bertha is there, since Turnip becomes a beloved (if somewhat unusual) part of the family

1906—In April, Casey's railroading job takes him to San Francisco, where he has a few days layover. He decides to see some of the sights, but manages to cover only a part of the waterfront when he notices the landscape beginning to quiver. The quiver quickly becomes all-out shaking, and Casey, miraculously escaping injury, retreats to the railroad yard in an attempt to find his fellow workers.

The next few days are a nightmare, but Casey distinguishes himself during the great fire and subsequent rescue efforts. Tired to the bone, and realizing that "Home is where the hogs is," Casey catches the next train back to Iowa.

1910—Incessantly badgered by his sons JayJay and Gladys, T.J. forms the first Boy Scout troop in Iowa, following the founding of the national organization on February 8th. It becomes the only Boy Scout troop ever to award a merit badge for excellence in hog calling.

1917—In April, the war with Germany is declared. JayJay enlists immediately, after a recruiter tells him that in the army there are no hogs to slop, you can eat all you want, and there are lots of good fishin' holes in France. Upon hearing of his older brother's enlistment, Baby Gladys joins up too (after a lengthy and somewhat physical discussion with the recruiter concerning his proper name). Gladys feels that with his strength, he should be there to protect his brother. Both boys are shipped off to France, and JayJay spends the entire war fishing the streams and ponds of that country while Baby Gladys digs trenches around him and keeps watch with a rifle.

1920—A new era is ushered in for the Weepeeple family, as Brentwood graduates from high school and enrolls in the Rolla School of Mines at Rolla, Missouri.

1921—Discovering that he has a strong dislike for the underground, Brentwood transfers to the University of Missouri at Columbia. There, he majors in math and meets a charming and beautiful freshman who attends Stephens College. Amanda Collingwood is the epitome of the "new woman," who wears cloche hats, short skirts, silk stockings, and has bobbed hair. Brentwood is charmed. Victoria is, of course, appalled. Casey is in Texas. Together, Brentwood and Amanda learn the Charleston, the black bottom, and the shimmy, attend Valentino movies, and occasionally swallow a goldfish or two just to be able to say they did.

1924—The fun comes to an end when Brentwood graduates from Mizzou and takes a job at Boatman's Bank in St. Louis. Amanda remains in Columbia to complete her senior year, much to the chagrin of her mother who warns Amanda that there are "loose and conniving women" in St. Louis.

1925—Loose women notwithstanding, Brentwood and Amanda tie the knot as soon as her graduation ceremonies are over. They settle in St. Louis, but Brentwood discovers that he has a strong dislike for wood paneling and tellers' cages. Casting about for a more exciting career that will utilize his mathematics (cipherin') degree, Brentwood's imagination is captured by a newspaper article about Dr. Robert H. Goddard, who has demonstrated the practicality of rockets. Convincing Amanda that this is where his future lies, Brentwood packs up the household and they move "down east."

Upon their arrival in Auburn, Massachussetts, Brentwood contacts Dr. Goddard and lands a job assisting the great scientist. However, because the job does not pay much, Amanda decides to supplement the family income by accepting a typist position with the Smithgood, Hearthstone, Yarrow, Smithgood, Turnbull, Everheart, and Riddinghouse law firm. (For obvious reasons, the firm never uses its acronym.)

1929—Amanda is suddenly out of a job due to the collapse of the stock market and the subsequent demise of Smithgood, Hearthstone, Yarrow, Smithgood, Turnbull, Everheart, Riddinghouse, and several law clerks. Fortunately, by this time Brentwood's incisive mind and hard work have resulted in a series of promotions within Dr. Goddard's organization and he is able to resume his place as sole breadwinner of the household.

1930—Amanda takes to heart her new role as housewife, and in November gives birth to their first son, Edward. In the same year, Gal is rewarded for thirty years of hard work when she wins the motion picture academy's award for best performance by an actress.

1934—The Weepeeple family reunion is held at Maude and Barney's farm in Council Bluffs. As one celebrant remarks, "We could apply for statehood, what with all the folks who've showed up!"

Barnard Zachary (Barney) Weepeeple

Born: May 4, 1849

Perhaps the most telling personal characteristic that Barney exhibits is his affinity for a good hog. Obviously, his parents could not have foreseen this lifelong attraction when they gave Barney his middle name in honor of America's then new Whig president, Zachary Taylor. President Taylor was, of course, quite well known as a courageous and successful military leader. Not so well known was his abiding passion for hogs, both on the hoof and a la carte.

Over the years, Barney developed quite a talent for hog calling. In fact, he was State Hog Calling Champion twice running, and was naturally expected to attend the National Hog Callers Contest. But there was a slight problem.

One would assume that a national contest for a skill as truly midwestern as hog calling would be held in Iowa, or at least in a neighboring state. And for many years it was—until a wealthy southern plantation owner craftily devised a not-so-aboveboard scheme (Barney called it "an out-and-out boondoggle") in which large amounts of money quietly changed hands.

This resulted in a change of venue for the nationals—from their former home in Iowa to Halagaloo, Alabama, as unlikely a place as could be imagined! The plantation owner, who shall remain nameless in deference to his innocent descendants, bribed the local newspaper editor to run a front-page banner headline on the occasion of the first Alabama contest proclaiming, "Halagaloo and Hog Calling Too!"

True to his courageous nature, Barney assembled the midwestern hog farmers to devise a strategy for bringing the contest back where it ought to have stayed. Rallying round the motto, "There ain't no call for hogs in Alabama," this determined band of farmers brought the contest back home. Their hastily fashioned flag, portraying the coiled tail of a prize hog and the admonition "Don't Slop on Me!" is still on display at the Weepeeple homestead.

That little anecdote highlights another of Barney's most evident traits—his downright stubbornness. For years he refused to admit that he could hardly see past his own nose, and has to this day resisted suggestions that he visit an eye doctor. Maude did manage to convince him to pick out some "readin' spectacles" at the general store, but she says he wears them on top of his head as often as over his eyes.

Asked if he would sum up his philosophy of life for us, Barney at first said, "No." But Gal took him aside and whispered something (she told me later that she just explained what "philosophy" meant), and Barney came back smiling. In his own words, Barney's philosophy of life is this; "I work hard and play hard too. Why live to be a hundred if you can do it in fifty?"

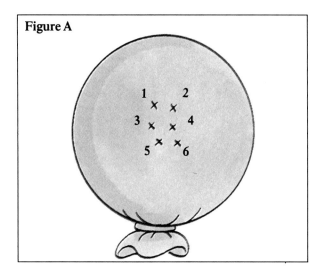

Figure A

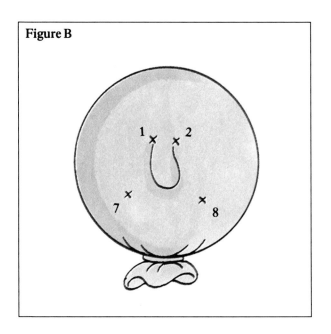

Figure B

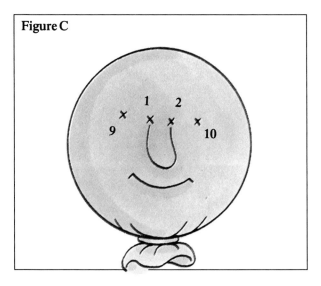

Figure C

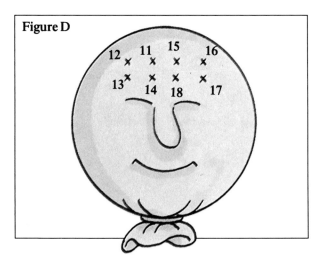

Figure D

Materials and Tools

Metric equivalents in centimeters are indicated in parentheses.

½ yard (0.46 m) of navy blue and white striped cotton fabric, at least 36 inches (90) wide

½ yard (0.46 m) of plaid cotton flannel

6-inch (15) length of 1-inch (2.5) wide seam binding in a color to coordinate with the shirt

½ yard (0.46 m) of flesh-colored cotton knit fabric

¼ yard (0.23 m) of black vinyl fabric

Sewing thread to match the shirt and overall fabrics

Heavy-duty and regular flesh-colored thread

Six small white buttons

Two ½-inch (1.3) diameter metal buttons (or 1-inch [2.5] wide buckle fixtures) for the overall straps, and two metal buttons for the overall sides

½ pound (227 g) of polyester fiberfill

One leg cut from a pair of regular weave flesh-tone pantyhose (or one nylon stocking)

Small gray wiglet (or substitute gray yarn)

Two tiny (no larger than ¼-inch [0.6] diameter) eye beads (sold in hobby stores for use as doll eyes)

2-foot length (61) of flexible single strand copper wire

Light brown fine felt-tip marker, pale pink powdered cheek blusher, and white glue

Long sharp needle, scissors, straight pins, and a sewing machine (optional)

Turn to page 154 and make a body for Barney, following the instructions for Making the Arms, Making Legs with Boots, and Making the Torso. (Barney was once heard to say that he wouldn't be caught dead, "with my bare feet showing, or wearing them fancy boots with flaps," so be sure to skip over the sections on Adding the Boot Flaps and Making Legs with Feet.) Since Barney is obviously an adult, use the adult-size scale drawings (Figure A, page 155) to make the full-size patterns.

Making the Head

1. Cut a 6-inch (15.2) length from the upper portion of the pantyhose leg or stocking, and slit it lengthwise so that you have a flat rectangle.

2. Wrap the rectangle around a large handful of fiberfill. Gather the edges of the hose together and twist, to create a head form. The twisted ends will be at the back of the head, just above the neck. (Detailed instructions for stuffing and forming a head are given in the Soft Sculpturing Tips section of this book.) Barney's head should be approximately 12 inches (30.5) in circumference, measuring around the nose and ear line. It should be at least 4½ inches (11.4) in diameter from top to bottom. Add or remove fiberfill until the head is the correct size, then wrap the twisted hose tightly with heavy-duty thread.

3. Use a long sharp needle and a 36-inch length (91) of heavy-duty flesh-colored thread to sculpture the facial features. To form Barney's nose, follow the entry and exit points illustrated in Figure A. (You may be interested to know that Barney's nose attained its unique curve in a somewhat unpleasant encounter with a problem pig many years ago. Barney says that the problem was quickly cured, making mighty fine bacon.)

   a. Enter where the hose is tied at the neck, pass through the center of the head, and exit at point 1. Pinch up a vertical ridge, approximately ½ inch (1.3) high, between points 1 and 2. (This will be the bridge of the nose.)

   b. Reenter at 1 and exit at 2. Reenter at 2 and exit at 1, pulling the thread tightly. Keep the thread pulled tightly as you take an additional stitch underneath the surface between points 1 and 2 in order to secure the ridge. Exit at 1.

   c. Pinch up the nose ridge between points 3 and 4. (These points should be approximately ½ inch [1.3] directly below points 1 and 2.) Pull the thread across the surface, enter at 3 and exit at 4. Pull the thread across the surface, enter at 2 and exit at 1.

   d. Hold the thread with one hand near point 1 to maintain the tension, reenter at 1 and exit at 5. (Points 5 and 6 should be about ½ inch [1.3] below and slightly to the right of points 3 and 4, but not any lower than the center line of the head.) Pull the thread across the surface, enter at 6 and exit at 2. Pull the thread until the end of the nose appears (between points 5 and 6).

   e. Holding the thread taut, reenter at 2 and exit at 3. Hold the thread tension near point 3, pull the thread across the surface, enter at 6 and exit at 4. Pull the thread across the surface, enter at 5 and exit at 1.

   f. Tighten and hold the thread as you take one or two stitches back and forth under the surface between points 1 and 2 to secure the nose form. Exit at 2.

4. Continue working with the same thread to create Barney's smile, following the entry and exit points illustrated in Figure B. (Asked what he is always smiling about, Barney recently replied, "I'm tired of hearin' about that furrin lady named Mona. We got some durn good grins in Iowa, too!") Points 7 and 8 will be the corners of the mouth. They should be 1½ inches (3.8) apart, on a line approximately 1 inch (2.5) below the end of the nose.

   a. Reenter at 2 and exit at 7. Pull the thread across the surface, enter at 8 and exit at 1.

   b. Pull the thread until a smile appears. With one hand, hold tension on the thread near point 10. With the other hand use the tip of the needle to lift additional fiberfill into the upper lip and into the chin area, forming the chin shape.

   c. Reenter at 1 and take one or two stitches under the surface between points 1 and 2 to secure the stitches. Exit at 1.

5. To form the eyes, follow the entry and exit points illustrated in Figure C. Point 9 will be the outside corner of the closed right eye. It should be approximately 1 inch (2.5) directly to the left of point 1. Point 10, the corner of the left eye, should be 1 inch (2.5) directly to the right of point 2.

   a. Pull the thread across the surface, enter at 9 and exit at 2. Pull the thread across the surface, enter at 10 and exit at 1.

   b. Pull the thread gently until eye lines appear. Hold the thread taut, and stitch one or two times under the surface between points 1 and 2 to secure the eyes. Exit at 1.

6. To form the eyebrow ridges, follow the entry and exit points illustrated in Figure D. The following list of measurements will help you mark the points correctly.

Between points 1 and 11 = ⅞ inch (2.2).
Between points 11 and 12 = ¾ inch (1.9).
Between points 12 and 13 = ⅜ inch (1).
Between points 13 and 14 = ¾ inch (1.9).
Points 15 through 18 mirror points 11 through 14.

   a. To form the right eyebrow ridge, reenter at 1 and exit at 11. Pull the thread across the surface, enter at 12 and exit at 13.

   b. Pull the thread across the surface, enter at 14 and exit at 11. Pull the thread gently until a ridge appears. Hold the thread taut and stitch back and forth one or two times under the surface between points 11 and 14 to secure the ridge. Exit at 11.

   c. To form the left eyebrow ridge, reenter at 11 and exit at 15. Pull the thread across the surface, enter at 16 and exit at 17.

   d. Pull the thread across the surface, enter at 18 and exit at 15. Pull the thread gently until an eyebrow ridge appears. Hold the thread taut and stitch back and forth one or two times under the surface between points 15 and 18 to secure the ridge. Exit at 15.

7. To form the forehead wrinkle, follow the entry and exit points illustrated in Figure E. (Barney at first objected to our calling it a wrinkle, but when the only alternative we could think of was a character line, he relented and said he'd rather people thought he was old and wrinkled than a character.) The following list of measurements will help you mark the points correctly on Barney's head.

Between points 11 and 19 = ¾ inch (1.9).
Between points 15 and 20 = ¾ inch (1.9).
Between points 20 and 21 = ¼ inch (0.6).
Between points 21 and 22 = ½ inch (1.3).
Between points 19 and 23 = ¼ inch (0.6).
Between points 23 and 24 = ¼ inch (0.6).
Between points 22 and 25 = ¼ inch (0.6).

   a. Use the tip of the needle to lift extra fiberfill up into a forehead ridge just above the eyebrow ridges. It should be about 1½ inches (3.8) long and ¼ inch (0.6) deep. Reenter at 15 and exit at point 19.
   b. Pull the thread across the surface, enter at 20 and exit at 21. Pull the thread across the surface, enter at 22 and exit at 23.
   c. Pull the thread across the surface, enter at 24 and exit at 25. Pull the thread gently until the forehead wrinkle appears. Hold the thread taut as you pull it across the surface, enter at 22 and exit at 23.
   d. Hold the thread taut, reenter at 23 and guide the needle through the interior of the head to the point where the hose is tied. Exit, pull the thread tightly, lock the stitch, and cut the thread.

8. Brush powdered cheek blusher on the cheeks. (This will reproduce his rosy color, a natural result of clean country living.) Glue small eye beads next to the nose, over the eye lines. To create eyebrows, either draw them on the eyebrow ridges using a light brown felt-tip marker, or cut two short pieces from the wiglet and glue them on.

9. Follow the entry and exit points illustrated in Figure F to sculpture the ears.

   a. Enter at the neck and exit at 26. (Point 26, which will be the top of the ear, should be even with the lower end of the nose.) Pinch up a small curved ridge, as shown, just below point 26.
   b. Stitch back and forth under the ridge, moving toward point 27 with each stitch. Pull the thread gently until an ear forms. Exit at 27.
   c. Lock the stitch behind the ear, reenter at 27, and exit at the neck.
   d. Lock the stitch and cut the thread.
   e. Repeat steps a through d on the opposite side of the head.

10. Twist the copper wire into the shape of glasses, as shown in Figure G.

11. Cut portions of the gray wiglet and glue them to the sides and back of Barney's head so that he has a large bald spot on top. ("And proud of it," says Barney. "Nobody but sissies who never need a hat git through this life with all their hair.") Glue a small amount of hair across the top of Barney's forehead, where the normal hairline would be if he hadn't had to wear a hat so much (Figure H).

Attaching the Head to the Body

1. Turn a narrow seam allowance to the inside on the neck opening of the body. Gather the neckline ¼ inch (0.6) from the folded edge using heavy-duty, flesh-colored thread. Pull the gathering threads until the opening measures approximately 1 inch (2.5) across.

2. Center the head over the opening, inserting the tied neck portion of the head under the back edge of the neck opening. Whipstitch completely around the neck several times to secure the head to the body. (Barney has asked that you do this carefully, as he hates to think of Barney dolls with loose heads that bob and loll about, "lookin' like that disgraceful sot, old Zeke Weepeeple, who we don't talk about much.")

Making the Overalls

1. Scale drawings of the sewing patterns for the overall, bib, and pocket are given in Figure I. Enlarge the drawings to full-size paper patterns.

2. Fold the blue and white striped fabric as shown in Figure J. Cut two overall pieces, placing the pattern along a fold of the material where indicated. (Do not cut along the fold line.) Place the pocket pattern on the doubled material as shown and cut two pockets.

3. Unfold the fabric. Place the bib pattern on the fabric, paying attention to the direction of the stripes, and cut one fabric bib. In addition, cut two straps, each 10 × 3 inches (25.4 × 7.6) with the stripes running lengthwise, and cut one bib pocket, 3 × 2½ inches (7.6 × 6.4). (Barney says he bought a bargain pair of overalls one time that had the stripes running crossways instead of up and down. Claims he was fair game for the jokesters of three counties for about a year. He finally threw the overalls away the day that he was mistaken for an escaped convict and shot at by the county sheriff, who should have known better. Legend has it that Barney shed those overalls on the spot—just outside the Council Bluffs General Store & Grain Emporium—and gave several local ladies the shock of their lives when he walked inside to purchase a proper pair. Barney says he was perfectly decent-looking, maybe even a handsome figure of a man, in his one-piece long johns.)

4. On each of the two large pockets, fold a ¼-inch (0.6) seam allowance to the wrong side on all edges, clipping the curved edges so they lie flat. Press. Pin one pocket to each of the overall pieces, following the pocket placement lines shown on the scale drawing for the overall pattern. Topstitch the pockets in place.

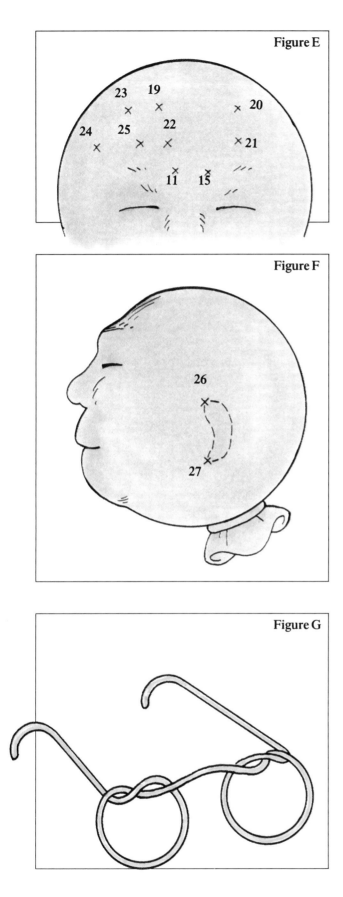

Figure E

23 19
×   ×   × 20
24 25   22
×   ×   ×   × 21
        × 11   15

Figure F

26
×
27
×

Figure G

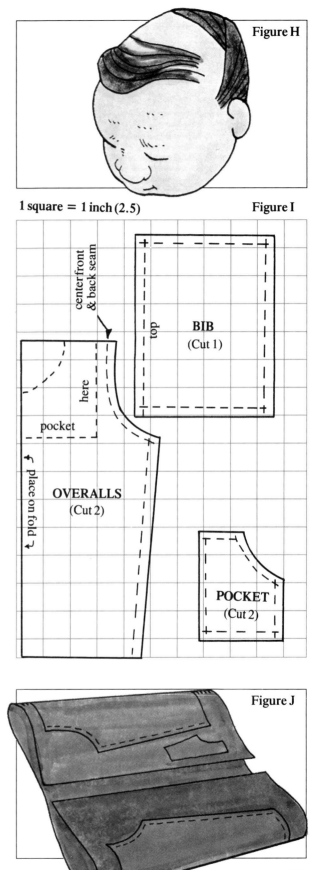

Figure H

1 square = 1 inch (2.5)   Figure I

center front
& back seam

top   BIB
(Cut 1)

here

pocket

place on fold   OVERALLS
(Cut 2)

POCKET
(Cut 2)

Figure J

21

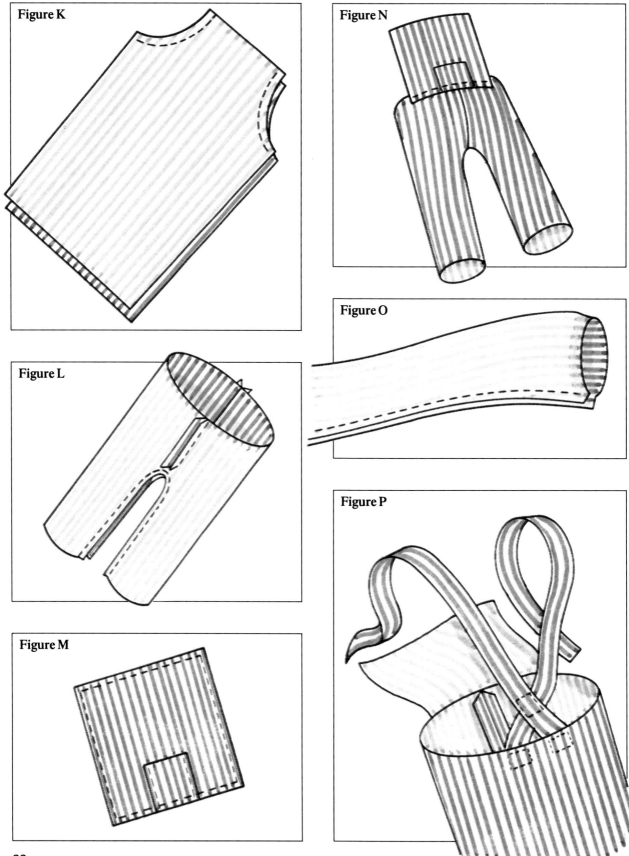

Figure K

Figure N

Figure L

Figure O

Figure M

Figure P

5. Pin the two overall pieces right sides together, and stitch the center front and back seams as shown in Figure K. (All seams are ⅜ inch [1] unless otherwise specified.) Refold the overalls, matching the center front and back seams, and stitch the inner leg seam (Figure L).

6. Fold a ⅜-inch (1) hem allowance to the wrong side around the entire waist edge and topstitch.

7. Fold a ⅜-inch (0.6) hem allowance to the wrong side on all four edges of the bib pocket and press. Fold a ⅜-inch (1) hem allowance to the wrong side on all four edges of the bib and press. Place the bib right side up on a flat surface. Pin the bib pocket (right side up) over the bib with lower edges even, centering the pocket between the sides of the bib (Figure M). Topstitch around all four edges of the bib and down the two side edges of the bib pocket as shown.

8. Center the bib over the front of the overall (Figure N) so that the lower bib edge overlaps the overall by ¾ inch (1.9). Topstitch.

9. Fold one strap in half lengthwise, right sides together. Stitch ⅜ inch (1) from the long edge, and from one short edge (Figure O). Turn the sewn strap right side out and press. Repeat for the remaining strap.

10. Pin the unstitched end of one strap at an angle underneath the waistline, just to one side of the center back seam (Figure P). Pin the unstitched end of the remaining strap in place, overlapping the straps as shown in Figure P, and topstitch through all thicknesses. The finishing work on the overalls will be done after the shirt has been made and the clothing can be fitted to Barney's fine figure of a man.

Making the Shirt

1. Scale drawings for the shirt back, shirt front, sleeve, collar, and cuff patterns are given in Figure Q. Enlarge the drawings to full-size paper patterns.

1 square = 1 inch (2.5)   **Figure Q**

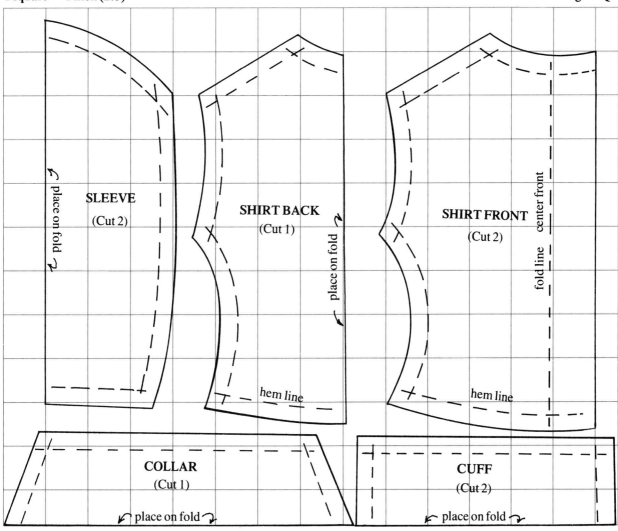

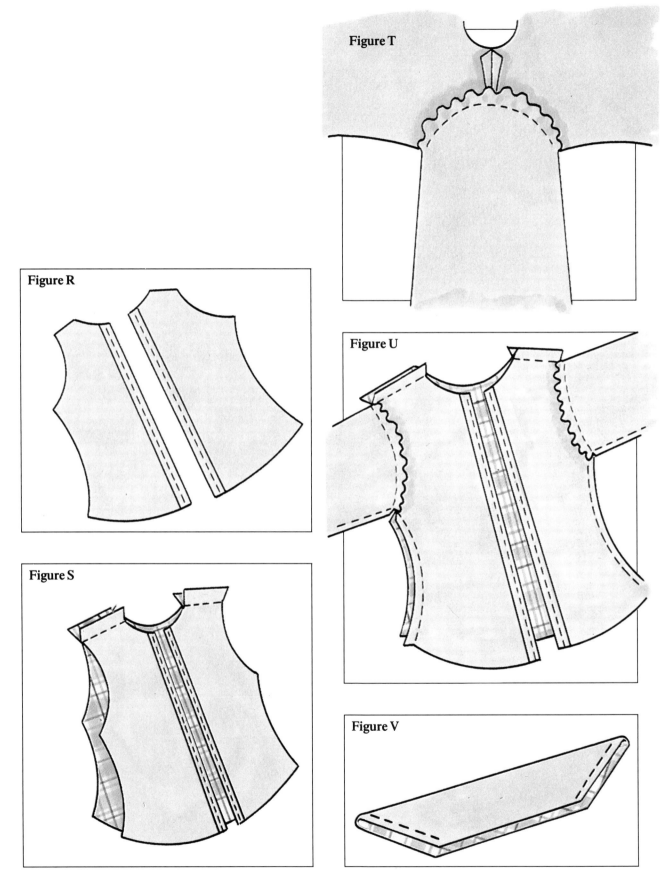

Figure R

Figure S

Figure T

Figure U

Figure V

2. Fold the plaid flannel fabric and pin the patterns in place, paying attention to the "place on fold" notations. Cut one shirt back, two shirt fronts, two sleeves, one collar, and two cuffs.

3. Fold the front hem allowance to the wrong side of the fabric on each shirt front and topstitch the hem allowances in place (Figure R).

4. Place the shirt back and shirt fronts right sides together. Stitch the shoulder seams (Figure S).

5. Sew the curved edges of the sleeves to the armhole edges of the shirt with right sides together (Figure T), easing the sleeves to fit.

6. Fold the shirt right sides together and stitch the side and underarm seam on each side (Figure U).

7. Fold the collar in half right sides together and stitch the seams along the two short edges (Figure V), leaving the remaining long edge open and unstitched. Clip the corners, turn the collar right side out, and press. Press the seam allowances to the inside on the remaining raw edges.

8. Pin the collar around the shirt neckline on the right side of the fabric, fitting it between the open front edge (Figure W). Topstitch the collar in place.

9. Fold one cuff right sides together and stitch the seams along the two short edges, leaving the remaining edge open and unstitched (Figure X). Trim the corners and turn the stitched cuff right side out. Press the seam allowances to the inside on the unstitched raw edges.

10. Gather the lower end of one sleeve along the gathering line. Pull up the gathers until the edge of the sleeve fits inside the open edge of the cuff (Figure Y). Pin the cuff in place and topstitch through all three layers, close to the edge of the cuff. Repeat steps 9 and 10 for the remaining cuff.

11. You can work buttonholes on each cuff and down the shirt front, or simply sew buttons on one side and tack the cuffs and shirt front together after you have put the shirt on Barney. (That will make it hard for Barney to get out of his clothes to take a bath, but he says he never was very fond of "all-over washing" more than about once a year anyway.)

Finishing Details

Dress Barney in his shirt and overalls. Pull the overall straps to the front and tack the ends of the straps over the upper edge of the bib. Sew a metal button to each strap (or add the buckle).

Unless you have made a very fat Barney, the waist edge of the overalls will be larger than the doll's waist. Fold the excess fabric into a pleat at each side of the waist, making the pleats as even as possible. Tack the pleats in place, and sew a metal button over each.

Hem the lower edge of each overall leg to fit Barney's leg. (He says he likes them kind of short so his nice new boots will show, and so he won't have to roll them up every time he slops the pigs.)

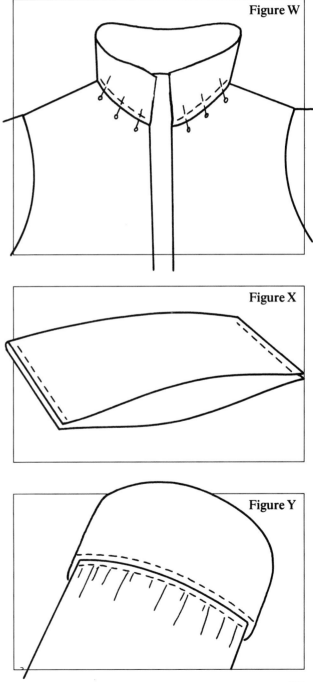

Figure W

Figure X

Figure Y

Mathilda (Maude) Perkins Weepeeple

Born: August 24, 1853

Maude is best known for her industriousness and talent in the kitchen, and for her avid interest in the Pottawatomie County Fair. Actually, it was her culinary talent that was responsible for the very existence of the county fair.

Shortly after Barney and Maude were married, a neighbor stopped in to welcome the Weepeeple to Council Bluffs. Maude brought out hot biscuits and her best persimmon jam, and offered tea. Corrine said the jam was the best she had ever tasted, and that Maude should really enter it in the county fair.

Maude liked the idea, but since the nearest fair was forty-six miles away and since "a body hasn't got time to travel by horse for two days to win a ribbon," she decided to "bring the mountain to Maude." Under her forceful guidance, the local women organized the Pottawatomie County Fair, which continues to this day.

Although no one disputes Maude's talents in the kitchen, there is a general consensus around the county that the same superlatives do not apply to her musical ability. Maude's mother (rest her soul) willed her pump organ to Maude, and Maude generously had it installed in the Mount Olive church where she plays it each and every Sunday, much to the anguish of the congregation. But since Maude retains ownership of the organ, grounds for protest are mighty slim.

Maude's organ playing does mercifully keep her out of the choir. Perhaps the only thing that Maude does less well than play the pump organ is sing. Although she is totally unaware of the fact, she is absolutely tone deaf, and only knows that the *Star Spangled Banner* is playing because everyone stands up.

Musical ability aside, Maude is capable of performing well in almost any situation. She was raised on a hog farm and learned to call hogs at her grandfather's knee. Unfortunately, her grandfather was not fond of wearing his dentures on a regular basis, so his call sounded more like "phooey" than "soo-ey." Maude has continued the tradition of yelling "phooey," and her hogs all respond.

Maude is really at her best in the midst of crisis. Several years ago, the hog farm was hit by a tornado. Maude was not upset, since the only thing it took was one small pig and the outhouse. "Nobody was in it at the time, and it was time to move it anyway" was her only comment on the matter.

After four days of tramping about the countryside, Maude found the still slightly dazed pig in the neighbor's lower forty acres. She carried him home. After administering several home remedies, Maude pronounced the pig healthy, but remarked later that "to this day that pig has a funny hitch to his git-along."

Maude has the distinction of being the first woman to almost become sheriff of Council Bluffs. Although she turned down the offer, she certainly had the qualifications for the job. As it happened, a city slicker accosted Maude outside the dry goods store one day. Maude immediately beat him senseless with her umbrella and sat on him until help arrived. The fellow considered himself lucky that Maude was then pushing sixty-five, or he probably would not have lived through the ordeal.

Figure A

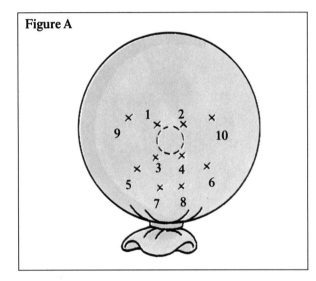

Figure B

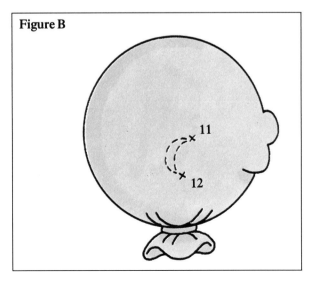

Figure C

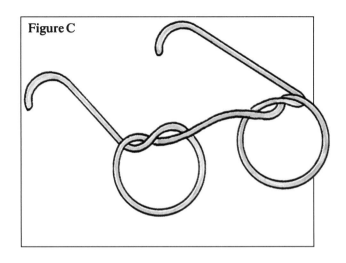

Materials and Tools

Metric equivalents in centimeters are indicated in parentheses.

1½ yards (1.4 m) of 36-inch (90) wide calico or small print fabric

1 yard (0.9 m) of white cotton fabric

1 yard (0.9 m) of white lace trim

½ yard (0.46 m) of flesh-colored cotton knit fabric

¼ yard (0.23 m) of black vinyl fabric

Regular and heavy-duty flesh-colored sewing thread

One leg cut from a pair of regular weave flesh-tone pantyhose (or one nylon stocking)

White sewing thread and sewing thread to match the calico fabric

Small gray wiglet (or substitute gray yarn)

Two tiny (no larger than ¼-inch [0.6] diameter) eye beads (sold in hobby stores for use as doll eyes)

2-foot (61) length of small diameter, flexible, single strand copper wire

½ pound (227 g) of polyester fiberfill

Light brown fine felt-tip marker, pale pink powdered cheek blusher, gray hairpins, and white glue

1 yard (0.9 m) of ¼-inch (0.6) wide elastic

One hook and eye closure

One small white pearl button

Long sharp needle, scissors, straight pins, and a sewing machine (optional)

Turn to page 154 and make a body for Maude, following instructions for Making the Arms, Making Legs with Boots, Adding Boot Flaps, and Making the Torso. Be absolutely certain to sew the waist carefully, as Maude is very particular about her waistline. She says she "ain't never worn one of them fool corsets, and don't intend to start now! The least that any worthwhile body should do is support isself." She is rather fond of her new boots with buttoned flaps, so don't skip that section. Use the scale drawings for adult-sized arm, leg, boot, boot flap, and torso (Figure A, page 155) to make the full-size patterns.

Making the Head

1. Tie the pantyhose leg or stocking into a tight knot near the open end, and cut the hose 6 inches (15) below the knot. Turn, so the knot is on the inside.

2. Stuff a generous amount of fiberfill inside the hose, manipulating the shape until a head is formed. (Detailed instructions for stuffing and forming a head are given in the Soft Sculpturing Tips section of this book). Maude's head should be at least 12 inches (31) in circumference, measuring around the nose and ear line. It should be approximately 4½ inches (11) in diameter from top to bottom. Tie the hose in a tight knot at the open end.

3. Use a long sharp needle and a 36-inch (90) length of heavy duty flesh-colored thread to sculpture the facial features. To form Maude's nose, follow the entry and exit points illustrated in Figure A. (As you may or may not be aware, Maude comes from a long line of perfect-nosed Perkins, and at the age of 11 she had the honor of being voted the prettiest nose in the Mount Olive Sunday School class. So if you stitch carefully, you will faithfully recreate Maude's prize-winning feature.)

   a. Enter where the hose is knotted at the neck, pass through the center of the head, and exit at point 1. Sew a clockwise circle of deep basting stitches approximately 1 inch (2.5) in diameter, and exit at point 2.

   b. Use the tip of your needle to carefully lift fiberfill within the circle just enough to make a small bulge. Gently pull the thread until a round nose appears inside the circle.

   c. Hold the thread with one hand and take another stitch, entering at 2 and exiting at 1.

   d. To form the nostrils, reenter at 1 and exit at 3. Reenter ¼ inch (0.6) above 3 and exit at 2.

   e. Pull the thread gently and maintain the tension while you reenter at 2 and exit at 4. Reenter ¼ inch (0.6) above 4 and exit at 1.

   f. Pull the thread gently and maintain the tension while you take another small stitch at point 1.

4. Continue working with the same thread to form the mouth. Maude's mouth is not a source of vanity for her, but she allows that it is "certainly a necessary item to round out a person's face."

   a. Enter at 1 and exit at 5. Pull the thread across the surface, enter at 6 and exit at 1. Pull the thread until a smile appears.

   b. Reenter at 1 and exit at 2. Reenter at 2 and exit at 7. Pull the thread across the surface, enter at 8 and exit at 2. Pull the thread gently to form Maude's lower lip.

5. To form the eyes, follow the entry and exit points illustrated in Figure A.

   a. Reenter at 2 and exit at 9. Pull the thread across the surface, enter at 1 and exit at 10.

   b. Pull the thread across the surface, enter at 2 and exit at 1. Gently pull the thread until the eye lines appear. Lock the stitch.

   c. Reenter at 1, guide the needle through the interior of the head to the knot at the top. Exit near the knot, pull the thread taut, lock the stitch, and cut the thread.

6. Brush powdered cheek blusher on Maude's cheeks, across the bottom of her mouth, and on the tip of her nose. Glue small eye beads next to the nose, over the eye lines. To create eyebrows, draw them using a light brown felt-tip marker, or cut short pieces from the wiglet and glue them in place. They begin above the inner corner of the eye, and continue in a quarter circle to the outer corner.

7. Unlike Barney, Maude has no wrinkles on her forehead, a fact she attributes pridefully to her regimen of religiously applying a special herbal facial every night. Her second-cousin-by-marriage Clara was the creator of this prized potion, and for many years kept her recipe a closely guarded secret. It was only after a long period of negotiation that Maude was successful in convincing Clara to trade the formula for Maude's Honeydew Cupcake recipe. Due to the effects produced by the herbal facial, Maude's youthful skin is devoid of wrinkles, and you can proceed directly to the ears. Follow the entry and exit points illustrated in Figure B to sculpture the ears.

   a. Enter at the neck knot and exit at 11. (Point 11, which will be the top of the ear, should be even with the lower portion of the nose.) Pinch up a small curved ridge at an angle, as shown, just below point 11.

   b. Stitch back and forth under the ridge, moving toward point 12 with each stitch, and pulling the thread gently until an ear forms. Exit at point 12.

   c. Lock the stitch behind the ear, reenter at that point, and exit at the neck knot.

   d. Lock the stitch and cut the thread.

   e. Repeat steps a through d on the opposite side of the head.

8. Twist the copper wire into the shape of eyeglasses, as shown in Figure C. Trim the wiglet to fit Maude's head and glue it in place. Gently comb the hair up into a soft bun, on top of Maude's head, and secure with hairpins. Don't worry if you can't get every hair to stay in place; it is Maude's opinion that a perfect hairdo is the sign of a life misspent.

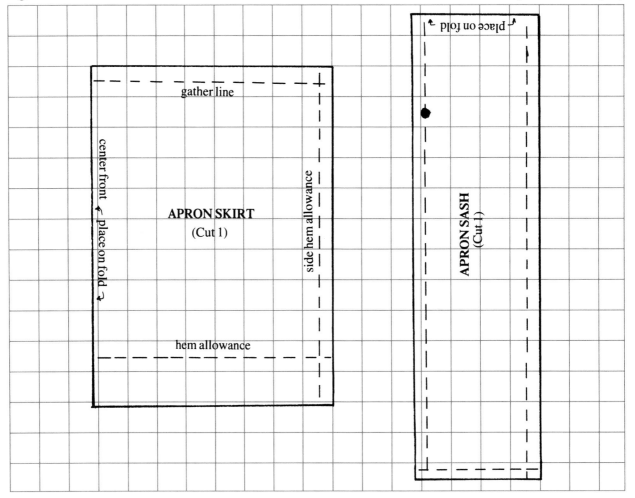

Attaching the Head to the Body

1. Turn a narrow seam allowance to the inside on the neck opening of the body. Gather the neckline ¼ inch (0.6) from the folded edge, using heavy-duty flesh-colored thread. Pull the gathering threads until the opening measures approximately 1 inch (2.5) across.

2. Center the head over the opening, inserting the tied neck portion inside the body. Whipstitch completely around the neck several times to secure the head to the body. (Maude's feelings about a body's neck are pretty much the same as those she has about corsets.)

Making the Apron

1. Even when wearing her Sunday dress, Maude is never without her practical white cotton apron. As Maude puts it, "There's no use in lolling around when there's pies to make and porches to sweep." So she only removes her apron once a week just before the trip to church, and dons it again immediately upon her return. To make the apron, enlarge the patterns for the apron skirt and sash given in Figure D. Cut one of each piece from white cotton fabric,

paying particular attention to the "place on fold" notations. Transfer the small placement circles to the fabric pieces, where indicated on the drawings.

2. Turn and stitch a ½-inch (1.3) hem along each side of the apron skirt. Turn and hem the bottom edge, 1½ inches (3.8) deep.

3. Gather the apron skirt ⅜ inch (1) from the top edge, using long basting stitches.

4. Lay the sash right side up on a flat surface. Place the apron skirt right side down on top of the sash, as shown in Figure E. Gently pull the gathers until the skirt fits between the small circles along the top edge of the seam allowance. Adjust the gathers evenly. Pin and then stitch the skirt to the sash along the gathering line.

5. Fold and press the remaining seam allowances on the sash to the wrong side (Figure F).

6. Fold the pressed sash in half lengthwise, sandwiching the gathered skirt between the two layers of the sash, as shown in Figure G.

7. Topstitch ¼ inch (0.6) from the edge completely around the sash.

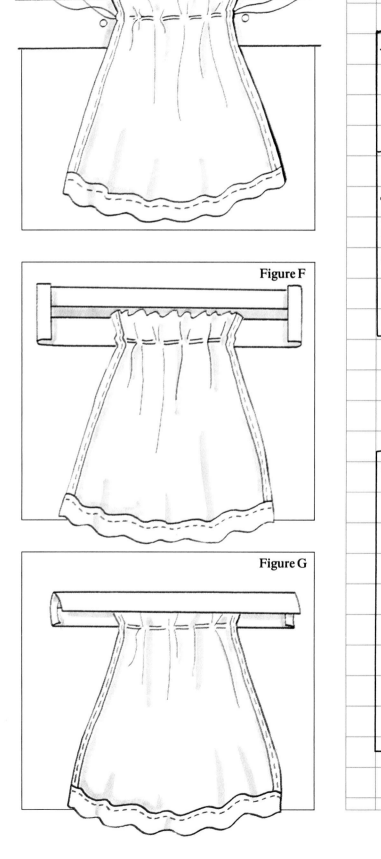

Figure E

Figure F

Figure G

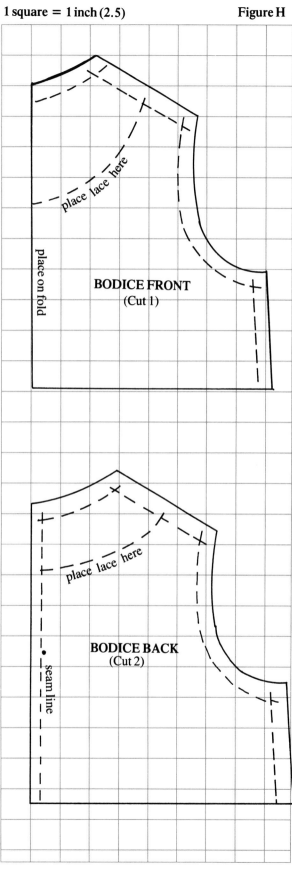

place lace here

place on fold

BODICE FRONT
(Cut 1)

place lace here

seam line

BODICE BACK
(Cut 2)

Figure H

1 square = 1 inch (2.5)

place on fold
hem
SKIRT
(Cut 1)
gather
center back seam

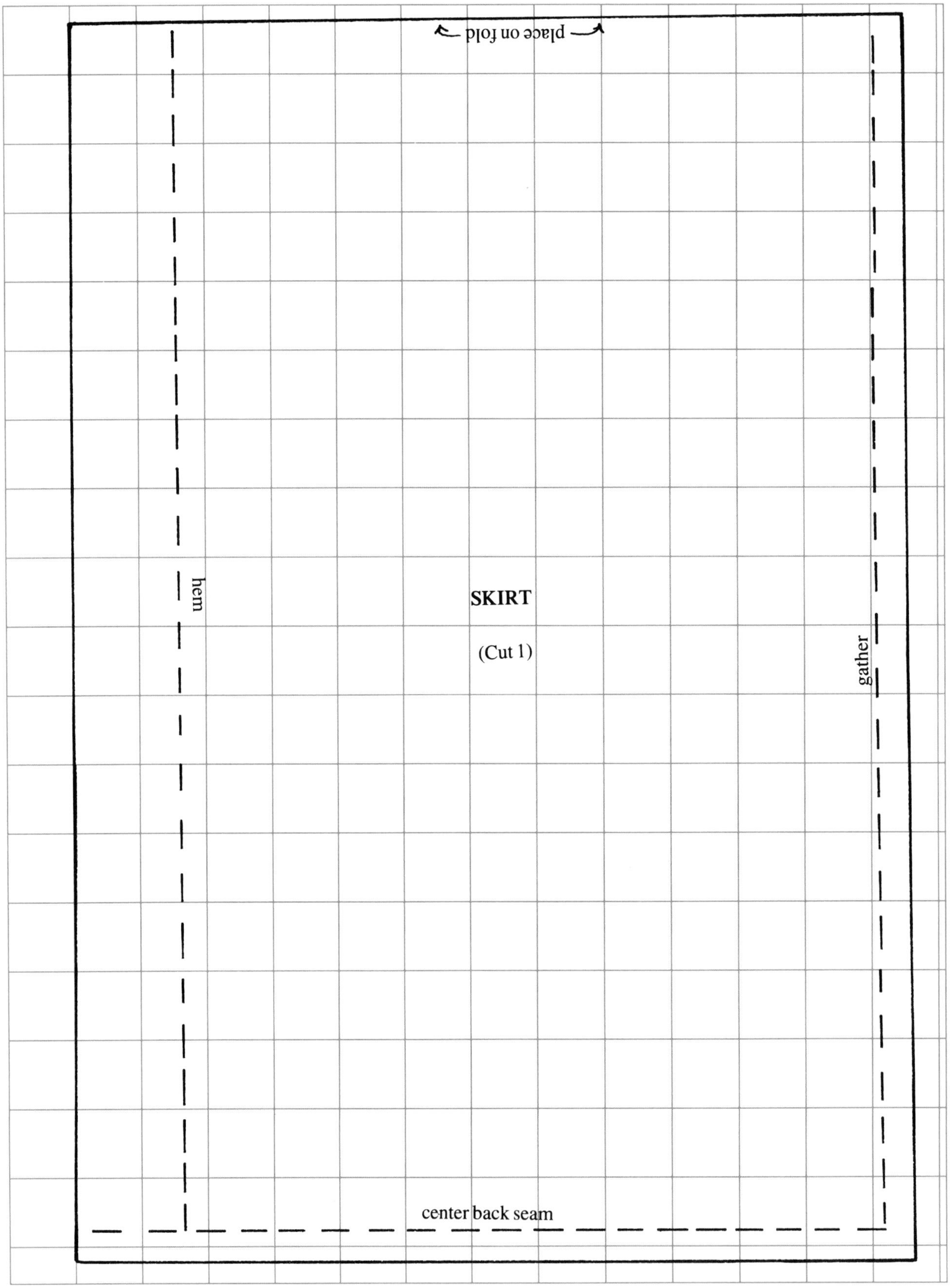

Figure H

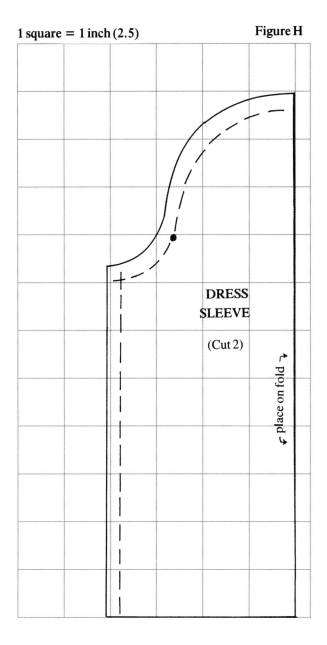

DRESS
SLEEVE

(Cut 2)

↙ place on fold ↗

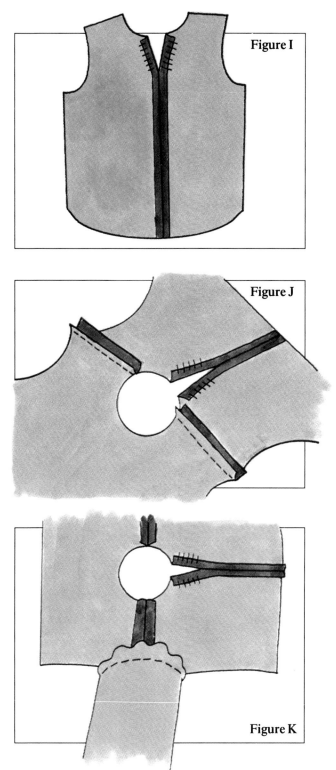

Figure I

Figure J

Figure K

Making the Dress

1. Enlarge the dress patterns given in Figure H, and cut the following pieces from calico fabric: one front bodice, two back bodices, two sleeves, and one skirt. Pay attention to the "place on fold" notations, and transfer the small circles to the pattern pieces.

2. Place the two bodice backs right sides together and stitch the center back seam from the bottom edge to the small circle. Leave the top portion of the seam open and unstitched. Press the seam open. Turn the raw edges under along the unstitched portion of the seam, and whipstitch in place (Figure I).

3. Pin the front and back bodices right sides together at the shoulder seams (Figure J). Stitch, then press the seams open.

4. Gather the top of the sleeve, ⅜ inch (1) from the raw edge between the small circles. Pin the gathered edge of the sleeve to the armhole edge of the bodice, adjusting the gathers evenly (Figure K). Stitch along the gathering line. Attach the remaining sleeve to the opposite side of the bodice in the same manner.

Figure L

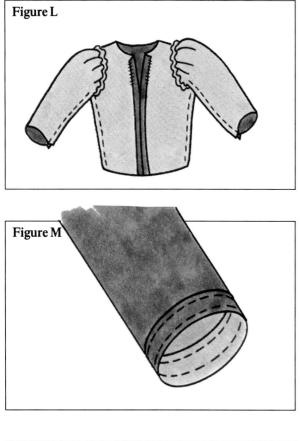

Figure M

Figure N

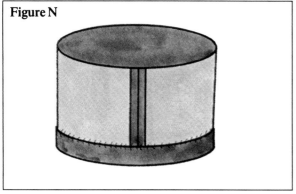

Figure O

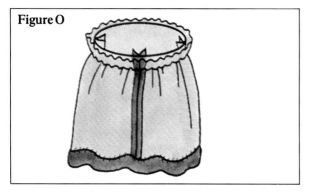

5. Fold the bodices right sides together, and stitch the underarm and side seams (Figure L).

6. To make casings for elastic in the sleeves, press the raw edges to the wrong side. Turn under a 1-inch (2.5) hem and stitch. Stitch the hem again ⅜ inch (1) from the first stitching, to form the casing (Figure M). Leave a small opening in the stitching to insert the elastic. Topstitch lace trim along the hemmed edge of each sleeve. (The dress you are making is Maude's Sunday-go-to-meeting best. Lace is scarce in Council Bluffs, and Maude is very proud of it. This particular lace originally adorned her stepmother's first wedding gown, which was custom made for her by the then famous couturier, Buford of St. Louis. The button has no such significant history, having been purchased at Sol's Dry Goods Emporium and Brush Hogging Service.)

7. Measure Maude's wrist and cut a piece of elastic 1 inch (2.5) longer. Thread the elastic through the sleeve casing. Stitch the ends of the elastic securely together, and pull it back inside the casing. Whipstitch the opening in the casing together.

8. Fold the skirt right sides together, and stitch the center back seam. Press the seam open. Turn and stitch a 1½-inch (3.8) deep hem along the lower edge (Figure N).

9. Gather the top edge of the skirt using long basting stitches. Insert the assembled bodice inside the gathered skirt, placing right sides together and matching center back seams (Figure O). Pull the skirt gathers until they fit evenly around the bottom of the bodice. Stitch the bodice to the skirt along the gathering line. Turn the dress right side out and press the waist seam.

10. To finish the neckline, turn under a ¼-inch (0.6) hem and topstitch. Topstitch lace trim over the hemmed edge. Topstitch lace trim over the placement lines to form a yoke, beginning and ending at the center back seam. Sew a small white button to the dress front, centering it on the yoke. Sew a hook and eye closure to the neckline at the back of the dress.

Making the Bloomers

1. Enlarge the bloomer pattern given in Figure P. Cut two bloomers from white cotton fabric.

2. Pin the two bloomer pieces right sides together, and stitch the center front and back seams (Figure Q).

3. Refold the bloomers right sides together, matching the center front and back seams. Stitch the inner leg seam (Figure R).

4. Make casings at the waist and leg edge of the bloomers, as you did for the dress sleeves. Measure and cut lengths of elastic, and thread them through the casings.

5. Topstitch lace trim around the bottom edges of the bloomer legs.

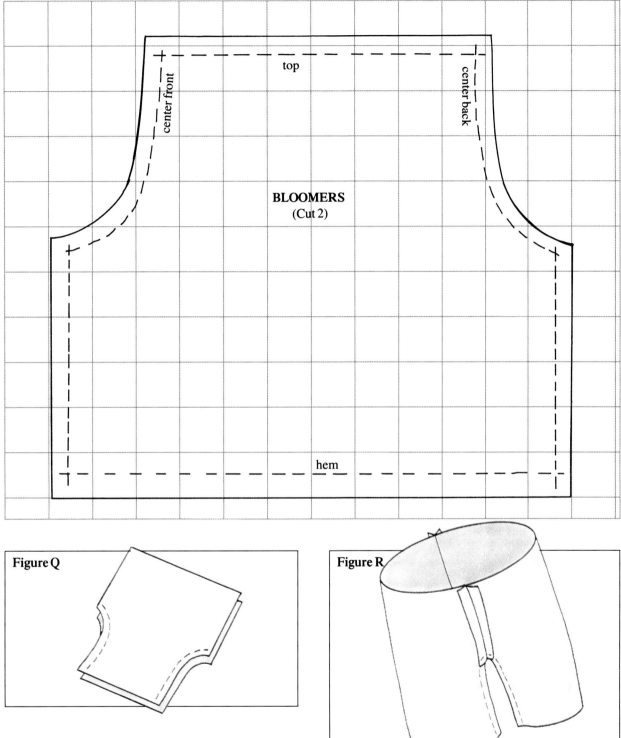

center front

top

center back

BLOOMERS
(Cut 2)

hem

Figure Q

Figure R

Finishing Details

Dress Maude in her bloomers, making sure to pull them up securely around her waist. (She says that proper women are never caught with their bloomers down, and won't even discuss the rumor that in the city some women are exposing their ankles.)

Pull Maude's dress over her head and hook it together at the back. Tie the apron around her waistline in a practical, no nonsense bow in the back.

Theobald Japheth (T.J.) Weepeeple

Born: Sepember 28, 1870

It will probably come as no surprise to you that very few people know T.J.'s full name. When T.J. was born, Barney and Maude wanted to name him after the famous Union Pacific engineer, T.J. Doyle. Being ignorant of Mr. Doyle's full name, Maude inquired and received suggestions from a traveling peddler who happened to be passing through Council Bluffs. The peddler, anxious to please, offered the most heroic names he knew. He was rewarded for his efforts when Maude named the baby and then bought the next-to-most-expensive apple peeler from the peddler's cart.

T.J. was an easy child to raise. At an early age he exhibited his love for the soil. As Maude later recalled, "You could put him on the ground, hand him a sturdy stick, and he'd stay there for hours. Sure was handy when a body was digging potatoes."

Despite his famous namesake, T.J. always felt the need to stay in one place. Throughout his life he traveled no farther than forty miles from home, believing that "there ain't much point in leaving someplace if you're just gonna turn around and come back."

When T.J. and Birdie married, most observers felt it was a marriage made in heaven; or more correctly Hog Heaven, which is what the newlyweds christened their new hog farm. T.J. was a devoted husband and worked hard to provide a good life for his family. His skills at diagnosing particularly rare hog infections were acclaimed throughout the county and there was a daily stream of hogs brought to T.J.'s door by farmers seeking his advice and ministrations. Birdie was justly proud of T.J's reputation and cheerfully cleaned up the daily stream.

T.J. was also an exceptionally fine father, spending many hours with his three children, teaching them the finer points of hog farming and such necessary facts of life as "always look where you're walking in a cow pasture," and "never trust anyone who has more than two arms." This last bit of philosophy was formulated by T.J. as a child after hearing one of the neighboring farmers talk about his trip to Kansas City and a "one-armed" bandit which he encountered. Somehow young T.J. interpreted the conversation to mean that the one arm was an additional appendage. This bit of information had stayed with him, and he felt it important enough to pass on to the next generation.

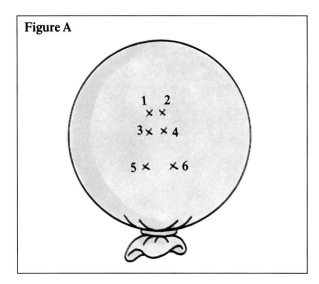

Figure A

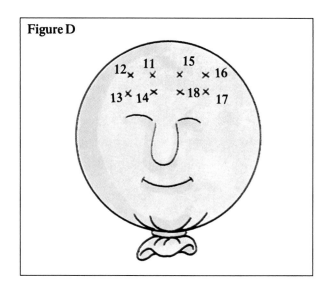

Figure D

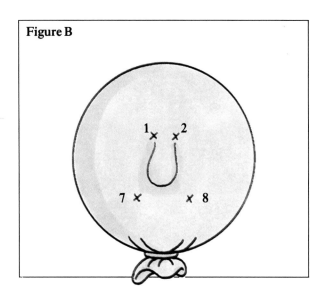

Figure B

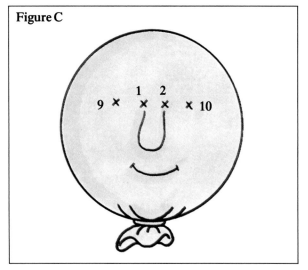

Figure C

Materials and Tools

Metric equivalents in centimeters are indicated in parentheses.

½ yard (0.46 m) of navy blue denim fabric, at least 36 inches (90) wide

½ yard (0.46 m) of white cotton knit fabric

½ yard (0.46 m) of flesh-colored cotton knit fabric

Heavy-duty and regular flesh-colored thread

6-inch (15) length of single-fold white 1-inch (2.5) wide seam binding

Two metal buttons for the overall sides

½ pound (227 g) of polyester fiberfill

One leg cut from a pair of regular weave flesh-tone pantyhose (or one nylon stocking)

Small brown wiglet (or substitute brown yarn)

Two tiny eye beads, ¼-inch (0.64) or smaller in diameter (sold in hobby stores as doll eyes)

Small straw hat (also available in hobby shops)

Pale pink powdered cheek blusher, and white glue

Long sharp needle, scissors, straight pins, and a sewing machine (optional)

Turn to page 154 and make a body for T.J., following the instructions for Making the Arms, Making Legs with Boots, and Making the Torso. Following T.J.'s admonition concerning the number of arms on a trustworthy character, be sure to give him only one on each side of his body. And because hog farming is not without its share of unexpected pitfalls, make certain that you sew the boots sturdily so that T.J.'s feet are safely protected on trips to the hog pen. Of course, omit the decorative flaps on the boots; they would most certainly be inappropriate in a sty. Use the adult body patterns to make T.J. (Figure A. page 155), but sew the arm seams slightly more narrow. Although T.J. is not often given to personal vanity, he is proud of his muscular arms, which are a result of "years of good, honest hog slopping."

Making the Head

1. Tie the pantyhose leg or stocking in a tight knot near the open end and cut across the hose 6 inches (15) below the knot. Turn the hose so that the knot is on the inside.

2. Stuff a generous amount of fiberfill inside the hose, manipulating the shape until a head is formed. (Detailed instructions for stuffing and forming the head are given in the Soft Sculpturing Tips.) T.J.'s head should be at least 12 inches (30.5) in circumference, measuring around the nose and ear line. It should be at least 4½ inches (11.4) in diameter from top to bottom. Tie the hose in a knot at the open end. (This will be the neck.)

3. Use a long sharp needle and a 36-inch (91) length of heavy-duty flesh-colored thread to sculpture the facial features. To form T.J.'s nose, follow the entry and exit points illustrated in Figure A. (T.J. and his father originally possessed almost identical noses. After Barney's encounter with the pig, however, T.J. became the sole member of the family to retain what some have called the classic Weepeeple nose.)

a. Enter where the hose is tied at the neck, pass through the center of the head, and exit at point 1. Pinch up a vertical ridge, approximately ½ inch (1.3) high, between points 1 and 2. (This will be the bridge of the nose.)

b. Reenter at 1 and exit at 2. Reenter at 2 and exit at 1, pulling the thread tightly. Keep the thread pulled tightly as you take an additional stitch underneath the surface between points 1 and 2 to secure the ridge. Exit at 1.

c. Pinch up the nose ridge between points 3 and 4. (These points should be approximately ¼ inch [0.65] directly below points 1 and 2.) Pull the thread across the surface, enter at 3 and exit at 4. Pull the thread across the surface, enter at 2 and exit at 1.

d. Hold the thread taut, reenter at 1 and exit at 5. (Points 5 and 6 should be about ½ inch [1.3] below and slightly to the right of points 3 and 4, but not any lower than the line of the head.) Pull the thread across the surface, enter at 6 and exit at 2. Pull the thread until the end of the nose appears (between points 5 and 6).

e. Hold the thread taut, reenter at 2 and exit at 3. Pull the thread across the surface, enter at 6 and exit at 4. Pull the thread across the surface, enter at 5 and exit at 1.

f. Tighten and hold the thread as you take one or two stitches back and forth under the surface between 1 and 2 to secure the nose. Exit at 2.

4. Continue working with the same thread to form T.J.'s mouth, following the entry and exit points illustrated in Figure B. (T.J., being of a serious nature, lacks the broad smile which always brightens his father's face. Since his wife Birdie smiles almost continually, it is probably just as well.) Points 7 and 8 will be the corners of the mouth. They should be 1 inch (2.5) apart, on a line approximately 1 inch (2.5) below the end of the nose.

a. Reenter at 2 and exit at 7. Pull the thread across the surface, enter at 8 and exit at 1.

b. Pull the thread until the mouth appears. With one hand, hold tension on the thread near point 1, and with the other hand use the tip of the needle to lift a very small amount of additional fiberfill first into the upper lip and then into the chin area. The chin should not be prominent; T.J. has never been one to stick his chin out.

c. Reenter at 1 and take one or two stitches under the surface between points 1 and 2 to secure the stitches. Exit at 1.

5. To form the eyes, follow the entry and exit points illustrated in Figure C. Point 9 will be the outside corner of the closed right eye. It should be approximately 1 inch (2.5) directly to the left of point 1. Point 10, the corner of the left eye, should be 1 inch (2.5) directly to the right of point 2.

a. Pull the thread across the surface, enter at 9 and exit at 2.

b. Pull the thread across the surface, enter at 10 and exit at 1.

c. Pull the thread gently until eye lines appear. Hold the thread taut and stitch one or two times under the surface between points 1 and 2 to secure the eyes. Exit at 1.

6. To form the eyebrow ridges, follow the entry and exit points illustrated in Figure D. The following list of measurements will help you mark the points correctly.

Between points 1 and 11 = ⅞ inch (2.2)
Between points 11 and 12 = ¾ inch (1.9)
Between points 12 and 13 = ⅜ inch (1)
Between points 13 and 14 = ¾ inch (1.9)
Points 15 through 18 are mirror images of points 11 through 14.

a. To form the right eyebrow ridge, reenter at 1 and exit at 11. Pull the thread across the surface, enter at 12 and exit at 13.

b. Pull the thread across the surface, enter at 14 and exit at 11. Pull the thread gently until an eyebrow ridge appears. Hold the thread taut and stitch back and forth one or two times under the surface between points 11 and 14 to secure the ridge. Exit at 11.

c. To form the left eyebrow ridge, reenter at 11 and exit at 15. Pull the thread across the surface, enter at 16 and exit at 17.

d. Pull the thread across the surface, enter at 18 and exit at 15. Pull the thread gently until an eyebrow ridge appears. Hold the thread taut and stitch back and forth one or two times under the surface between points 15 and 18 to secure the ridge. Exit at 15.

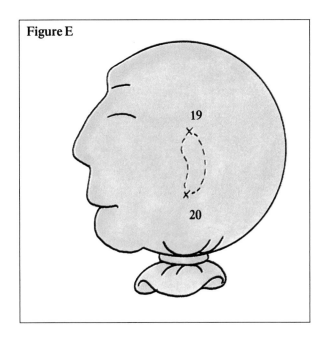

Figure E

19

×

×

20

b. Stitch back and forth under the ridge, moving toward point 20 with each stitch. Pull the thread gently until an ear forms. Exit at 20.

c. Lock the stitch behind the ear, reenter at that point, and exit at the neck.

d. Lock the stitch and cut the thread.

e. Repeat steps a through d on the opposite side of the head.

9. Trim the brown wiglet and glue it to T.J.'s head. It should cover the head but not his ears. Birdie regularly trims T.J.'s hair with the kitchen shears. (T.J. says, "Only them traveling salesmen wear their hair parted and pasted down with all that gooey stuff," so don't make the haircut perfect.)

Attaching the Head to the Body

1. Turn a narrow seam allowance to the inside on the neck opening of the body. Gather the neckline ¼ inch (0.6) from the folded edge using heavy-duty, flesh-colored thread. Pull the gathering threads until the opening measures approximately 1 inch (2.5) across.

2. Center the head over the opening, inserting the tied neck portion of the head inside the neck opening. Whipstitch completely around the neck several times to secure the head to the body. (Even though T.J. rarely sticks his chin out, he holds his head proudly.)

Making the Overalls

T.J.'s overalls are made in the same manner as Barney's, but are cut from navy blue denim. T.J. used to wear the same kind of striped overalls that Barney adopted after his career with the railroad, but soon discarded them as being too hard to keep looking good after a day of tending the hogs. Turn to page 20 and follow the instructions for Making the Overalls, steps 1 through 10, substituting T.J.'s denim for the blue and white striped fabric Barney wears.

Making the Shirt

1. Scale drawings for the shirt back, shirt front, sleeve, collar, and cuff patterns are given in Figure F. Enlarge the drawings to full-size paper patterns.

2. Fold the white cotton knit fabric and pin the patterns in place, paying attention to the "place on fold" notations for each of the patterns. Cut the following pieces: one shirt back, one shirt front, two sleeves, one collar, and two cuffs. Be sure to slit the shirt back at the top neckline, as this serves two practical purposes. It will enable you to fit the completed shirt over T.J.'s head and it makes it possible for Birdie to tell the difference between the neckline and the cuffs.

7. Brush powdered blusher lightly on T.J.'s cheeks. (T.J. doesn't mind a bit having you put blusher on his doll. He says it's "really 'bout the same as rubbin' around in red clay." That, he explains, is an old hog doctor's trick for getting close to the patients. Seems a hog will trust a man more if he's closer to hog color. Strange as it sounds, T.J. swears by this technique, and everyone says he knows best where hogs are concerned.) Glue small eye beads next to the nose, on top of the eye lines. To create eyebrows, cut two short pieces from the wiglet and glue them over the eyebrow lines. To make the mustache, cut another piece from the wiglet and glue it above the mouth.

8. To sculpture the ears, follow the entry and exit points illustrated in Figure E.

a. Enter at the neck and exit at 19. (Point 19, which will be the top of the ear, should be even with the lower end of the nose.) Pinch up a small curved ridge, as shown, just below point 19.

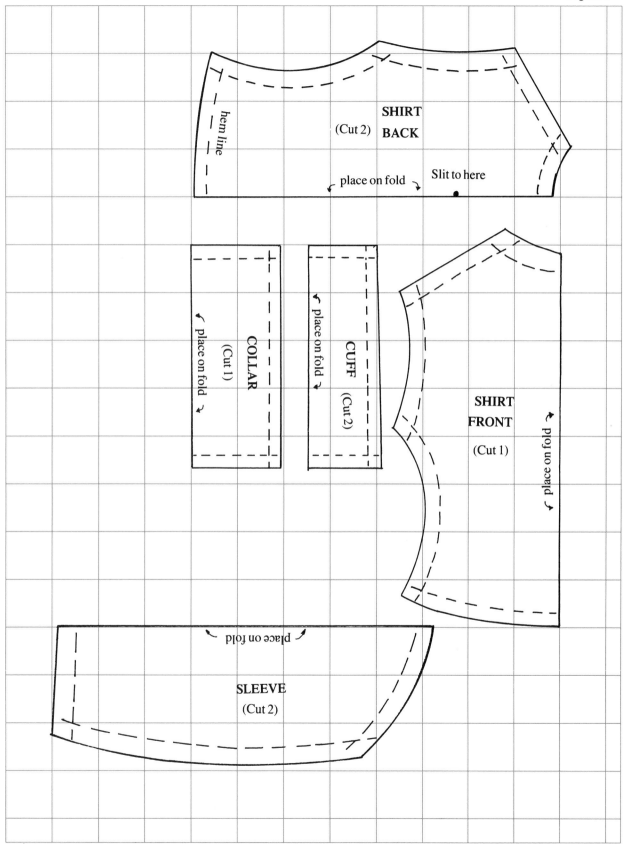

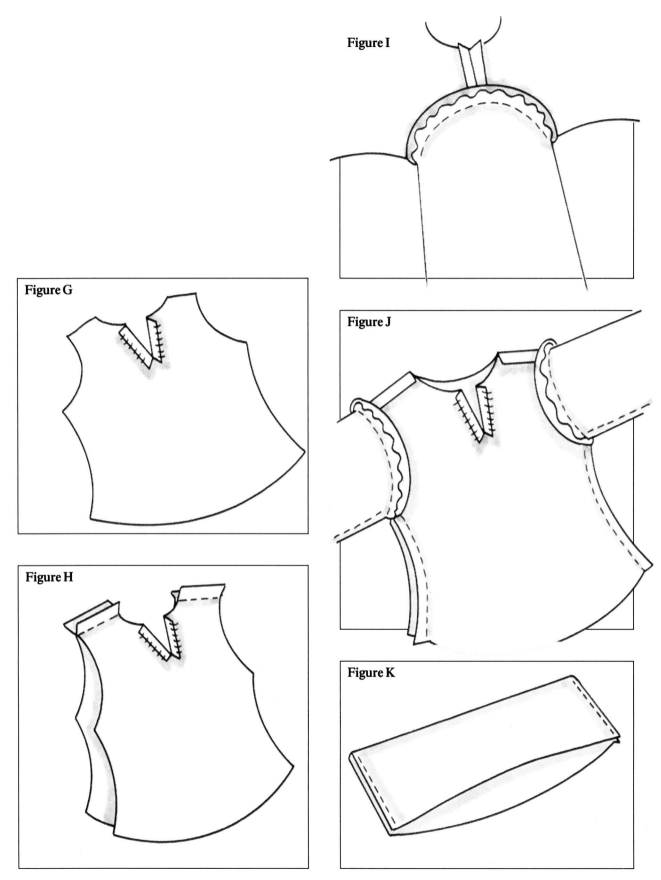

Figure I

Figure G

Figure J

Figure H

Figure K

3. Turn a ¼-inch (0.65) wide hem to the wrong side along both sides of the slit in the shirt back and whipstitch them in place (Figure G). Place the shirt back and shirt front right sides together. Stitch the shoulder seams (Figure H).

4. Sew the curved edges of the sleeves to the armhole edges of the shirt with right sides together (Figure I), easing the sleeves to fit.

5. Fold the shirt right sides together and stitch the side and underarm seam on each side (Figure J).

6. Fold the collar in half lengthwise, placing right sides together and stitch across the short ends (Figure K), leaving the long raw edges open and unstitched. Clip the corners, turn the collar right side out, and press.

7. Pin the collar around the shirt neckline on the right side of the fabric (Figure L). Topstitch the collar in place and stitch seam binding over the lower raw edge of the collar.

8. Fold the cuff right sides together widthwise. Stitch along the two raw edges. (Figure M). Turn the stitched cuff right side out, fold it in half (Figure N), and press the seam allowance to the inside on the unstitched raw edges.

9. Gather the lower end of one sleeve along the gathering line. Pull up the gathers until the edge of the sleeve fits inside the open edge of the cuff (Figure O). Pin the cuff in place and topstitch through all three layers, close to the edge of the cuff. Repeat these procedures to make the remaining cuff.

10. You can sew snaps at the top and bottom of the collar in the back of the shirt, or simply whipstitch the ends of the collar together after you have put the shirt on T.J. (Since they are without indoor plumbing, T.J. usually jumps in the hog trough fully clothed to wash anyway. He says washing his body and clothes at the same time "saves a lot of fuss and bother, not to mention soap. Besides," he adds, "when a body smells all soapy and unnatural it discommodes the hogs.")

Finishing Details

Dress T.J. in his shirt and overalls. Pull the overall straps to the front and tack the ends over the upper edge of the bib. Remove the overalls and stitch the ends of the straps in a secure square stitch pattern.

Redress T.J. in his overalls, and fold the excess fabric at his waistline into a pleat at each side, making the pleats as even as possible. Tack the pleats in place and sew a metal button over each.

Hem the lower edge of each overall leg to fit T.J.'s leg length. (One overall leg is just a little bit shorter than the other, since Birdie hemmed them originally.)

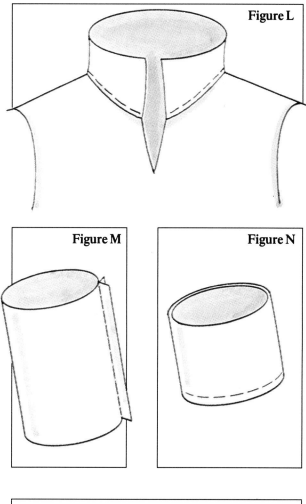

Figure L

Figure M

Figure N

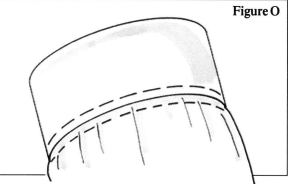

Figure O

Parthenia (Birdie) Floyd Weepeeple

Born: January 22, 1874

Although Birdie has an exceptionally warm and generous spirit and is full of good intentions, she is (as Maude puts it) "one banana short of a full bunch." Obviously, this is not a trait that can (or should) be overlooked by even one's closest and dearest kinfolk. And each and every one of Birdie's family and friends makes allowances.

There are, however, those in the community who make observations of a less-than-kind nature, including one member of the Mount Olive sewing circle who was recently heard to say that "the butter has slipped off of Birdie's noodles." Birdie vaguely acknowledges to herself that things do tend to get away from her on occasion and firmly resolves to do better in the future. As hard as she may try to avoid it, however, every day seems to bring another crisis. For instance, T.J. has time and time again reminded Birdie that the lock on the smokehouse door is prone to stick. His admonitions notwithstanding, Birdie has several times been done to a near turn before T.J. returned from the fields to slop the hogs and released her.

Her older children (having grown up with the situation) take their mother's eccentricities pretty much in stride. They now accept peanut butter and jelly sandwiches without bread in the normal course of events, and early learned to cut their own meat as a precaution against their mother handling sharp knives.

T.J. loves his wife even more than he loves his hogs—so much, in fact, that he wears shirts lacking sleeves without comment. The shirts were unintentionally disfigured one winter when they froze on the clothesline and Birdie broke off the sleeves in an attempt to remove them. To give Birdie credit, she tried to recover by using the sleeves as ironing boards. Unfortunately, they thawed before she was able to perfect her idea.

Unusual situations just naturally seem to gravitate toward Birdie. One evening, when T.J. had not yet returned from the fields, a census taker arrived at the front door. Birdie patiently answered his questions to the best of her ability until he asked whether her children were boys or girls. She indignantly replied, "Of course! And furthermore, you can take your tasteless questions down the road to the Johnson farm, where they go in for that sort of thing!" The census taker later said that was the turning point in establishing his career as a vacuum cleaner salesman.

Birdie's one area of unquestioned expertise and competence is in the care and feeding of prize hens. She treats them as equals and has a relationship with them built on mutual respect. Birdie talks to her chickens, which is a good thing since they are the only ones who appear to understand her completely. At any rate, she has won as many ribbons at the Pottawatamie County Fair with her hens as Maude has collected with her jams and quilts.

True to her compassionate nature, Maude accepts and defends Birdie, often remarking that "Half a wit beats having none at all."

Materials and Tools

Metric equivalents in centimeters are indicated in parentheses.

1½ yards (1.4 m) of 36-inch (90) wide calico or small print fabric

1 yard (0.9 m) of white cotton fabric

1 yard (0.9 m) of white lace trim

½ yard (0.46 m) of flesh-colored cotton knit fabric

¼ yard (0.23 m) of black vinyl fabric

Regular and heavy duty flesh-colored sewing thread

One leg cut from a pair of regular weave flesh-tone pantyhose (or one nylon stocking)

White sewing thread and sewing thread to match the calico fabric

Small brown wiglet (or substitute brown yarn)

Two tiny (no larger than ¼-inch [0.6] diameter) eye beads (sold in hobby stores for use as doll eyes)

½ pound (227 g) of polyester fiberfill

Light brown fine felt-tip marker, pale pink powdered cheek blusher, brown hairpins, and white glue

1 yard (0.9 m) of ¼-inch (0.6) wide elastic

One hook and eye closure

Six tiny black beads for the boot flap buttons.

Long sharp needle, scissors, straight pins, and a sewing machine (optional)

Turn to page 154 and make a body for Birdie, following instructions for Making the Arms, Making Legs with Boots, Adding Boot Flaps, and Making the Torso. Although there is a general consensus in Council Bluffs that Birdie may not have "all the pieces to her puzzle," she is physically unimpaired. Stitch carefully so you don't add any physical deformities to her woes. Birdie's black boots with buttoned flaps were a gift from T.J. last Christmas, so don't skip that section. Be sure to position the flaps on the outside of each boot, as Birdie can't seem to distinguish left from right otherwise. Use the scale drawings for adult-sized arm, leg, boot, boot flap, and torso (Figure A, page 155) to make the full-size patterns.

Making the Head

1. Tie the pantyhose leg or stocking into a tight knot near the open end, and cut the hose 6 inches (15) below the knot. Turn, so that the knot is on the inside.

2. Stuff a generous amount of fiberfill inside the hose, manipulating the shape until a head is formed. (Detailed instructions for stuffing and forming a head are given in the Soft Sculpturing Tips section of this book). Birdie's head should be at least 12 inches (31) in circumference, measuring around the nose and ear line. It should be approximately 4½ inches (11) in diameter from top to bottom. Tie the hose in a tight knot at the open (neck) end.

3. Use a long sharp needle and a 36-inch (90) length of heavy duty flesh-colored thread to soft sculpture the facial features. Although Birdie and Maude are not related except by marriage, many people remark that they do bear a resemblance to one another. Nothing could please Birdie more, since she strives to emulate Maude. To form Birdie's nose, follow the entry and exit points illustrated in Figure A.

    a. Enter where the hose is knotted at the neck, pass through the center of the head, and exit at point 1. Sew a clockwise circle of deep basting stitches approximately 1 inch (2.5) in diameter, and exit at point 2.

    b. Use the tip of your needle to carefully lift fiberfill within the circle just enough to make a small bulge. Gently pull the thread until a round nose appears inside the circle.

    c. Hold the thread with one hand and take another stitch, entering at 2 and exiting at 1.

    d. To form the nostrils, reenter at 1 and exit at 3. Reenter ¼ inch (0.6) above 3 and exit at 2.

    e. Pull the thread gently and maintain the tension while you reenter at 2 and exit at 4. Reenter ¼ inch (0.6) above 4 and exit at 1.

    f. Pull the thread gently and maintain the tension while you take another small stitch at point 1.

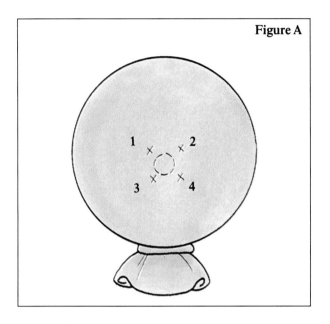

Figure A

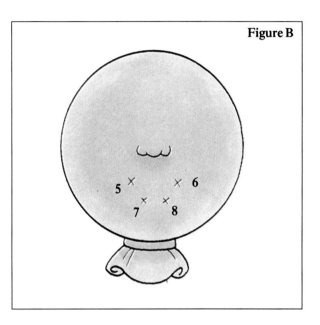

Figure B

4. Form the mouth, following entry and exit points in Figure B.

   a. Enter at 1 and exit at 5. Pull the thread across the surface, enter at 6 and exit at 1. Pull the thread until a smile appears.

   b. Reenter at 1 and exit at 2. Reenter at 2 and exit at 7. Pull the thread across the surface, enter at 8 and exit at 2. Pull the thread gently to form Birdie's lower lip. Do this carefully, as Birdie has a very small mouth (some say that's a good thing), of which she is quite proud.

5. To form the eyes, follow the entry and exit points illustrated in Figure C.

   a. Reenter at 2 and exit at 9. Pull the thread across the surface, enter at 1 and exit at 10.

   b. Pull the thread across the surface, enter at 2 and exit at 1. Gently pull the thread until the eye lines appear. Lock the stitch.

   c. Reenter at 1, guide the needle through the interior of the head to the knot at the top. Exit near the knot, pull the thread taut, lock the stitch, and cut the thread.

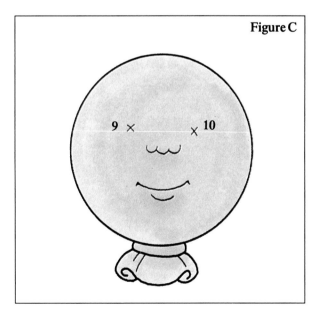

Figure C

Figure F

Figure D

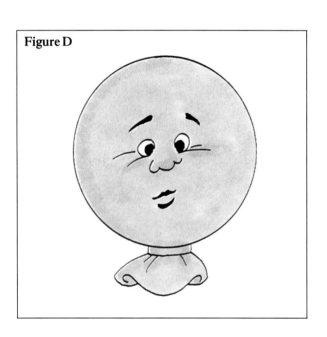

Figure E

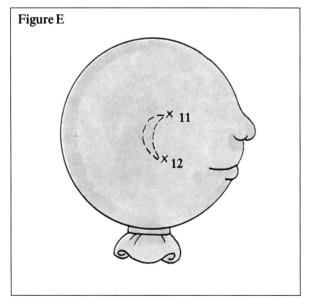

6. Birdie's face is illustrated in Figure D. Brush powdered cheek blusher on Birdie's cheeks and on the tip of her nose. Apply a goodly amount of blusher to her mouth, as Birdie wears a bit of lipstick ever since she began her subscription to *Lydia Morgenthaller's Guide to Lovely Living*. Glue small eye beads next to the nose, over the eye lines. Draw the eyebrows using a light brown felt-tip marker. Birdie's eyebrows are drawn at an angle, and have no arch. They begin above the inner corner of the eye, and end above the outer corner.

7. Follow the entry and exit points illustrated in Figure E to sculpture Birdie's ears.

    a. Enter at the neck knot and exit at 11. (Point 11, which will be the top of the ear, should be even with the lower portion of the nose.) Pinch up a small curved ridge at an angle, as shown, just below point 11.

    b. Stitch back and forth under the ridge, moving toward point 12 with each stitch, and pulling the thread gently until an ear forms. Exit at point 12.

    c. Lock the stitch behind the ear, reenter at that point, and exit at the neck knot.

    d. Lock the stitch and cut the thread.

    e. Repeat steps a through d on the opposite side of the head.

8. Trim the wiglet to fit Birdie's head and glue it in place. Comb the hair up into a tight bun on top. Secure the bun well with hairpins, as Birdie's grasp on things in general seems to have a direct relationship to the neatness of her hair arrangement. She does, however, usually have one stray lock that curls across her forehead (Figure F).

Attaching the Head to the Body

1. Turn a narrow seam allowance to the inside on the neck opening of the body. Gather the neckline ¼ inch (0.6) from the folded edge, using heavy-duty flesh-colored thread. Pull the gathering threads until the opening measures approximately 1 inch (2.5) across.

2. Center the head over the opening, inserting the tied neck portion inside the body. Whipstitch completely around the neck several times to secure the head to the body. (Secure the head well, because even though Birdie's mind flops on occasion, her head does not.)

Making the Apron

Birdie has a white cotton apron just like Maude's, which Maude made as a gift for Birdie on her birthday. After Maude repeated the instructions three different times, Birdie finally caught on and now wears her apron with the sashes tied in back. To make the apron, turn to page 30 and follow the instructions for Making the Apron.

Making the Dress

Almost everyone in the Council Bluffs sewing circle has a best dress similar to this one. Birdie's was made for her by the group, after she herself had attempted the project without success. Initially, it appeared satisfactory. A few days later, however, Birdie's dress looked very much like T.J.'s sleeveless shirt. Maude consoled her by explaining that the ability to set in sleeves was a special gift from The Creator, which not everyone receives. Turn to page 33 and follow the instructions for Making the Dress. The only difference is that Birdie's dress does not have a lace yoke or a button, so omit these additions.

Making the Bloomers

Although Birdie more often than not forgets to put her bloomers on in the morning, go ahead and make them anyway, just in case. Turn to page 34 and follow the instructions given for Making the Bloomers.

Finishing Details

Dress Birdie and fasten her clothing securely, as she is not always aware when something gets loose or even when she loses it entirely. T.J. says he admires her ability to concentrate only on what she is doing, and not on how she looks while doing it, as is the case with most womenfolk. But he tends to keep a quiet eye on her, and will quickly step in with a helpful hand when a hook or sash starts to come undone (Figure G).

Figure G

Penelope Delphinia (Gal) Weepeeple

Born: March 3, 1890

Gal was firstborn to Birdie and T.J. and the recipient of a rather unusual middle name, owing to the book Birdie read during the course of her pregnancy. The book, which took Birdie the entire nine months to read, was a little known forty-eight-page masterpiece by the famous eighteenth-century author Lewis P. Bumpus. It was entitled, *The Anguished Life of Delphinia Hedgeripple or Can an Aristocratic Orphan Find Happiness in the Coal Mines of East Wales?*

Being the eldest child of a competent-but-busy father and a sincere-but-somewhat-discombobulated mother, Gal assumed much of the household work at an early age. Perhaps because of the tedious demands of her everyday life and inspired by her own elegant given names, she became enamored of the excitement in the lives of the great and famous. She determined to become an actress.

Gal's most cherished heroine was the English actress Lily Langtry, who she actually saw in the flesh at a performance of *Lady Windermere's Fan* on the stage in Kansas City. This all came about because one spring Gal's Aunt Victoria and Uncle Casey visited the farm on their way back from New York City. Victoria was "simply appalled at the lack of cultured atmosphere away out here in the backwash of civilization!" She promptly bundled Gal off to Kansas City for a month of intensive "cultural uplifting."

Back at the farm, Gal's fantasies returned to the excitement of the stage while she set about putting things right in the Weepeeple household. Gal determined that one day when she was older she would seek her fortune in the theater, become rich and famous, and liberate her mother from the bondage of farm life. To this, Birdie was once heard to reply, "I got no earthly desire to be liberate, cause my readin's as good as anybody's."

Gal, undaunted, continued to refine her acting skills through a rigorous daily schedule of practice in the barnyard. At first none of the animals paid much heed and, in fact, expressed what might be aptly described as disdain for the carryings on in their previously peaceful domain. As Gal's performances blossomed, however, the audience grew. At first, small groups of assorted denizens began to congregate. And then she began to pack the barnyard regularly, necessitating Standing Room Only signs to be posted nightly in the chicken coop.

Gal turned to her long-time friend and advisor, Turnip the pig, for guidance and crowd control. Never one to ignore a friend in need, Turnip handled the seating arrangements and auditioned supporting cast members. In return, Gal gave a benefit performance for the orphaned piglets on Mr. Beecham's farm, whose unfortunate father had the day before hammed it up for the final time.

Later in life, when she had fulfilled her dreams of greatness, Gal acknowledged her debt to her barnyard friends in a touching tribute delivered in her acceptance speech before the Motion Picture Academy.

Materials and Tools

Metric equivalents in centimeters are indicated in parentheses.

1½ yards (1.4 m) of 36-inch (90) wide calico or small print fabric

1 yard (0.9 m) of white cotton fabric

1 yard (0.9 m) of white eyelet trim, 1 inch (2.5) wide

½ yard (0.46 m) of flesh-colored cotton knit fabric

¼ yard (0.23 m) of black vinyl fabric

½ ounce (14 g) of dark brown weaver's fiber or yarn

One leg cut from a pair of regular-weave flesh-tone pantyhose, or one nylon stocking

Regular and heavy-duty flesh-colored thread

½ pound (227 g) of polyester fiberfill

1 yard (0.9 m) each of ¼-inch (0.6) and ¾-inch (1.9) wide satin ribbon to coordinate with the calico or print fabric

1 yard (0.9 m) of ¼-inch (0.6) wide elastic

One hook and eye closure

Long sharp needle, scissors, light brown felt-tip marker, pins, and a sewing machine (optional)

Turn to page 154 and make a body for Gal, following instructions for Making the Arms, Making Legs with Boots, Adding Boot Flaps, and Making the Torso. (Gal has been dieting for quite some time, because she's tired of always being cast as the heavy in the community plays. She'll love you forever if you exaggerate the effects of the diet when you stitch her body.) Use the scale drawings for child-sized arm, leg, boot, boot flap, and torso (Figure B, page 156) to make the full-size patterns.

Making the Head

1. Tie the pantyhose leg or stocking into a tight knot near the open end, and cut the hose 6 inches (15) below the knot. Turn, so that the knot is on the inside.

2. Stuff a generous amount of fiberfill inside the hose, manipulating the shape until a head is formed. (Detailed instructions for stuffing and forming a head are given in the Soft Sculpturing Tips section of this book). Gal's head should be slightly more round than Barney's or Maude's, and at least 12 inches (31) in circumference, measuring around the nose and ear line. It should be approximately 4½ inches (11) in diameter from top to bottom. Tie the hose in a tight knot at the open (neck) end.

3. Use a long sharp needle and a 36-inch (90) length of heavy-duty flesh-colored thread to sculpture the facial features. To form Gal's nose, follow the entry and exit points illustrated in Figure A. (Obviously, Gal has inherited the "perfect Perkins proboscis," as Barney is fond of calling it. Gal remains uncertain about the word "proboscis," and can't imagine where on earth her grandfather picked it up, so she concentrates on the "perfect" part of the phrase and tries to ignore the rest.)

    a. Enter where the hose is knotted at the neck, pass through the center of the head, and exit at point 1. Sew a clockwise circle of basting stitches 1 inch (2.5) in diameter, and exit at 2.

    b. Use the tip of your needle to carefully lift fiberfill within the circle just enough to make a small bulge. Gently pull the thread until a round nose appears inside the circle.

    c. Hold the thread with one hand and take another stitch, entering at 2 and exiting at 1.

    d. To form the nostrils, reenter at 1 and exit at 3. Reenter ¼ inch (0.6) above 3 and exit at 2.

    e. Pull the thread gently and maintain the tension while you reenter at 2 and exit at 4. Reenter ¼ inch (0.6) above 4 and exit at 1.

    f. Pull the thread gently and maintain the tension while you take another small stitch at point 1.

4. Continue working with the same thread to form the mouth, referring to Figure A.

    a. Enter at 1 and exit at 5. Pull the thread across the surface, enter at 6 and exit at 1. Pull the thread until a smile appears.

    b. Reenter at 1 and exit at 2. Reenter at 2 and exit at 7. Pull the thread across the surface, enter at 8 and exit at 2. Pull the thread gently to form Gal's lower lip.

5. To form the eyes, follow the entry and exit points illustrated in Figure A, working with the same thread.

    a. Reenter at 2 and exit at 9. Pull the thread across the surface, enter at 1 and exit at 10.

    b. Pull the thread across the surface, enter at 2 and exit at 1. Gently pull the thread until the eye lines appear. Lock the stitch.

    c. Reenter at 1, guide the needle through the interior of the head to the knot at the top. Exit near the knot, pull the thread taut, lock the stitch, and cut the thread.

6. Brush powdered blusher lightly on Gal's cheeks,

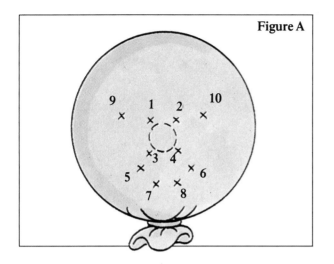

Figure A

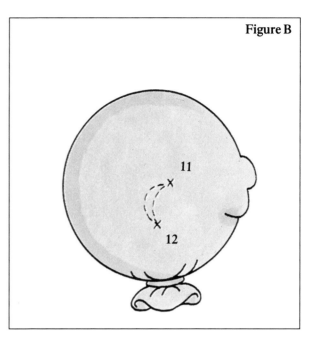

Figure B

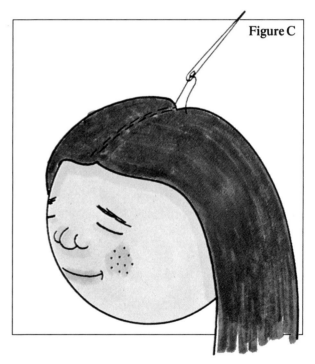

Figure C

across her mouth, and on the tip of her nose. Use the light brown marker to draw eyelashes along the eye lines and large freckles on her cheeks and nose. (It really seems a shame to do this, since Gal can often be heard bemoaning her freckled fate and one time, in fact, nearly disfigured herself for life trying to remove the freckles using Malvina Morris' famous lye soap along with some sandpaper. When that didn't work, she spent an entire summer sunbathing her face, hoping that eventually the freckles would merge into one large tan. This, however, only resulted in a painful sunburn. As Birdie often says, "We musn't fool with what nature give us.")

7. Follow the entry and exit points illustrated in Figure B to sculpture Gal's ears.

   a. Enter at the neck knot and exit at 11. (Point 11, which will be the top of the ear, should be even with the lower portion of the nose.) Pinch up a small curved ridge at an angle, as shown, just below point 11.

   b. Stitch back and forth under the ridge, moving toward point 12 with each stitch, and pulling the thread gently until an ear forms. Exit at point 12.

   c. Lock the stitch behind the ear, reenter at that point, and exit at the neck knot.

   d. Lock the stitch and cut the thread.

   e. Repeat steps a through d on the opposite side of the head.

8. To make Gal's thick, lustrous hair (of which she is understandably proud), first cut the fiber or yarn into 20-inch (50) lengths. Center the fibers across Gal's head and stitch them in place along her center part, from front to back, using a backstitch (Figure C). Place the fibers as close together as possible. Trim some of the fibers to form bangs in the front. Divide and braid the remaining fiber on each side, and tie the ends of the braids with short lengths of fiber. Cover each fiber tie with a length of narrow satin ribbon tied in a bow. To finish, glue or hand stitch the hair to Gal's head around her hairline to hold it in place.

Attaching the Head to the Body

1. Turn a narrow seam allowance to the inside on the neck opening of the body. Gather the neckline ¼ inch (0.6) from the folded edge, using heavy-duty flesh-colored thread. Pull the gathering threads until the opening measures approximately 1 inch (2.5) across.

2. Center the head over the opening, inserting the tied neck portion inside the body. Whipstitch around the neck several times to secure the head to the body.

53

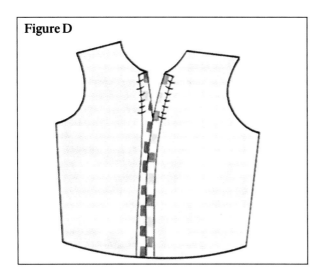

Figure D

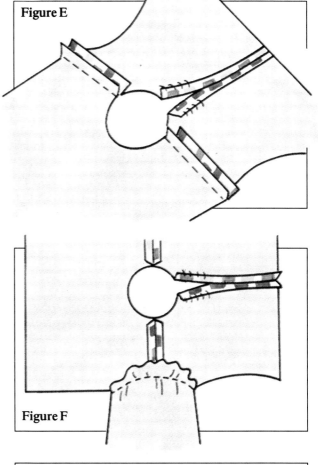

Figure E

Figure F

Making the Dress

1. Enlarge the dress patterns given in Figure H, and cut the following pieces from calico fabric: one front bodice, two back bodices, two sleeves, and one skirt. Pay attention to the "place on fold" notations, and transfer the small circles to the fabric pieces.

2. Place the two bodice backs right sides together and stitch the center back seam from the bottom edge to the small circle. Leave the top portion of the seam open and unstitched. Press the seam open. Turn the raw edges under along the unstitched portion of the seam, and whipstitch in place (Figure D).

3. Pin the front and back bodices right sides together at the shoulder seams (Figure E). Stitch, then press the seams open.

4. Gather the top of one sleeve, ⅜ inch (1) from the raw edge between the small circles. Pin the gathered edge of the sleeve to the armhole edge of the bodice, adjusting the gathers evenly (Figure F) and placing right sides together. Stitch along the gathering line. Attach the remaining sleeve to the opposite side of the bodice in the same manner. Press the seam allowances toward the bodice on both sides.

5. Fold the bodices right sides together, and stitch the underarm and side seams (Figure G).

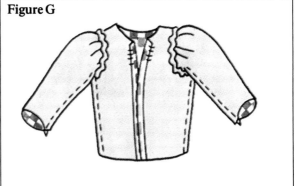

Figure G

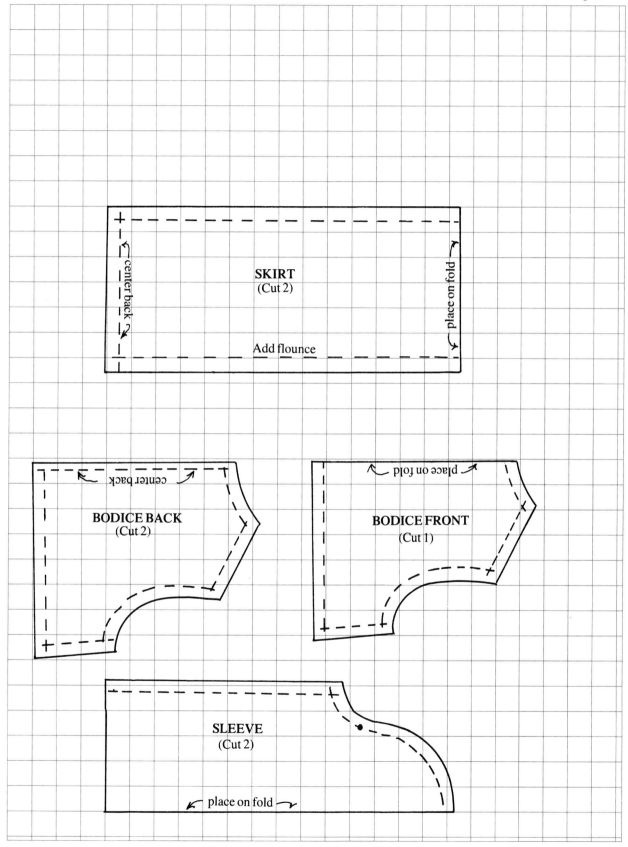

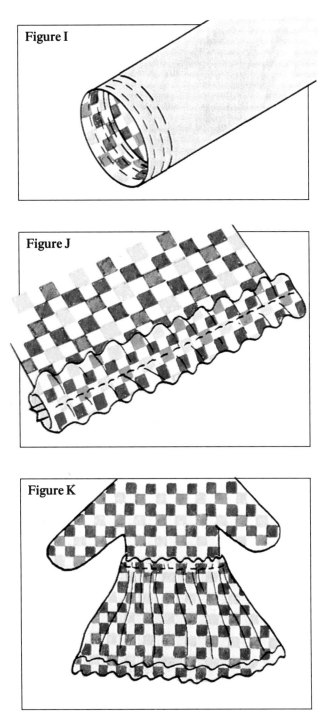

Figure I

Figure J

Figure K

6. To make casings for elastic in the sleeves, press the raw edges to the wrong side. Turn under a 1-inch (2.5) hem and stitch. Stitch the hem again ⅜ inch (1) from the first stitching to form the casing (Figure I). Leave a small opening in the stitching to insert the elastic. Topstitch eyelet trim along the hemmed edge of each sleeve. Turn the bodice right side out.

7. Measure Gal's wrist and cut a piece of elastic 1 inch (2.5) longer. Thread the elastic through the sleeve casing. Stitch the ends of the elastic securely together and pull it back inside the casing. Whipstitch the opening in the casing together.

8. Turn and stitch a 1½-inch (3.8) deep hem along the lower edge of the skirt. Turn and stitch a ¼-inch (0.6) deep hem along the upper edge.

9. To make the ruffle for the bottom of the dress, cut and piece together 5-inch-wide strips of calico to a length of 86 (218) inches. Fold the strip in half lengthwise, right sides together, and stitch a ½-inch (1.3) wide seam along the doubled raw edges. Turn the stitched ruffle right side out and press so that the seam runs down the center. The seam will be placed on the underside of the ruffle when it is attached to the dress.

10. Gather the ruffle with long basting stitches placed over the seam line. Fit and pin the gathered ruffle to the lower hemmed edge of the skirt. The raw edges of the ruffle should be placed even with the raw side edges of the skirt. Adjust the gathers evenly. Topstitch the ruffle to the dress (Figure J).

11. Fold the skirt right sides together, matching center back seam lines. Stitch the seam, from the top of the skirt to the bottom of the ruffle. Press the seam open.

12. Turn the skirt right side out and gather the waistline using a long basting stitch. Fit the dress over the bottom edge of the completed bodice, placing the gathering line ½ inch from the lower edge of the bodice (Figure K). Pull the gathers to fit and adjust them evenly. Topstitch the skirt to the bodice.

13. To finish the neckline, turn under a ¼-inch (0.6) hem and topstitch. Topstitch eyelet trim over the hemmed edge. Tie narrow satin ribbon over the eyelet trim on each wrist, ending with a bow. Tie a small bow of the same ribbon and whipstitch it to the center front of the dress neckline. (Gal is very fond of her eyelet trim and satin ribbons. In fact, she begged that a great deal more be added, pointing out that Lily Langtry's dresses were literally covered with lace and bows. Maude and Birdie agreed that Lily's dresses were indeed beautiful, but also observed that Lily's performances were limited to the indoors, and that her dresses were not subjected to quite as many barnyard pitfalls as were Gal's.)

1 square = 1 inch (2.5)   **Figure L**

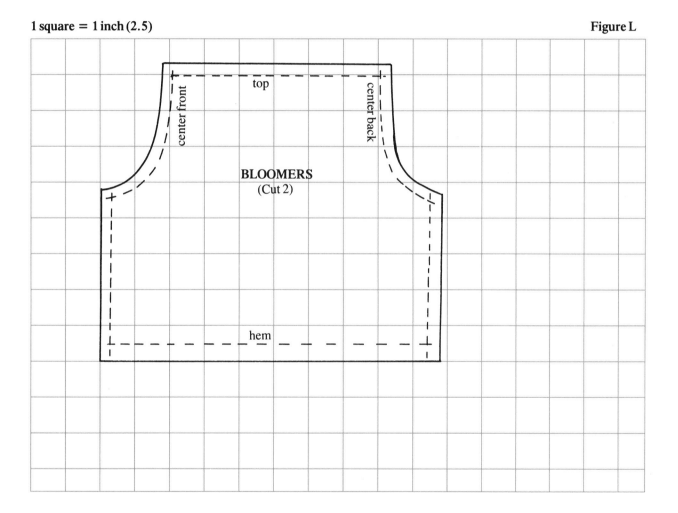

center front

top

center back

BLOOMERS
(Cut 2)

hem

Making the Bloomers

1. Enlarge the bloomer pattern given in Figure L and cut two bloomers from white cotton fabric.

2. Gal's bloomers are sewn together in the same manner as Maude's (see page 34). Substitute eyelet on Gal's bloomers for the lace that is sewn around the bottom edges of Maude's.

Finishing Details

Dress Gal in her bloomers and dress. Tie the ¾-inch-wide length of satin ribbon around her waistline. Gal prefers that the ribbon be tied in a double bow at the back, to hide the safety pins. The pins are necessary to hold the empty flour sacks which Gal stuffs underneath the back of her skirt, thereby producing a mound that vaguely resembles Lily Langtry's fashionable bustle.

Jeremiah Jeremiah (JayJay) Weepeeple

Born: December 18, 1892

JayJay's double name was the result of quite a family feud. It seems that T.J. and Birdie each had a beloved ancestor named Jeremiah, for whom each wished to name the new baby. It was one of the few occasions during their marriage when T.J. and Birdie both stood their ground, unable to agree for which ancestor the baby would be named. A neighbor, unable to sleep through the ruckus, intervened and suggested a compromise solution—that they name the baby for both ancestors. Birdie was secretly pleased, since she was convinced that it was her ancestor's name that was first.

As in most families, the second child born to Birdie and T.J. was not at all like their first. While Gal dreams of a different life, JayJay remains content and aspires to nothing more than a continuation of the hog farming tradition. While Gal assumes responsibility around the home, JayJay spends the greater part of his days sitting on the creek bank baited for walleye.

His one ambition is to perfect his stink-bait formula, which has caused some consternation in the community when the wind is from the south. JayJay once approached his grandfather Barney to underwrite the stink-bait business, but their discussion ended abruptly during the formula-mixing demonstration and JayJay was never successful in reopening the negotiations.

JayJay is rarely seen wearing a shirt or shoes, and in fact was nearly six years old before Birdie could convince him to wear a stitch. He still sometimes forgets to dress, much to Gal's dismay, because she likes to have the local girls over for tea and a spot of impromptu theater. Birdie knows immediately what the problem is when she hears Gal's plaintive, "Mo-ther!!!"

JayJay possesses many of the traits of both his mother and father. Like T.J., he loves the farm and the hogs. Like his mother, he experiences some difficulties with everyday life. He would probably have more luck with his stink bait, for instance, if he applied it to the lure rather than to the handle of his fishing pole.

Probably the most distressing daily problem that JayJay faces is his inability to remember where he is going or why—a problem compounded by the fact that Birdie rarely remembers where she sent him. On a recent excursion to town, JayJay visited the dry goods store, the bakery, the blacksmith, and spent several hours on the creek bank before returning home. When T.J. inquired as to his whereabouts, Birdie replied that she thought she had sent him to the bank, or maybe to the Johnson farm for a new shirt pattern with stronger sleeves. Fortunately, JayJay has a voracious appetite and prefers Birdie's cooking to any other, so he always manages to make it back home by meal time.

Later in his life, JayJay combines his two greatest loves in his choice of profession when he opens JayJay's Bait Shop and Beanery.

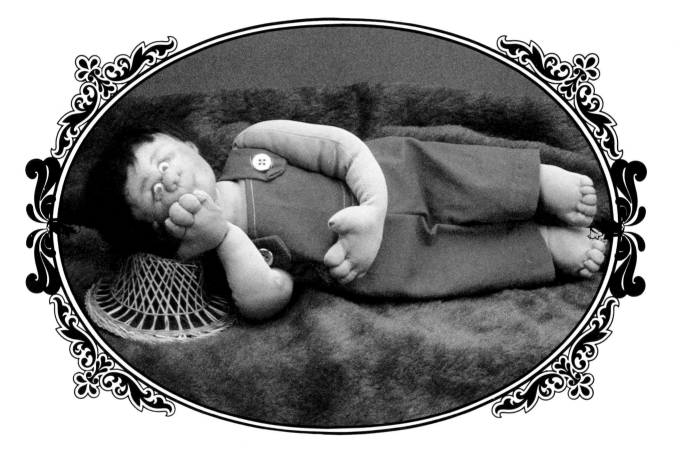

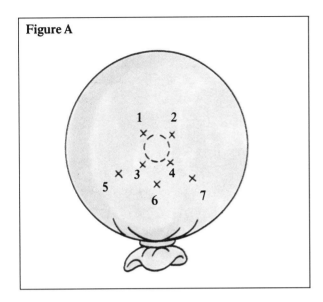

Figure A

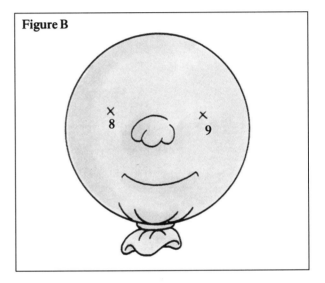

Figure B

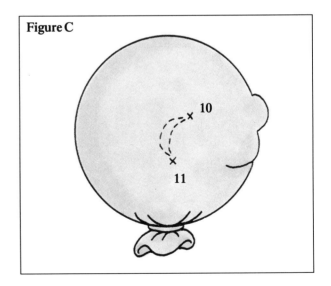

Figure C

Materials and Tools

Metric equivalents in centimeters are indicated in parentheses.

½ yard (0.46 m) of blue cotton fabric, at least 36 inches (90) wide

½ yard (0.46 m) of flesh-colored cotton knit fabric

Heavy-duty and regular flesh-colored thread

Two ¾-inch (1.9) diameter buttons (or 1-inch [2.5] wide buckle fixtures) for the overall straps and two metal buttons for the overall sides

½ pound (227 g) of polyester fiberfill

One leg cut from a pair of regular weave flesh-tone pantyhose (or one nylon stocking)

¼ ounce (7 g) of dark brown weaver's fiber or yarn

Two eye beads, ¼ inch (0.6) or smaller in diameter (sold in hobby stores as doll eyes)

Small straw hat (also available at hobby stores)

Light brown fine felt-tip marker, pale pink powdered cheek blusher, and white glue

Long sharp needle, scissors, straight pins, and a sewing machine (optional)

Turn to page 154 and make a body for JayJay, following the instructions for Making the Arms, Making Legs with Feet, and Making the Torso. Although he is normally a forgiving soul, JayJay will be out of sorts for weeks if you try to make boots for him, so be sure to skip over Making Legs with Boots. Use the scale drawings for child-size arm, leg, foot parts, and torso (Figure B, page 156) to make the full-size patterns.

Making the Head

1. Tie the pantyhose leg or stocking into a tight knot near the open end, and cut the hose 6 inches (15) below the knot. Turn, so that the knot is on the inside.

2. Stuff a generous amount of fiberfill inside the hose, manipulating the shape until a round head is formed. (Detailed instructions for stuffing and forming a head are given in the Soft Sculpturing Tips section of this book.) JayJay's head should be at least 12 inches (31) in circumference, measuring around the nose and ear line. It should be approximately 4½ inches (11) in diameter from top to bottom. Tie the hose in a tight knot at the open (neck) end.

3. To create JayJay's facial features, use a long sharp needle and a 36-inch (90) length of heavy-duty flesh-colored thread. Begin with his nose, following the entry and exit points illustrated in Figure A. (Many friends and neighbors have remarked that JayJay is "the spittin' image of his ma." JayJay is quite pleased that he so closely resembles such a lovely lady. But he is secretly incensed that people believe he would spit anywhere near his mother.)

    a. Enter where the hose is knotted at the neck, pass through the center of the head, and exit at point 1. Sew a clockwise circle of deep basting stitches approximately 1 inch (2.5) in diameter, and exit at point 2.

    b. Use the tip of your needle to carefully lift fiberfill within the circle just enough to make a small bulge. Gently pull the thread until a round nose appears inside the circle.

    c. Hold the thread with one hand and take another stitch, entering at 2 and exiting at 1.

    d. To form the nostrils, reenter at 1 and exit at 3. Reenter ¼ inch (0.6) above 3 and exit at 2.

    e. Pull the thread gently and maintain the tension while you reenter at 2 and exit at 4. Reenter ¼ inch (0.6) directly above 4 and exit at 1.

    f. Pull the thread gently and maintain the tension while you take another small stitch at point 1.

4. Continue working with the same thread to form the mouth, referring to Figure A.

    a. Enter at 1 and exit at 5. Pull the thread across the surface, enter at 6 and exit at 7.

    b. Pull the thread across the surface, enter at 6 and exit at 1. Pull the thread until the smile appears.

    c. Take a stitch under the surface between points 1 and 2 to secure the smile, and exit at 2.

5. To form the eyes, follow the entry and exit points illustrated in Figure B.

    a. Reenter at 2 and exit at 8. Pull the thread across the surface, enter at 1 and exit at 9.

    b. Pull the thread across the surface, enter at 2 and exit at 1. Gently pull the thread until the eye lines appear. Lock the stitch.

    c. Reenter at 1 and guide the needle through the interior of the head to the knot at the top. Exit near the knot, pull the thread taut, lock the stitch, and cut the thread.

6. Brush powdered blusher lightly on JayJay's cheeks. Glue the eye beads next to the nose, over the eye lines. Draw the eyebrows and the upper eyelid lines, using the light brown felt-tip marker. JayJay's eyebrows have very little arch. Dot large freckles on his cheeks.

7. Follow the entry and exit points illustrated in Figure C to sculpture JayJay's ears.

    a. Enter at the neck knot and exit at 10. (Point 10, which will be the top of the ear, should be even with the lower portion of the nose.) Pinch up a small curved ridge at an angle, as shown, just below point 10.

    b. Stitch back and forth under the ridge, moving toward point 11 with each stitch, and pulling the thread gently until an ear forms. Exit at point 11.

    c. Lock the stitch behind the ear, reenter at that point, and exit at the neck knot.

    d. Lock the stitch and cut the thread.

    e. Repeat steps a through d on the opposite side of the head.

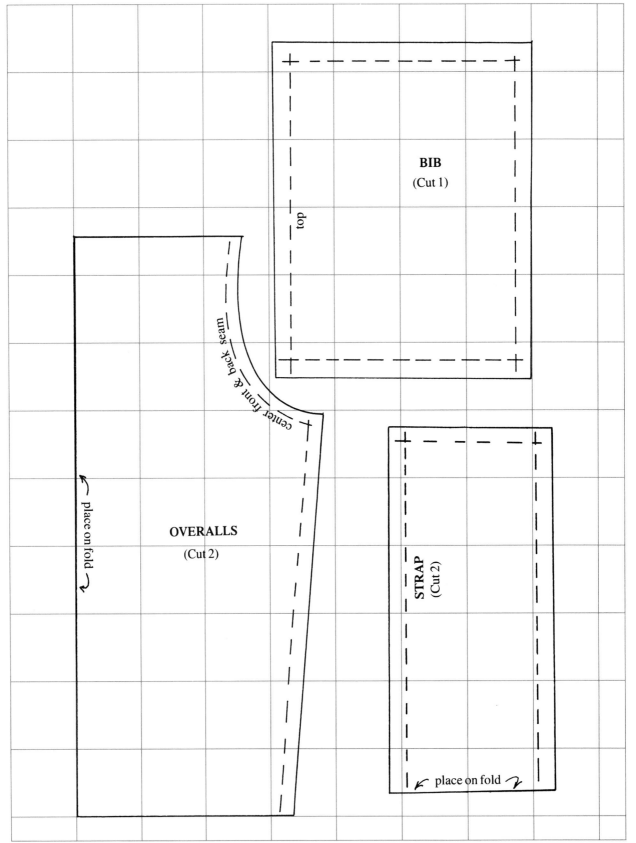

BIB
(Cut 1)

top

center front & back seam

place on fold

OVERALLS
(Cut 2)

STRAP
(Cut 2)

place on fold

8. To make JayJay's hair, cut the fiber or yarn into 8-inch (20) lengths. Center the fibers across JayJay's head and stitch them in place along his center part, from front to back (Figure E). Place the fibers as close together as possible. Comb out the fibers carefully and then trim short bangs in the front. Refer to the photograph of JayJay at the beginning of this section as you give him a proper haircut. Then glue the fiber to the head around the hairline. (T.J. usually places a bowl over JayJay's head as a guide when cutting his hair. Although most hair-cutting is done by the womenfolk, JayJay prefers that his father do the honors. This is understandable, since Birdie's skills with sharp instruments are questionable. In order to avoid any injury to her son when cutting his hair, Birdie proceeds with the greatest caution. The most recent session lasted a little over two hours, and Birdie had only finished trimming JayJay's bangs. Ever since that time, T.J. has been the family barber.)

Attaching the Head to the Body

1. Turn a narrow seam allowance to the inside on the neck opening of the body. Gather the neckline ¼ inch (0.6) from the folded edge, using heavy-duty thread. Pull up the gathers until the opening measures approximately 1 inch (2.5) across.

2. Center the head over the opening, inserting the tied neck portion inside the body. Whipstitch around the neck several times to secure the head to the body.

Making the Overalls

1. Scale drawings of the sewing patterns for the overall and bib and strap are given in Figure D. Enlarge the drawings to full-size paper patterns.

2. Cut two overall pieces (note "place on fold"), one bib and two straps from the blue cotton fabric.

3. JayJay's overalls are made in the same manner as Barney's, except that they have no pockets. (This might seem somewhat strange, but there's a very good reason. As you know, JayJay is an avid fisherman. Early in his angling career, he discovered that his overall pockets were a perfect place to store both worms and his famous stink bait. However, because he rarely remembered to remove the leftovers when the overalls went into the washing pile, Birdie's laundry began to draw an alarming number of flies. She remedied the situation in her own inimitable manner—by removing the pockets from every pair of JayJay's overalls.) To make JayJay's pocketless overalls, turn to page 20, and follow the instructions for making Barney's, ignoring all references to pockets.

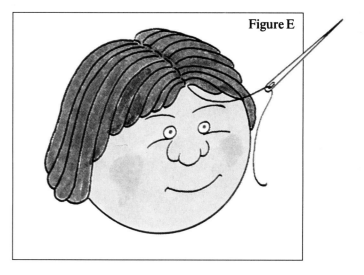

Figure E

Finishing Details

Dress JayJay in his overalls. Pull the straps to the front and tack the ends over the upper edge of the bib. Sew a button to each strap, or, if you prefer, add the buckles.

Fold the excess fabric into a pleat at each side of the waist, making the pleats as even as possible. Tack the pleats in place and sew a metal button over each. Hem the lower edge of each overall leg.

Put JayJay's straw hat on his head. He'll feel much more at ease if you will make him a fishing pole from a small tree twig (or a length of wooden dowel rod) and some string. But you'll have to keep an eye on him if you provide a pole, as he's likely to wander off to the local fishing hole—or even worse, he'll start concocting a batch of stink bait in your kitchen sink!

Gladstone Fred (Baby Gladys) Weepeeple

Born: August 16, 1897

The circumstances of Baby Gladys' birth have been well documented in the Weepeeple family saga. Fortunately, since Birdie was not attended by Lucybelle Sloane, the birth had not been officially recorded when the case of mistaken identity was discovered. It was therefore determined (by a meeting of all the family members) that a more appropriate formal name be given to the child, although within the family the baby boy was by then and would always remain Baby Gladys.

The formal name was of such import that the entire family was called in to discuss the matter. Various names were bandied about, Gal insisting all the while that she had been cheated out of a baby sister and if the name had to be changed at all it should be changed to Susan. Maude proposed a more suitable and masculine name—Buford, after the famous St. Louis couturier—because like Buford, Gladys was completely bald.

The family finally settled on Gladstone, in hope that this choice would cover for the original error. Birdie added the middle name, since it "just naturally flows with such a highfalutin' first name."

Owing to the fact that everyone in the family continued to call him Gladys (despite his fancy new name), and the community of Council Bluffs was relatively small in those days, the boy learned the manly art of self defense at an extremely tender age. As near as Birdie can recall, he was about eighteen months old when he engaged in fisticuffs with another youngster who had just learned the word "sissie." That unfortunate toddler never uttered the offending word again, and indeed never said anything at all for the next six months.

Gladys took to weight lifting early in life, as a natural extension of his defensive requirements, and before his sixth birthday could (and regularly did) bench press the outhouse, much to the dismay of the current occupant. After several unfortunate incidents the family grew accustomed to this display. But on one occasion, a traveling peddler (who was ignorant of Gladys' need to display his strength) received a permanent trauma when his concentration was interrupted in midstream.

Over the course of his life, Gladys' sense of humor grew and his need to physically defend his manhood diminished.

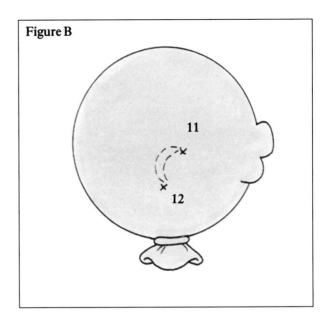

Figure B

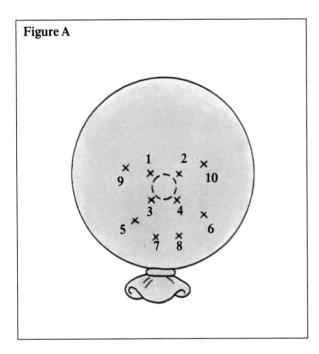

Figure A

Materials and Tools

Metric equivalents in centimeters are indicated in parentheses.

¼ yard (0.23 m) of flesh-colored cotton knit fabric

½ yard (0.46 m) of white cotton fabric

One leg cut from a pair of regular weave flesh-tone pantyhose (or one nylon stocking)

2 x 3-inch (5.1 x 7.6) piece of white cotton fabric

1 yard (0.9 m) of ¼-inch (0.6) wide white lace trim

½ yard (0.46 m) of ¼-inch (0.6) wide white ribbon

¼ pound (113 g) of polyester fiberfill

Regular and heavy-duty flesh-colored sewing thread

White sewing thread, pale pink powdered cheek blusher, and two tiny safety pins

One small snap closure

Light brown fine felt-tip marker, long sharp needle, scissors, pins, and a sewing machine (optional)

Making the Head

1. Cut a 6-inch (15) length from the upper portion of the pantyhose leg or stocking and slit it lengthwise so that you have a flat rectangle.

2. Wrap the rectangle around a small handful of fiberfill. Gather the edges of the hose together and twist, to create a head form. (Detailed instructions for stuffing and forming a head are given in the Soft Sculpturing Tips section of this book.) Gladys' head should be approximately 7½ inches (19) in circumference, measuring around the nose and ear line. It should be at least 2½ inches (6.35) in diameter from top to bottom. Add or remove fiberfill until the head is the correct size. Then wrap the twisted hose tightly with heavy-duty thread. Cut off most of the excess hose below the thread.

3. Use a long sharp needle and a length of heavy-duty flesh-colored thread to sculpture the facial features. To form Gladys' nose, follow the entry and exit points illustrated in Figure A. (Although Baby Gladys is a much loved member of the family, he is most definitely not the best looking of the Weepeeple clan. Although Birdie was not attended by Lucybelle during the birth, Lucybelle did visit the new arrival when she returned to the county and managed to cover her embarrassment when she mistook Baby Gladys for one of the also newborn piglets. Of course, no one has mentioned it to Birdie, who thinks that her youngest is absolutely beautiful, and the family is careful to cover Gladys' face with blankets during church so as not to encourage comments from the congregation.)

    a. Enter where the hose is knotted at the neck, pass through the center of the head, and exit at point 1. Sew a clockwise circle of deep basting stitches approximately ½ inch (1.3) in diameter, and exit at point 2.

b. Use the tip of your needle to carefully lift fiberfill within the circle just enough to make a small bulge. Gently pull the thread until a little round nose appears inside the circle.

c. Hold the thread with one hand and take another stitch, entering at 2 and exiting at 1.

d. To form the nostrils, reenter at 1 and exit at 3. Reenter just barely above 3 and exit at 2.

e. Pull the thread gently and maintain the tension while you reenter at 2 and exit at 4. Reenter just barely above 4 and exit at 1.

f. Pull the thread gently and maintain the tension while you take another tiny stitch at point 1.

4. Continue working with the same thread to form the tiny mouth, referring to Figure A.

a. Enter at 1 and exit at 5. Pull the thread across the surface, enter at 6 and exit at 1. Pull the thread until a smile appears. Although it is tiny in size, Baby Gladys already displays his mother's temperament and has a much bigger smile inside.

b. Reenter at 1 and exit at 2. Reenter at 2 and exit at 7. Pull the thread across the surface, enter at 8 and exit at 2. Pull the thread gently to form Gladys' lower lip.

5. To form the eyes, follow the entry and exit points illustrated in Figure A.

a. Reenter at 2 and exit at 9. Pull the thread across the surface, enter at 1 and exit at 10.

b. Pull the thread across the surface, center at 2 and exit at 1. Gently pull the thread until Gladys' tiny closed eyes appear. Lock the stitch.

c. Reenter at 1, guide the needle through the head to the knot at the bottom. Exit near the knot, pull the thread taut, lock the stitch, and cut the thread.

6. Brush a small amount of powdered blusher on Gladys' cheeks, across his mouth, and on the tip of his nose. (Ugliness notwithstanding, Gladys has a perfect skin tone and is an extremely healthy baby. Later in life, this robust health will provide Gladys with the physical strength necessary to ward off many attacks that will be precipitated by his somewhat unusual name.) Draw eyelashes along the closed eye lines, using the felt-tip marker.

7. Follow the entry and exit points illustrated in Figure B to sculpture Gladys' ears.

a. Enter at the neck knot and exit at 11. (Point 11, which will be the top of the ear, should be even with the lower portion of the nose.) Pinch up a small curved ridge at an angle, as shown, just below point 11.

b. Stitch back and forth under the ridge, moving toward point 12 with each stitch, and pulling the thread gently until an ear forms. Exit at point 12.

c. Lock the stitch behind the ear, reenter at that point, and exit at the neck knot.

d. Lock the stitch and cut the thread.

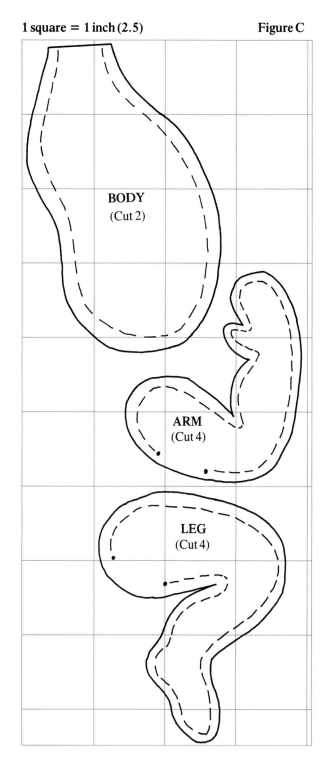

1 square = 1 inch (2.5) Figure C

BODY (Cut 2)

ARM (Cut 4)

LEG (Cut 4)

e. Repeat steps a through d on the opposite side of the head.

8. Since Baby Gladys is totally bald, there is no need to add hair. Birdie is sure that it is a temporary condition and is not concerned. Not many other folks have even noticed it, since Gladys is almost always completely covered with blankets.

Figure C   1 square = 1 inch (2.5)

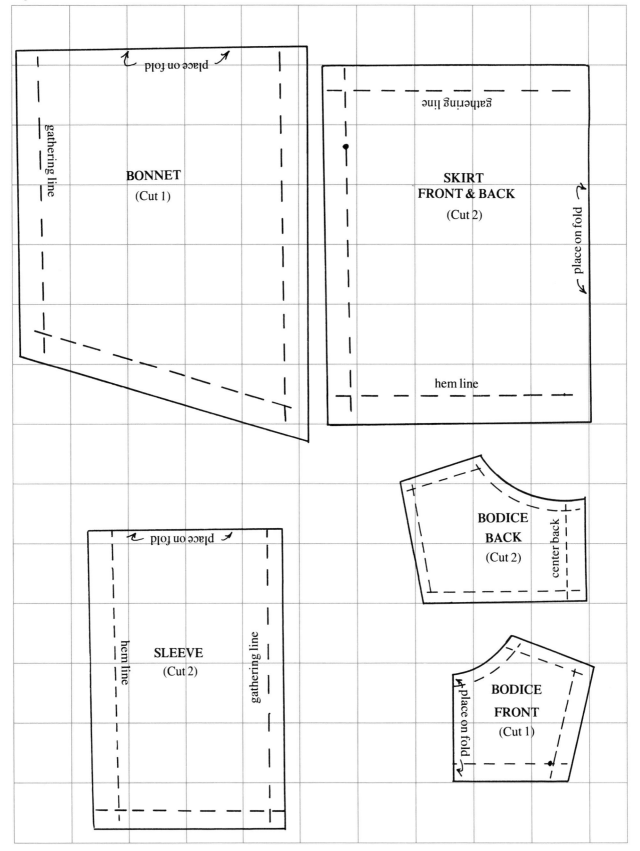

BONNET

(Cut 1)

place on fold

gathering line

gathering line

**SKIRT
FRONT & BACK**

(Cut 2)

place on fold

hem line

**BODICE
BACK**

(Cut 2)

center back

place on fold

SLEEVE

(Cut 2)

hem line

gathering line

place on fold

**BODICE
FRONT**

(Cut 1)

Making the Body

Gladys' body is constructed differently than the bodies of the other Weepeeple because he is still a baby. (There has been talk in Council Bluffs that all of Birdie's babies are constructed differently, but that rumor is spread only by the most unkind members of the community. There is some evidence to support the theory that rumors of this sort almost always originate with Agatha Dahlrimple, a spinster lady living at the edge of town in the Victorian home she inherited from her parents. Maude is not at all concerned with the rumors and chalks it up to the fact that many years ago Barney spurned young Agatha's improper advances.)

1. Scale drawings for Gladys' body and clothes are given in Figure C. Enlarge the patterns to full size and cut the following body pieces from flesh-colored cotton knit fabric: two torsos, four arms, and four legs.

2. Place the two torso pieces right sides together and sew a ¼-inch (0.6) wide seam around all edges, leaving the neck edge open and unstitched (Figure D).

3. Clip the curves, turn the torso right side out, and press. Stuff the torso gently but firmly, working through the neck opening. Leave the top ¼ inch (0.6) at the neck opening unstuffed.

4. Place two arm pieces right sides together and sew around the outer edges, leaving the upper arm open and unstitched between the small circles (Figure E).

5. Clip the curves, turn the arm right side out, and press. Stuff the arm firmly, working through the unstitched opening. Turn the seam allowance to the inside on both sides of the opening and whipstitch the folded edges together with tiny invisible stitches. Repeat the procedure to make the other arm.

6. Turn to page 157 and follow the instructions for sculpturing the hands. Use a sharp needle and heavy-duty flesh-colored thread.

7. Place two leg pieces right sides together, and sew a ¼-inch (0.6) wide seam around the outer edges, leaving the upper leg open and unstitched between the placement circles (Figure F).

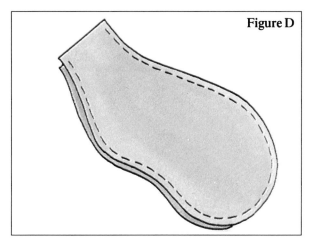

Figure D

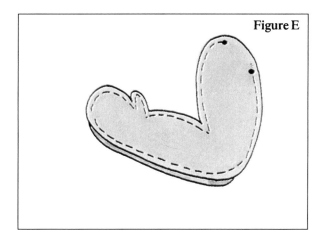

Figure E

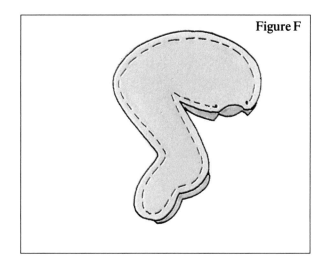

Figure F

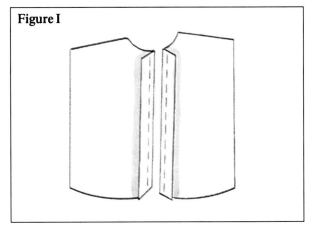

Figure I

8. Clip the curves, turn the leg right side out and press. Stuff the leg firmly, working through the unstitched opening. Turn the raw edges to the inside on both sides of the opening and whipstitch the folded edges together with tiny invisible stitches. Follow the same procedure to make the second leg.

9. Turn to page 159 and follow the instructions for sculpting the feet. Use a sharp needle and heavy-duty flesh-colored thread.

Assembling the Body

1. Turn a narrow seam allowance to the inside on the neck opening of the body. Gather the neckline ¼ inch (0.6) from the folded edge, using heavy-duty flesh-colored thread. Pull the gathering threads until the opening measures approximately ½ inch (1.3) across.

2. Center the head over the opening, inserting the tied neck portion inside the body. Whipstitch around the neck several times to secure the head to the body.

3. Place the arms on each side of the body as shown in Figure G. Use heavy-duty flesh-colored thread to sew the arms to the body. Insert the needle through the center of the upper shoulder portion of one arm, push it straight through the body, and through the corresponding portion of the second arm. Reverse the procedure, ending where you began (Figure H). Repeat this entire procedure several times to secure the arms firmly to the body. Lock the stitch and cut the thread.

4. Place the legs on either side of the lower portion of the body and stitch them in place using the same procedure used to attach the arms.

Figure G

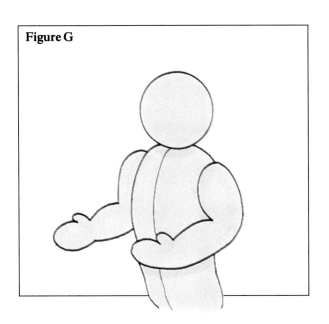

Figure H

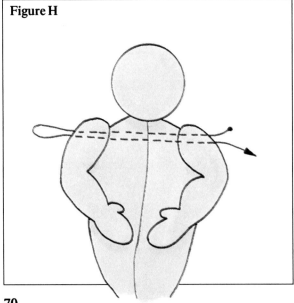

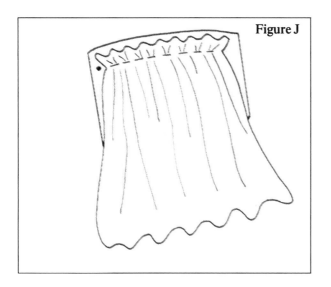

Making the Gown

The gown that Baby Gladys wears is not a new one. It was originally made by Ma Weepeeple for her first born son, Barney, back in 1849, and it has been worn by Weepeeple babies ever since. Baby Gladys continues to wear the gown, although it is becoming a little short for him. However, Birdie can't quite remember where she stored the next-biggest little boy outfit, and so is unable to update his clothing.

1. Enlarge the gown patterns given in Figure C, and cut the following pieces from white cotton fabric: one front bodice, two back bodices, two sleeves, and two skirts. Pay attention to the "place on fold" notations, and transfer the small placement circles to the fabric pieces.

2. Turn a ¼-inch (0.6) wide hem to the wrong side along the center back of each back bodice and stitch, as shown in Figure I.

3. Turn a ¼-inch (0.6) wide hem to the wrong side on the bottom edge of each skirt piece and stitch. Gather the top edge of each skirt piece using basting stitches.

4. Place the front bodice and one gathered skirt right sides together. Pull the gathering threads until the skirt fits between the small circles along the bottom edge of the bodice (Figure J). Sew the front bodice and the skirt together, stitching across the gathering line.

5. Attach the two bodice back pieces to the remaining skirt piece in the same manner used to attach the front. Overlap the hemmed center back edges of the bodice backs to create a neck opening (Figure K).

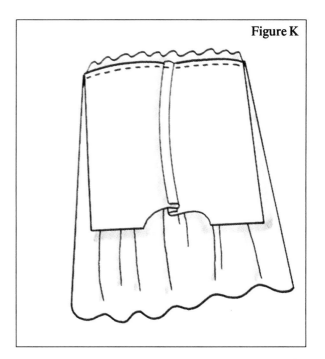

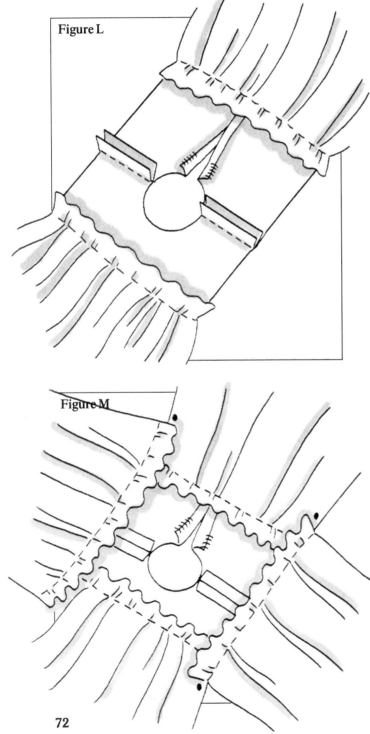

Figure L

Figure M

Figure N

6. Pin the front and back bodices right sides together at the shoulder seams (Figure L). Stitch, and press the seams open.

7. Turn a ¼-inch (0.6) wide hem to the wrong side along the bottom edge of one sleeve and stitch. Topstitch lace trim over the hemmed edge. Gather the top of the sleeve ¼ inch (0.6) from the raw edge, between the small circles. Pin the gathered edge of the sleeve to one armhole edge of the bodice, placing right sides together and adjusting the gathers evenly (Figure M). Stitch along the gathering line. Attach the remaining sleeve to the opposite side of the bodice in the same manner.

8. Fold the bodices right sides together, and stitch the underarm and side seams (Figure N). Topstitch lace trim around the bottom hemmed edge of the gown.

9. To finish the neckline, turn under a ¼-inch (0.6) wide hem and topstitch. Topstitch lace trim over the front bodice/skirt seam, and add another length of trim just above it.

Making the Bonnet

1. Enlarge the drawing for the bonnet pattern given in Figure C. Cut one bonnet piece from white cotton fabric. Turn under a ¼-inch (0.6) wide hem along the long front edge of the bonnet and topstitch. Topstitch lace trim over the hemmed edge. Turn under a ¼-inch (0.6) wide hem along both the short ends of the bonnet and topstitch.

2. The bonnet is pulled together in the back with a length of ribbon run through a casing. To make the casing, turn under a ⅜-inch (1) wide hem on the remaining raw edge of the bonnet. Topstitch close to the casing edge (Figure O). Cut a 6-inch (15) length of ¼-inch (0.6) wide white ribbon and thread it through the casing. Gather the bonnet along the ribbon, and tie the ribbon in a bow at the bottom back of the bonnet (Figure P).

3. Cut a 3-inch (7.5) length of white ribbon. Turn one end under and tack it to the front corner of the bonnet. Cut and attach another length of ribbon to the opposite side of the bonnet.

Finishing Details

Baby Gladys is no doubt rather cold, since you've left him undressed all this time. The piece of white cotton fabric will serve as a diaper. Use your own prefered diapering fold and secure with the two tiny safety pins.

Slip the gown over Gladys' head. Sew one half of the snap closure to each side of the back neck opening, and snap them closed. Gather the sleeves ½ inch (1.6) from the bottom edges, using a long basting stitch. Pull the threads until the sleeve ends fit Gladys' wrists, and secure the threads. Put the bonnet on Gladys' head and tie the ribbon ends in a bow underneath his chin.

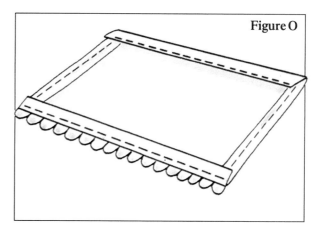

Figure O

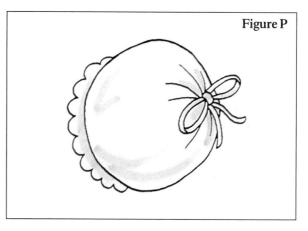

Figure P

Casanova Barnyard (Casey) Weepeeple

Born: March 23, 1872

Casey's legal name is an unusual combination (to say the least), which was produced by two totally unrelated occurrences. Searching for a more formal first name for Casey, Maude noticed the cover of a book entitled *History of My Life*, by Giovanni Jacopo Casanova.

The book had been lent to her by Second-Cousin Wilhelmina, a woman of probable moral turpitude who lived in New York City. Wilhelmina sent the book along with a note recommending it as "a volume of enlightenment." And indeed, when Maude read the book some months later, she was thoroughly enlightened. Had Maude progressed beyond the cover before she named him, Casey would undoubtedly have been called something less suggestive than Casanova.

Casey's middle name was the result of a slightly hard-of-hearing official at the courthouse and of Maude's wish that Casey be named for his father. It seems that when Maude said "Barnard" the clerk heard "Barnyard" and so it was recorded.

This was unknown to anyone outside the family until Casey was required to produce his official birth record on the occasion of his marriage to Victoria Mortimer. Victoria was the only child of an extremely wealthy and socially prominent mortician in Kansas City who, along with his wife, was none too pleased at the prospect of having a son-in-law who made his living with the railroad. Mr. and Mrs. Mortimer had naturally assumed that Victoria would become the bride of one Jonathan Morganstern Brightly III, son of another prominent mortician, and thereby unite the empire. After much pleading they finally acceded to Victoria's wishes, but Mrs. Mortimer drew the line at sending out engraved ivory invitations proclaiming the marriage of her beloved only daughter to a man whose official name was Casanova Barnyard.

After weeks of Victoria's wailings and Mrs. Mortimer's desperate hand-wringing, Mr. Mortimer saved the day by financing a stylish but quiet elopement. Mrs. Mortimer was then able to send out informal announcements on her personalized pale-pink stationery (with the white lilies and gilt rosebuds emblazoned about her initials), and thus tranquilize her abused sensibilities.

Casey and Victoria settled down in a stylish cottage (thanks to Mrs. Mortimer), unstylishly located (thanks to Casey's work) near the railroad tracks. Casey persevered and before his fortieth birthday had achieved the rank of chief engineer.

In spite of their diverse backgrounds, Casey and Victoria had many things in common. She was impressed by social standing, and his work required that he stand most of the time; she thought that it broadened one's outlook to travel, and his work required that he travel most of the time; she felt that people with "new money" were almost always tasteless, and his salary potential prohibited that possibility for them.

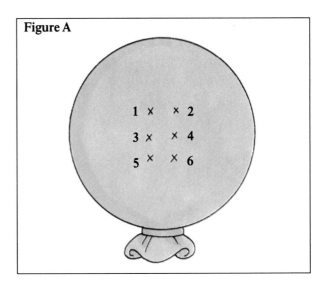

Figure A

Materials and Tools

Metric equivalents in centimeters are indicated in parentheses.

½ yard (0.46 m) of light blue denim fabric, at least 36 inches (90) wide

¼ yard (0.23 m) of navy blue and white striped cotton fabric, at least 36 inches (90) wide

½ yard (0.46 m) of red cotton fabric

6-inch (15) length of single-fold red seam binding, 1 inch (2.5) wide

½ yard (0.46 m) of flesh-colored cotton knit fabric

¼ yard (0.23 m) of black vinyl fabric

Red and white sewing thread

Heavy-duty and regular flesh-colored thread

Six small white buttons

Two 1-inch (2.5) wide buckle fixtures for the overall straps and two metal buttons for the overall sides

½ pound (227 g) of polyester fiberfill

One leg cut from a pair of regular weave flesh-tone pantyhose (or one nylon stocking)

Small brown wiglet (or substitute brown yarn)

Triangular piece of red bandanna fabric, measuring 12 inches (31) along the longest side

2-inch (5) square piece of light weight cardboard or vinyl fabric

Small amount of white paint and a small paint brush (or substitute typewriter correction fluid)

Dark brown and black fine felt-tip markers, pale pink powdered cheek blusher, and white glue

Long sharp needle, scissors, straight pins, and a sewing machine (optional)

Turn to page 154 and make a body for Casey, following the instruction for Making the Arms, Making Legs with Boots, and Making the Torso. Since boot flaps are definitely not regulation railroad issue, skip over the section on Adding the Boot Flaps. Use the scale drawings for the adult-size arm, leg, boot, and torso (Figure A, page 155) to make the full-size patterns.

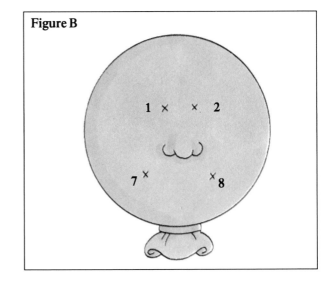

Figure B

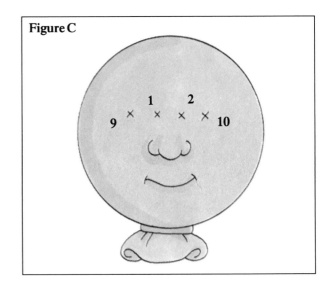

Figure C

Making the Head

1. Cut a 6-inch (15) length from the upper portion of the pantyhose leg or stocking and slit it lengthwise so that you have a flat rectangle.

2. Wrap the rectangle around a large handful of fiberfill. Gather the edges of the hose together and twist to create a head form. The twisted ends will be at the back of the head, just above the neck. (Detailed instructions for stuffing and forming a head are given in the Soft Sculpturing Tips section of this book.) Casey's head should be approximately 12 inches (31) in circumference, measuring around the nose and ear line. It should be at least 4½ inches (11.4) in diameter from top to bottom. Add or remove fiberfill until the head is the correct size, and then wrap the twisted hose tightly with heavy-duty thread.

3. Use a long sharp needle and a 36-inch (91) length of heavy-duty flesh-colored thread to sculpture the facial features. To form Casey's nose, follow the entry and exit points illustrated in Figure A. (Although Casey's nose resembles his father's, it is somewhat straighter. This is due in part to avoiding encounters with hogs, but also in part to his great-great uncle, Jeffrey Perkins, who Maude says was "quite a dandy in his time, owing to the clearness of his eyes and the strength of his nose lines." No one in the family ever mentions that while Jeffrey may have been clear of eye and straight of nose, he was three times tarred, feathered, and run out of town on a rail due to the undue amount of less-than-respectful attention which he paid to certain womenfolk.)

    a. Enter where the hose is tied at the neck, pass through the center of the head, and exit at point 1. Pinch up a vertical ridge, approximately ½ inch (1.3) high, between points 1 and 2. (This will be the bridge of the nose.)

    b. Reenter at 1 and exit at 2. Reenter at 2 and exit at 1, pulling the thread tightly. Keep the thread pulled tightly as you take an additional stitch underneath the surface between points 1 and 2 to secure the ridge. Exit at 1.

    c. Pinch up the nose ridge between points 3 and 4. (These points should be approximately ½ inch [1.3] directly below points 1 and 2.) Pull the thread across the surface, enter at 3 and exit at 4. Pull the thread across the surface, enter at 2 and exit at 1.

    d. Hold the thread with one hand near point 1 to maintain the tension, reenter at 1 and exit at 5. (Points 5 and 6 should be about ½ inch [1.3] below and slightly to the right of points 3 and 4,

but not any lower than the center line of the head.) Pull the thread across the surface, enter at 6 and exit at 2. Pull the thread until the end of the nose appears (between points 5 and 6).

    e. Holding the thread taut, reenter at 2 and exit at 3. Hold the thread tension near point 3, pull the thread across the surface, enter at 6 and exit at 4. Pull the thread across the surface, enter at 5 and exit at 1.

    f. Tighten and hold the thread as you take one or two stitches back and forth under the surface between points 1 and 2 to secure the nose form. Exit at 2.

4. Continue working with the same thread to form Casey's smile, following the entry and exit points illustrated in Figure B. Points 7 and 8 will be the corners of the mouth. They should be 1½ inches (3.8) apart, on a line approximately 1 inch (2.5) below the end of the nose.

    a. Reenter at 2 and exit at 7.

    b. Pull the thread across the surface, enter at 8 and exit at 1.

    c. Pull the thread until a slight smile appears. (Casey considers it thoroughly unprofessional for a chief engineer to smile broadly, but he's a friendly person, so it still peeks through on most occasions.) With one hand, hold tension on the thread near point 1, and with the other hand use the tip of the needle to lift a small amount of additional fiberfill into the upper lip, and into the chin area, forming the chin shape.

    d. Reenter at 1 and take one or two stitches under the surface between points 1 and 2 to secure the stitches. Exit at 1.

5. To form the eyes, follow the entry and exit points illustrated in Figure C. Casey's eye lines are stitched first and then his open eyes are painted on. (Like his great-great uncle, Casey has bright clear eyes. This clearness of eye is no doubt in part responsible for his rise to greatness in railroading. One of the most desirable qualities in a chief engineer is a decisive and confident glance—a take charge appearance—which will enable him to command and direct, and to insure that those in his command will follow him without question in times of great peril. As Barney says, "I ain't never seen a chief engineer with shifty eyes.") Point 9 will be the outside corner of the closed right eye. It should be approximately 1 inch (2.5) directly to the left of point 1. Point 10, the outside corner of the left eye, should be 1 inch (2.5) directly to the right of point 2.

    a. Pull the thread across the surface, enter at 9 and exit at 2.

    b. Pull the thread across the surface, enter at 10 and exit at 1.

    c. Pull the thread gently until eye lines appear. Hold the thread taut and stitch one or two times under the surface between points 1 and 2 to secure the eyes. Exit at 1.

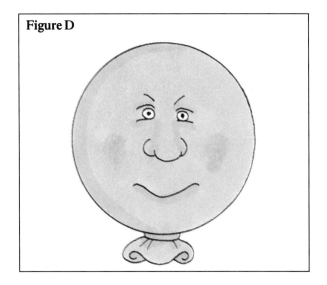

Figure D

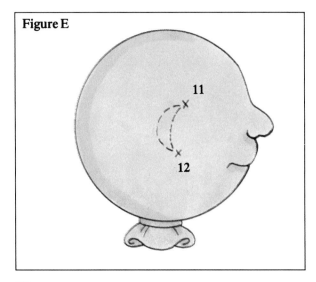

Figure E

11

12

6. Paint a small white circle, about ⅜-inch (1) in diameter, slightly off center on the eye line, closer to the nose than to the outside of the line. Let the paint dry, then add a tiny black circle in the center of the white one. Draw a black line straight across the top of the black circle, as shown in Figure D.

7. Brush powdered blusher on the cheeks. Be sparing with the blusher, since Casey's cheeks are quite a bit less ruddy than they were before his promotion. Now that he has earned the title of chief engineer, he no longer has the duty of sticking his face outside the train window to check the tracks ahead. To create eyebrows, draw them over the eyes using a light brown felt-tip marker.

8. Follow the entry and exit points illustrated in Figure E to sculpture the ears.

> **a.** Enter at the neck and exit at 11. (Point 11, which will be the top of the ear, should be even with the lower end of the nose.) Pinch up a small curved ridge, as shown, just below point 11.
> **b.** Stitch back and forth under the ridge, moving toward point 12 with each stitch. Pull the thread gently until an ear forms. Exit at 12.
> **c.** Lock the stitch behind the ear, reenter at that point, and exit at the neck.
> **d.** Lock the stitch and cut the thread.
> **e.** Repeat steps a through d on the opposite side of the head.

9. Trim the brown wiglet to fit Casey's head, thinning it out at the top. Casey is showing the first signs of balding, which he points to with great pride. Having seen pictures of many great leaders, he observes that almost all of them are bald, and so is pleased with his own progress in that direction. Victoria has noticed the thinning with much less enthusiasm, but consoles herself with the hope that others will simply assume Casey married a much younger woman.

Attaching the Head to the Body

1. Turn a narrow seam allowance to the inside on the neck opening of the body. Gather the neckline ¼ inch (0.6) from the folded edge using heavy-duty, flesh-colored thread. Pull the gathering threads until the opening measures approximately 1 inch (2.5) across.

2. Center the head over the opening, inserting the tied neck portion of the head under the back edge of the neck opening. Whipstitch completely around the neck several times to secure the head to the body. (It would most certainly not do to have a chief engineer who couldn't hold his head up!)

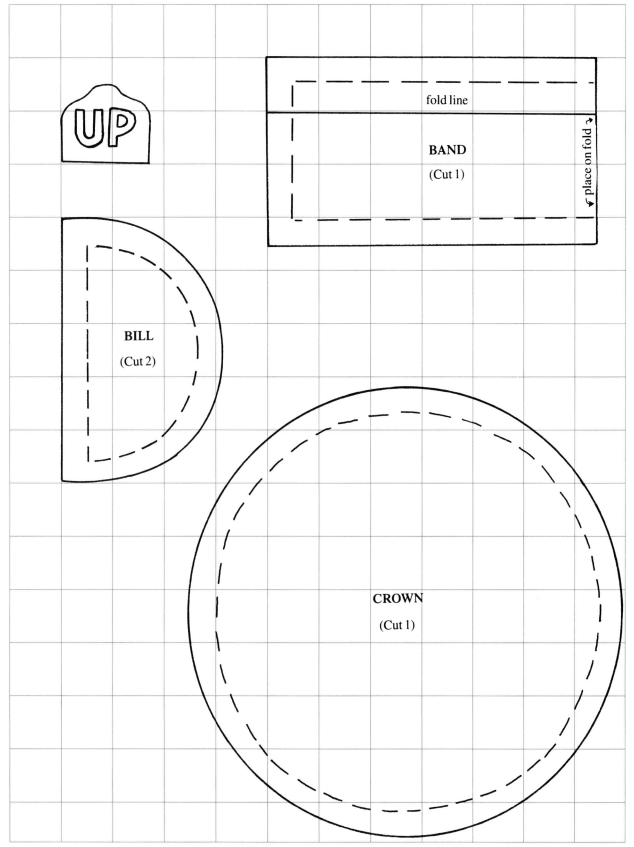

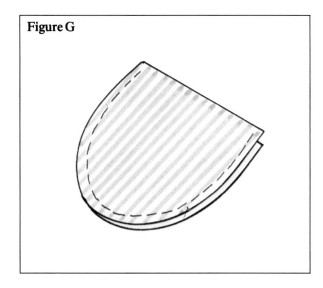

Figure G

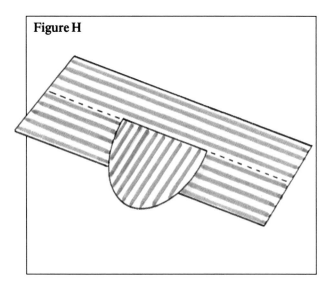

Figure H

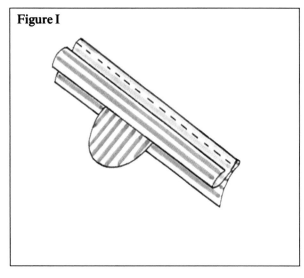

Figure I

Making the Overalls

Casey wears railroading overalls. They are sewn from the same pattern as Barney's and are complete with buckles on the straps. Casey has departed from regulation in only one matter—he absolutely insists that the front pockets be omitted from his overalls. Casey says, "A bib pocket is okay, 'cause you need somewhere to put your railroading pocket watch, but you give a man front pockets and he spends the whole day standing around with his hands inside them. True railroading men keeps them hands working." Turn to page 20 and follow the instructions for making the overalls, substituting light blue denim for the blue and white striped fabric and disregarding all references to front pockets.

Making the Shirt

Casey's shirt is made exactly like Barney's, although it is cut from red cotton fabric. Casey's wardrobe includes two of these shirts, so he always appears in the train yard looking his best. Turn to page 20 and follow the instructions for Making the Shirt, substituting red cotton fabric for Barney's plaid flannel.

Making the Hat

1. Scale drawings for Casey's hat are given in Figure F. Cut the following pieces from blue and white striped cotton fabric: one crown, one band, and two bills. Be sure to transfer the fold line to the band. The railroad officials are most testy about any departure from regulation stripe direction and once summarily dismissed an engineer who insisted on wearing a cap with stripes running diagonally across the bill, so pay particular attention to the grain arrows on the pattern pieces and Casey's stripes will all run in the regulation direction.

2. Place the two bill pieces right sides together and sew a ⅜-inch (1) seam around the entire curved edge (Figure G). Clip the curves, turn the bill right side out, and press.

3. Pin the bill to the center of the band, placing the unstitched edge of the bill along the fold line on the right side of the band fabric (Figure H).

4. Fold the band right sides together along the fold line and pin. Topstitch through all layers, ¼-inch (0.6) from the folded edge (Figure I). Unfold the band and press.

5. Fold the band in half widthwise, right sides together, and sew a ¼-inch (0.6) wide seam along the ends as shown in Figure J.

6. Sew basting stitches completely around the crown, ¼-inch (0.6) from the edge. Pull the threads to form even gathers, so that the crown fits inside the top edge of the brim and band assembly (Figure K). The all-important stripes on the crown should run in the same direction as those on the bill. Adjust the gathers evenly and stitch the crown in place.

7. Fold a ¼-inch (0.6) hem to the wrong side around the remaining raw edge of the band and topstitch. Turn the hat right side out.

8. Fold the band in half, wrong sides together, turning the hemmed edge to the inside, and press. Whipstitch the hemmed edge over the gathered edge of the crown inside the hat.

9. Cut a piece of cardboard or vinyl for the hat emblem. Carefully letter "UP" in the center of the emblem and outline the edges using a black felt-tip marker. Glue the emblem to the front of Casey's hat, just above the bill.

Finishing Details

Dress Casey in his shirt and overalls. Pull the overall straps to the front and tack the ends over the upper edge of the bib. Sew a buckle to each strap.

The waist edge of the overalls will be larger than Casey's waist. Every railroading man is proud of his physical conditioning and Casey is no exception. When he is between railroading trips, he works out at home by constantly moving and rearranging furniture for Victoria. As Casey remarked to a brakeman who admired his physical strength, "You move an armoire up and down three flights of stairs once a week, and you'll get in shape too!" Fold the excess fabric into a pleat at each side of the waist, making the pleats as even as possible. Tack the pleats in place, and sew a metal button over each.

Hem the lower edge of each overall leg to fit Casey's leg length.

Tie the red bandanna triangle around Casey's neck for a neckerchief. (Victoria insists that it is more properly called a cravat by gentlemen of refinement, to which Casey replies that the refined gentlemen can call it whatever they like — he figures the thing you use to wipe coal dust and sweat off your face is called a neckerchief.)

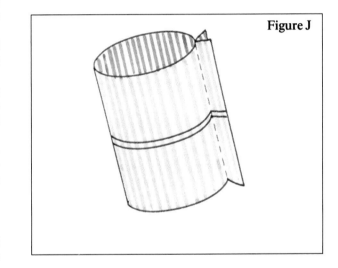

Figure J

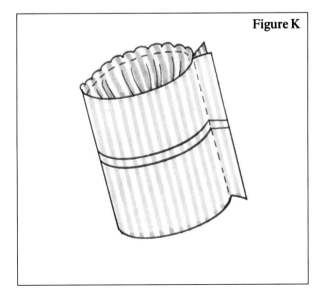

Figure K

Victoria Josephine Cleopatra (never Vicky) Mortimer Weepeeple

Born: May 17, 1875

On this date in history, two important events occurred. First and foremost was a birth in the household of the well- known and highly respected Mortimers of Kansas City. The lesser important event was the first running of the Kentucky Derby at Churchill Downs in Louisville, Kentucky.

The socially prominent Mortimers had been invited by the Governor of Kentucky to attend the opening ceremonies and subsequent thoroughbred horse race. Due to her delicate condition, however, Mrs. Mortimer was in her "period of confinement" and fortunately refused to leave the house.

Victoria, who was named after the reigning queen of Great Britain, was protected, pampered, and treated as royalty from birth. She was dressed in lace, had round-the-clock nurses, and (since her mother felt it would be socially unacceptable) never spit up in public.

At the tender age of four, Victoria was enrolled by her mother in Miss Chastity's School for Well-Bred Courteous Genteel and Refined Young Ladies. There she distinguished herself in needlework and table conversation, and never once had to be reprimanded for saying or doing anything useful. In addition, she took private lessons in organ playing and perfect posture from Miss Elvina Stoop.

When Victoria matriculated (with honors) from Miss Chastity's at the age of fifteen, Mrs. Mortimer began making plans for her daughter's social debut and subsequent marriage to Jonathan Morganstern Brightly III. The debut, Mrs. Mortimer decided, would begin with a series of tastefully intimate teas, to which everyone who was anyone would be invited by gilt engraved invitation. The season would culminate with a lavish cotillion, to be held in the newly completed and world famous Golden Swan Ballroom of the Royal Stockyards Hotel.

For months Mrs. Mortimer labored over every minute detail, making sure that the dance cards were printed correctly, that fittings were properly scheduled for Victoria's gown which was en route from Paris, and on and on. Flowers, of course, were not a major concern since there were always many lovely arrangements at Mr. Mortimer's place of business. The orchestra at one point looked as if it might be a problem, but in the end the Kansas City Philharmonic was able to reschedule its concert season to accommodate the Mortimers.

On the Sunday morning following the grand event, each and every one of the five thousand invited guests agreed that it was the crowning glory of the social season. Since Mr. Brightly III had not yet formally proposed, Mrs. Mortimer whisked Victoria away to tour the continent (European, of course), feeling certain that Mr. Brightly III would come to his senses during Victoria's absence. Victoria was most agreeable to the trip, since she was not at all fond of Mr. Brightly III, or of the prospect of spending the rest of her life as she had spent the first part—in the home of a mortician. Fortunately, the arrival of Casey changed Mrs. Mortimer's plans.

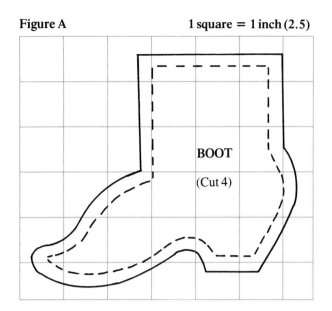

BOOT

(Cut 4)

Turn to page 154 and make a body for Victoria, following instructions for Making the Torso and Making Legs with Boots. Although the boots are assembled and attached to the legs in the same manner as Maude's, they are cut from an entirely different pattern, owing to the fact that they were custom-made in Kansas City and are of the latest fashion. It goes without saying that Victoria would never purchase ready-made boots which have been on the shelves and "subjected to being tried on by common everyday riffraff." So enlarge the pattern given in Figure A above and use it to cut the beige leather or vinyl pieces for Victoria's boots. In keeping with the stylish design, Victoria's boots have no flaps, so skip the section on Adding the Flaps. Follow the instructions for Making the Arms, but do not sculpture the fingers because Victoria always wears lace gloves.

Use the scale drawings for adult-sized arm, leg, and torso (Figure A, page 155) to make the full-size patterns, but sew the waistline a tiny bit smaller, as it is somewhat more petite after years of wearing a corset to bed. Victoria overheard that particular beauty secret while seated behind a rather bushy palm plant in an extremely posh restaurant. She never knew the source of the information, but has strictly adhered to the practice since that time. She finds that it is not terribly difficult to sleep wearing a corset, and over the years it has reduced her waistline by an entire $\frac{1}{8}$ (0.3) inch.

Materials and Tools

Metric equivalents in centimeters are indicated in parentheses

½ yard (0.46 m) of blue velvet (or substitute any equally ostentatious fabric)

¼ yard (0.23 m) of beige soft leather or textured vinyl

½ yard (0.46 m) of white eyelet fabric

8-inch (20) square of lace fabric

½ yard (0.46 m) of white taffeta

½ yard (0.46 m) of flesh-colored cotton knit fabric

One leg cut from a pair of regular weave flesh-tone pantyhose (or one nylon stocking)

Small blonde wiglet (or substitute pale yellow yarn)

12-inch (30) length of gold, bead, and lace trim 1½ inches (4) wide

6-inch (15) length of 2-inch (5) wide ornate trim—we used white pleated satin with lace on each side

½ yard (0.46 m) of 5-inch (13) wide white eyelet trim

White, black, and red acrylic paint and a fine-tipped artist's paint brush

½ yard (0.46 m) of 1-inch (2.5) or ¾-inch (1.9) wide white satin ribbon

Regular and heavy duty flesh-colored sewing thread

Regular and heavy duty white sewing thread

Royal blue sewing thread

½ pound (227 g) of polyester fiberfill

One hook and eye closure

Rhinestone earrings, pale pink powdered cheek blusher, blonde hairpins, and white glue

Long sharp needle, scissors, straight pins, and a sewing machine (optional)

Adding the Gloves

1. Cut the enlarged arm pattern just above the wrist, and use the hand portion to cut four glove pieces from the white lace fabric. Place two lace glove pieces right sides together and sew a ¼-inch (0.6) wide seam around the outer edges, leaving the wrist open and unstitched.

2. Turn the glove right side out, turn a tiny hem to the inside around the wrist, and whipstitch it in place. Fit the finished glove over Victoria's hand.

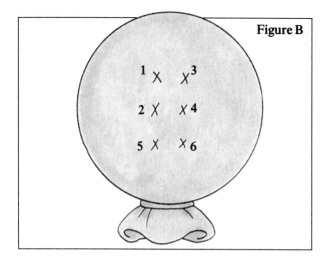

Figure B

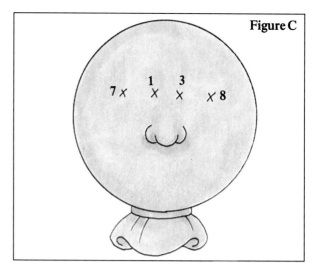

Figure C

3. Repeat the procedure to make the glove for the other hand. Proceed with the instructions to sculpture the fingers (over the gloves), substituting heavy-duty white thread for the usual flesh-colored.

Making the Head

1. Tie the pantyhose leg or stocking into a tight knot near the open end, and cut the hose 6 inches (15) below the knot. Turn, so that the knot is on the inside.

2. Stuff a generous amount of fiberfill inside the hose, manipulating the shape until a head is formed. (Detailed instructions for stuffing and forming a head are given in the Soft Sculpturing Tips section of this book.) Victoria's head should be at least 12 inches (31) in circumference, measuring around the nose and ear line. It should be approximately 4½ inches (11) in diameter from top to bottom. Tie the stuffed hose in a knot at the open (neck) end.

3. Use a long sharp needle and a 36-inch (90) length of heavy-duty flesh-colored thread to sculpture the facial features following the entry and exit points illustrated in Figure B. Since Victoria is a Weepeeple by marriage and not by blood relationship, her nose is noticeably different from the rest of the clan. She is quite vain about her nose, and speculates that the Mortimers were probably descended from the Greeks. (After all, she reasons, her nose is very much like the one on the genuine plaster bust in her mother's entry hall).

    a. Enter where the hose is knotted at the neck, pass through the center of the head, and exit at point 1. Pull the thread across the surface, enter at 2 and exit at 3. Enter at 4 and exit at 1. Pull the thread to form the straight Grecian bridge of the nose. Maintain the tension and lock the stitch.

    b. To form the nostrils, reenter at 3 and exit at 5. Reenter just slightly above 5 and exit at 3. Pull the thread firmly and lock the stitch. Reenter at 3 and exit at 6. Reenter just slightly above 6 and exit at 1. Pull the thread firmly and lock the stitch.

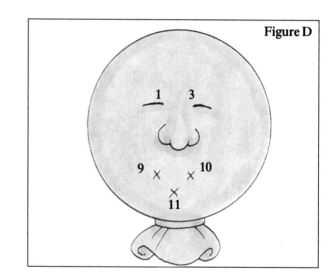

Figure D

4. Victoria's eye lines are stitched and then her open eyes are painted on. To stitch the eye lines, use the same length of thread, and follow the entry and exit points indicated in Figure C.

    a. Pull the thread across the surface, enter at 7 and exit at 3.

    b. Pull the thread across the surface, enter at 8 and exit at 1. Pull the thread to form the eye lines, maintain the tension, and lock the stitch.

5. Victoria's mouth is also shaped differently from the Weepeeple mouth. She uses lip rouge (to enhance her natural beauty), and is most careful to obtain just the right heart shape when she applies it. To form Victoria's mouth, follow the entry and exit points illustrated in Figure D.

    a. Reenter at 3 and exit at 9. Pull the thread across the surface, enter at 10 and exit at 1. Pull the thread firmly until the mouth line appears, and lock the stitch.

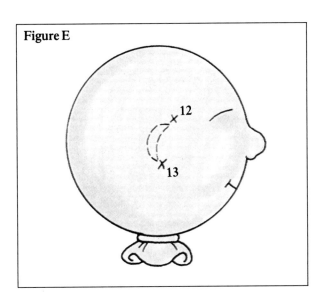

Figure E

Figure F

b. Victoria's bottom lip is formed by taking one additional stitch just below the mouth line. Reenter at 1 and exit at 11. Enter just barely to the left of point 11, and exit at 3. Pull the thread firmly, and lock the stitch.

c. Reenter at 3 and exit at the bottom of the neck near the tied knot. Lock the stitch and cut the thread.

6. Follow the entry and exit points illustrated in Figure E to sculpture Victoria's ears.

a. Enter at the neck knot and exit at 12. (Point 12, which will be the top of the ear, should be even with the lower portion of the nose.) Pinch up a small curved ridge at an angle, as shown, just below point 12.

b. Stitch back and forth under the ridge, moving toward point 13 with each stitch, and pulling the thread gently until an ear forms. Exit at point 13.

c. Lock the stitch behind the ear, reenter at that point, and exit at the neck knot.

d. Lock the stitch and cut the thread.

e. Repeat steps a through d on the opposite side of the head.

7. Trim the (naturally) blonde wiglet to fit Victoria's head and glue it in place. Comb the hair up to the top of the head, arrange it in a bun of curls, and secure it with hairpins. Victoria has her hair done once a week at the beauty salon just down the street from home. She would prefer to continue patronizing Monsieur Jacque's Salon of Beauty, which she frequented prior to her marriage to Casey (the same establishment which Mrs. Mortimer has visited on a weekly basis for many years). However, since Casey's salary precludes such excesses, she contents herself with a weekly visit to Sue's Haircut and Quick Message Delivery Service. She has, through the years, built up Sue's clientele by recommending her to the wives of other engineers, and so is treated in royal fashion.

8. Follow the illustration in Figure F to paint Victoria's eyes and mouth. Paint a softly edged triangle of white on the upper edge of each eyeline. Add a small black circle in the center of the white. Draw a short, straight, solid black line over the top of the circle, and lightly brush black over the entire upper edge of the white triangle, widening it over the outer corners of the eyes. Paint small arched eyebrows over the eyes. (For some inexplicable reason, although Victoria's hair is naturally blonde, she has black eyebrows). Finish her makeup by painting a small heart-shaped mouth using red paint.

Attaching the Head to the Body

1. Turn a narrow seam allowance to the inside on the neck opening of the body. Gather the neckline ¼ inch (0.6) from the folded edge, using heavy-duty flesh-colored thread. Pull the gathering threads until the opening measures approximately 1 inch (2.5) across.

2. Center the head over the opening, inserting the tied neck portion inside the body. Make certain that the head is positioned so that Victoria's nose points slightly upward, to enable her to look down it when necessary. Whipstitch completely around the neck several times to secure the head to the body.

Making the Blouse and Skirt

1. Although Victoria's clothes are obviously expensive, they are sewn from the same pattern as Maude's dress (a fact which Victoria does not wish to become common knowledge). A few crucial changes, however, must be made. Use the full-size patterns that you made from the scale drawings on pages 31 through 33, and cut one front bodice, two back bodices, and two sleeves from white eyelet fabric. Cut one skirt from blue velvet fabric. Follow the instructions for making Maude's dress on pages 33 and 34, steps 1 through 5.

2. Pin the 6-inch (15) length of wide satin and lace trim down the center front of the bodice and topstitch it in place along the edges of the satin.

3. To finish the neckline, turn under a ¼-inch (0.6) hem and topstitch. Topstitch the gold and lace neckline trim over the hemmed edge.

4. Turn under a ½-inch hem along the bottom edge of each sleeve and stitch. To make casings for the elastic, stitch wide white seam tape to the wrong side of each sleeve, even with the hemmed edge (Figure G). Stitch along both sides of the seam tape, leaving a small opening in the stitching to insert the elastic.

5. Measure Victoria's wrist and cut a piece of elastic 1 inch (2.5) longer. Thread the elastic through the sleeve casing. Stitch the ends of the elastic securely together and pull it back inside the casing. Whipstitch the opening in the casing together. Repeat on the other sleeve.

6. Dress Victoria in the bodice, so that it can be professionally fitted to her tastefully tiny waistline. Divide the excess fabric at the waist into six equal front pleats, placing three pleats on each side of the center trim (Figure H). Baste the pleats in place, and the fitting is complete.

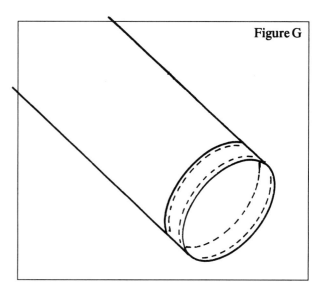

Figure G

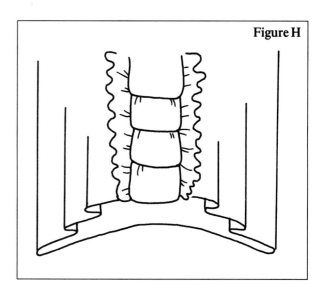

Figure H

Figure I

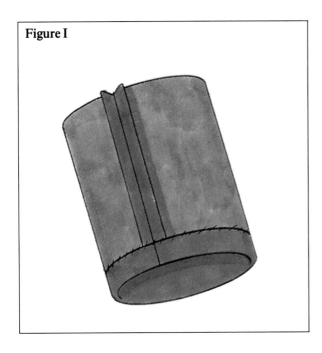

Figure K

Figure J

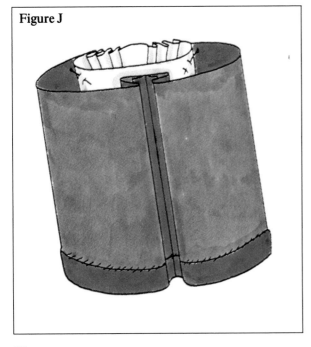

7. Fold the skirt right sides together, and stitch the center back seam. Press the seam open. Turn and stitch a 1½-inch (3.8) deep hem along the lower edge (Figure I).

8. Rather than being gathered evenly all the way around, Victoria's skirt is fitted straight across the front and pleated and gathered in the back. Pin the center front of the skirt to the center front of the bodice, placing right sides together. Smooth and pin the skirt flat against the bodice front. Pin the skirt to the side seams of the bodice. Fold a 2½-inch (6.4) wide double pleat in the skirt at the center back, as shown in Figure J. Gather the remaining skirt waistline (between the double pleat and the side seam of the bodice on each side), and ease the gathers to fit as shown in Figure K. Stitch the skirt to the bodice.

9. Turn the skirt and bodice right side out and press the waist seam toward the skirt. To create the swagged hemline, gently gather the left side of the skirt by running a long basting stitch from the bottom of the hem half way up the skirt. Pull the gathering thread and take another small stitch to anchor it in place. Tie the 1-inch (2.5) wide white satin ribbon in a bow and hand tack it to the skirt at the top of the gathers.

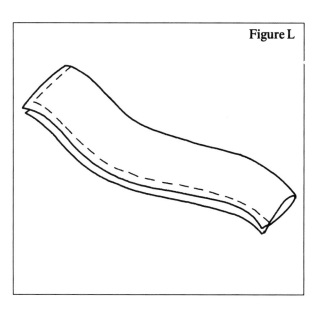

Figure L

Making the Slip

1. Victoria wears an eyelet-flounced slip underneath her blue velvet skirt. Use the same skirt pattern to cut the slip, but cut only one thickness for the slip, disregarding the "place on fold" notation on the pattern piece. This will make the slip only half as full as the skirt. Cut one slip from white taffeta fabric.

2. Fold the slip right sides together and stitch the center back seam. Press the seam open. To make a casing for the elastic at the waist, turn and stitch a ½-inch (1.3) wide hem around the top edge of the slip. Leave a small opening in the stitching to insert the elastic.

3. Measure Victoria's waist, and cut a piece of elastic 1 inch (2.5) longer. Thread the elastic through the waist casing. Stitch the ends of the elastic securely together and pull it back inside the casing. Whipstitch the opening in the casing together.

4. Topstitch the 5-inch (13) wide eyelet trim on the right side of the slip, placing the bottom of the trim even with the bottom raw edge of the slip. Trim away the excess taffeta underneath the stitched trim.

Making the Bloomers

Victoria's bloomers are sewn from the same pattern as Maude's, but they are cut from white taffeta fabric. Turn to page 34 and follow the instructions for making the bloomers, substituting the white taffeta for the cotton in the directions.

Making the Sash

1. To make the tie for the waist, cut a white taffeta rectangle 36 x 6 inches (90 x 15). Fold the rectangle lengthwise, right sides together, and stitch the raw edges, leaving one narrow end open and unstitched (Figure L).

2. Turn the sash right side out and press. Turn the remaining raw edges to the inside and whipstitch the opening together.

Finishing Details

Dress Victoria in her bloomers and slip. Sew the hook and eye closure to the back neckline of the bodice, and place it over her head (being most careful not to muss her coiffure). Tie the sash around her waist, ending with a soft double knot at the back. Blouse out the front of her bodice. (Although nature was certainly not generous with Victoria in this department, she accentuates what she does have.) To finish the illusion, glue or sew the rhinestone earrings to Victoria's ear lobes.

Brentwood Theodore Weepeeple

Born: July 24, 1902

Brentwood was the firstborn, long awaited, eagerly anticipated, only child of Victoria and Casey Weepeeple. He had a somewhat confusing early childhood. Half of it was spent happily tagging after his father in the train yard examining the undercarriages of railroad cars and engaging in other such grimy pastimes. The other half was spent in the front parlor at home, under the close scrutiny of his mother and Miss Stoop. Ordinarily, Miss Stoop did not accept young gentlemen students, but Victoria finally convinced her (with gentle pleas and thinly veiled threats) that Brentwood's upbringing would seriously suffer if he did not receive the benefits of Miss Stoop's long experience and vast knowledge.

Initially, Casey and Victoria had a number of fallings out concerning Brentwood's training and education. However, a compromise was reached whereby Brentwood would attend Mr. Smythe's School for Aspiring Gentlemen and Miss Stoop's organ and posture classes during the week. On the weekends, he would be tutored in the manly arts of hog slopping and railroading. This system worked quite well for a number of years. Brentwood was a flexible child and did his best to please both parents, which was no mean feat.

As Brentwood's high school graduation approached, however, the contrasting views of his parents began to reemerge. Victoria felt that the only choice to be made was between Harvard and Yale, whereas Casey was more inclined to think that his son would be happier going right to work for the railroad. Brentwood solved the problem by packing his bags and announcing his intention of attending the Rolla School of Mines. For a week Victoria was inconsolable. Casey was in Colorado.

Victoria slowly recovered, assisted by Casey's description of the benefits Brentwood would derive from his decision. In training as a future businessman, he would learn to relate to all kinds of people. He would meet the sons of the great mining magnates of America, who doubtless had eligible daughters of high standing. And then, he could always attend Yale graduate school at a later date.

The spell was broken when Brentwood returned home for the holidays. Doffing his racoon coat on the French provincial settee in the entrance hall, he kissed his mother loudly and excused his lateness by explaining that he and his roommate Paul had, "parked our dogs on the main drag, when a real Sheba invited us to a ritzy speak-easy. I told her, 'Nerts!' but Paul was keen on the idea and said it was hotsy-totsy with him. So we hopped in her struggle-buggy and told her we were ready to make some whoopee. We arrived at a swanky hotel, and were drinkin' really good hooch when the cops showed up and we had to scram." Whereupon, Victoria's eyes widened, then closed as she sank onto her best flowered carpet.

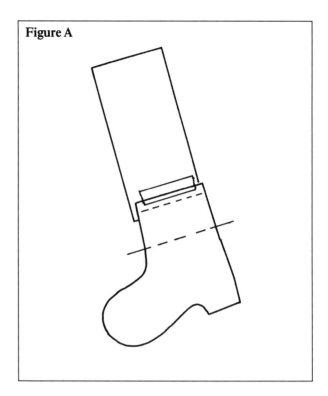

Figure A

Materials and Tools

Metric equivalents in centimeters are indicated in parentheses.

1 yard (0.9 m) of white cotton fabric, at least
36 inches (90) wide

6-inch (15) length of 1-inch (2.5) wide single-fold
white seam binding

½ yard (0.46 m) of flesh-colored cotton knit fabric

⅛ yard (0.15 m) of black vinyl fabric

¼ yard (0.23 m) of white cotton broadcloth (or other
heavy fabric)

Pair of adult-size argyle socks (from which the vest
will be made) in your choice of colors

½ yard (0.46 m) of ¾-inch (2) wide striped grosgrain
ribbon in a color to coordinate with the socks

White sewing thread

Six small white buttons

Heavy-duty and regular flesh-colored thread

½ pound (227 g) of polyester fiberfill

One leg cut from a pair of regular weave flesh-tone
pantyhose (or one nylon stocking)

Small dark brown wiglet (or substitute brown yarn)

White and black acrylic paint and an artist's fine-
tipped paint brush

Pale pink powdered cheek blusher and white glue

Long sharp needle, scissors, straight pins, and a
sewing machine (optional)

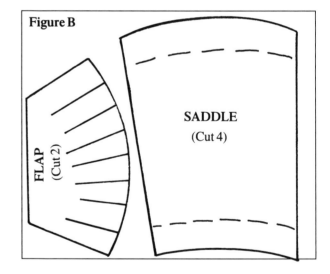

Figure B

Turn to page 154 and make a body for Brentwood, following the instructions for Making the Arms, and Making the
Torso. Since Brentwood is in college (voo-doo-dee-ohh),
use the full-size adult patterns. Brentwood wears saddle
shoes, so some adjustments must be made under the section entitled Making Legs with Boots.

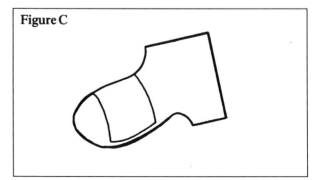

Figure C

1. Enlarge the adult boot and leg patterns to full size, and tape them together, overlapping the seam allowance, as shown in Figure A. Cut through the taped pattern at the ankle, to create two new patterns—a longer leg and a low-cut shoe.

2. Full-size patterns for the black "saddle" across Brentwood's shoe and the fringed flap are given in Figure B. Cut four saddles and two flaps from black vinyl. Cut the fringe on each of the flaps following the cutting lines provided on the patterns.

3. Cut four low-cut shoes from the white broadcloth and four legs from flesh-colored cotton knit. Glue the black saddle over the instep of the white shoe, matching seam allowances as shown in Figure C. Repeat the procedure to add the saddles to the remaining three shoe pieces.

4. Finish sewing the legs and shoes as described under Making Legs with Boots.

5. Glue a fringed flap over the top of each finished shoe. (Brentwood first became enamored of saddle shoes on a shopping trip in downtown Columbia. Stopping to window shop in front of a shoe store, Brentwood remarked, "I want those shoes in the window." To which Amanda immediately replied, "That's no problem, they already are in the window.")

Making the Head

1. Tie the pantyhose leg or stocking into a tight knot near the open end and cut the hose 6 inches (15) below the knot. Turn, so that the knot is on the inside.

2. Stuff a generous amount of fiberfill inside the hose, manipulating the shape until a head is formed (Detailed instructions for stuffing and forming a head are given in the Soft Sculpturing Tips section of this book.) Brentwood's head should be approximately 12 inches (31) in circumference (but no smaller), measuring around the nose and ear line. It should be at least 4½ inches (11.5) in diameter from top to bottom. Tie the stuffed hose in a tight knot at the open (neck) end.

3. Use a long sharp needle and a 36-inch (90) length of heavy-duty flesh-colored thread to sculpture the facial features. Since he is the son of Casey and Victoria, Brentwood's nose is a rather handsome combination of the two—somewhat smaller than his father's and much less upturned than his mother's. Follow the entry and exit points illustrated in Figure D.

    a. Enter where the hose is tied at the neck, pass through the center of the head, and exit at point 1. Pinch up a vertical ridge, approximately ½-inch (1.3) high, between points 1 and 2. (This will be the bridge of the nose.)

    b. Reenter at 1 and exit at 2. Reenter at 2 and exit at 1, pulling the thread tightly. Keep the thread pulled tightly as you take an additional stitch underneath the surface between points 1 and 2 to secure the ridge. Exit at 1.

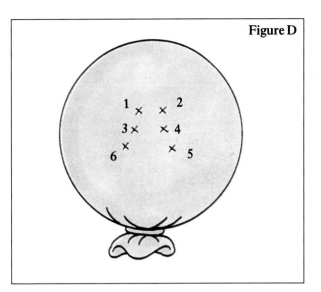

Figure D

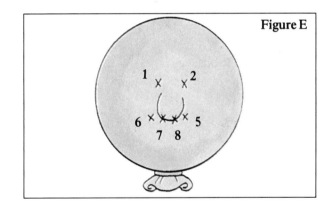

Figure E

    c. Pinch up the nose ridge between points 3 and 4. These points should be approximately ⅜ inch (1) directly below points 1 and 2. Pull the thread across the surface, enter at 3 and exit at 4. Pull the thread across the surface, enter at 2 and exit at 1.

    d. Hold the thread with one hand near point 1 to maintain the tension, reenter at 1 and exit at 5. (Points 5 and 6 should be about ½ inch [1.3] below and slightly wider apart than points 3 and 4). Pull the thread across the surface, enter at 6 and exit at 2. Pull the thread until the end of the nose appears (between points 5 and 6).

    e. Holding the threat taut, reenter at 2 and exit at 3. Hold the thread tension near point 3, pull the thread across the surface, enter at 6 and exit at 4. Pull the thread across the surface, enter at 5 and exit at 1.

    f. Tighten and hold the thread as you take one or two stitches back and forth under the surface between points 1 and 2 to secure the nose form. Exit at 2.

4. Continue working with the same thread to form the nostrils. Follow the entry and exit points shown in Figure E.

a. Reenter at 2 and exit at 8. Reenter slightly above 8 and exit at 2. Pull the thread until a nostril forms and lock the stitch.

b. Reenter at 2 and exit at 1. Reenter at 1 and exit at 7. Reenter slightly above 7 and exit at 1. Pull the thread until a second nostril appears, then lock the stitch.

c. Reenter at 1 and exit at 7. Pull the thread around the tip of the nose, enter at 6 and exit at 8. Pull the thread gently around the other side of the nose, enter at 5 and exit at 7. Pull the thread gently across the bottom of the nose, enter at 8 and exit at 2. Lock the stitch.

5. Continue working with the same thread to create Brentwood's smile, following the entry and exit points illustrated in Figure F.

a. Reenter at 2 and exit at 9.

b. Pull the thread across the surface, enter at 10 and exit at 1.

c. Pull the thread until a smile appears. With one hand, hold tension on the thread near point 1. With the other hand use the tip of the needle to gently lift the fiberfill above the smile and into the chin area.

d. Reenter at 1 and take one or two stitches under the surface between points 1 and 2 to secure the stitches. Exit at 1.

6. Brentwood's eye lines are first stitched, then his eyes are painted on. To form the eye lines, follow the entry and exit points illustrated in Figure G. Point 11 will be the outside corner of the right eye line. It should be approximately 1 inch (2.5) directly to the left of point 1. Point 12, the corner of the left eye line, should be 1 inch (2.5) directly to the right of point 2.

a. Pull the thread across the surface, enter at 11 and exit at 2.

b. Pull the thread across the surface, enter at 12 and exit at 1.

c. Pull the thread gently until the eye lines appear. Hold the thread taut and stitch one or two times under the surface between points 1 and 2 to secure the eyes, exiting at 1. Reenter at 1, exit at the neck knot, lock the stitch, and cut the thread.

7. Follow the illustrations given in Figure H to paint Brentwood's eyes and eyebrows. Paint a flat white oval above the eye line on each side of the nose. Paint a black circle in the center of each white oval. Paint a black line above each white oval at an angle, extending from the top of the inner eye to the outer corner.

8. Follow the entry and exit points illustrated in Figure I to sculpture Brentwood's ears.

a. Enter at the neck and exit at 13. (Point 13, which will be the top of the ear, should be even with the lower end of the nose.) Pinch up a small curved ridge, as shown, just below point 13.

b. Stitch back and forth under the ridge, moving toward point 14 with each stitch. Pull the thread gently until an ear forms. Exit at 14.

c. Lock the stitch behind the ear, reenter at that point, and exit at the neck.

d. Lock the stitch and cut the thread.

e. Repeat steps a through d on the opposite side of the head.

9. Brush a small amount of powdered cheek blusher on Brentwood's cheeks. Trim the wiglet to fit his head and glue it in place. (During his freshman year, Brentwood wore his hair in the classic center-part style and slicked it down with macassar oil. But he decided to change the style when an overzealous application of oil caused his hat to stick firmly in place for several days running. His currently preferred style is more of a dry look, but can't really be described as well-groomed, much to the dismay of his mother and to the delight of Amanda.)

Attaching the Head to the Body

1. Turn a narrow seam allowance to the inside on the neck opening of the body. Gather the neckline ¼ inch (0.6) from the folded edge using heavy-duty, flesh-colored thread. Pull the gathering threads until the opening measures approximately 1 inch (2.5) across.

2. Center the head over the opening, inserting the tied neck portion of the head inside the neck opening. Whipstitch completely around the neck several times to secure the head to the body.

Making the Trousers

Brentwood's trousers are fashionable "Oxford bags." The pleated waistline makes them comfortable, stylish, and convenient for concealing a hip flask, in which Brentwood assures Victoria he carries an emergency supply of buttermilk. When Victoria first discovered the flask, she confronted Brentwood with it, and informed him that whiskey kills more people than bullets. Brentwood replied that that's only because bullets don't drink.

1. Turn to page 21 and enlarge the scale drawing for the overalls to full size adding 1 inch (2.5) to the bottom of the leg to allow for the addition of a cuff. Use this pattern to cut two trousers pieces for Brentwood from white cotton, paying particular attention to the "place on fold" notation.

2. Follow step 5 on page 23 to assemble the trousers.

3. Fold and pin four equal pleats in the waistline, placing two pleats on each side of the center front seam. The pleated waistline should measure ½ inch (1.3) larger than Brentwood's waist. When the pleats are correct, topstitch around the waistline ¼ inch (0.6) from the edge.

4. Turn under a ¼-inch (0.6) wide hem around the waistline, and topstitch it in place. Turn under a 1-inch (2.5) hem along the lower edge of each leg, press, and stitch. Turn up a ½-inch (1.3) cuff and press.

Making the Shirt

Brentwood's shirt is made exactly like Barney's, although it is cut from white cotton fabric. Turn to page 23 and follow the instructions for Making the Shirt, substituting white cotton fabric for Barney's plaid flannel.

Making the Vest

You will be making Brentwood's vest from a pair of argyle socks. Brentwood's actual vest was knitted by Amanda, in her first (and last) attempt at needlework. Because of the complexity of knitting the argyle pattern, Amanda was forced to unravel and restart the knitting nine different times. On the tenth failure, Amanda's roommate directed her to Mrs. Goodfingers, a kindly local lady known for her knitting prowess. Mrs. Goodfingers was only too delighted to finish the project for a very reasonable fee. Amanda was relieved, to say the least. Brentwood was overjoyed. Victoria was in disgrace. Casey was in Newark.

1. Cut the top 9 inches (23) from one argyle sock above the ankle and slit it lengthwise so you have a flat rectangle. This will be the front of the sweater. Repeat the procedure on the remaining sock to cut a sweater back. On each of these pieces the ribbed upper edge of the sock will form the lower (waist) edge of the sweater.

2. On the sweater front, cut a V-shaped wedge in the middle of the upper edge to form the V-neck, as shown in Figure J.

3. Place the front and back pieces right sides together and stitch the shoulder seams. Stitch the side seams as shown in Figure K, leaving the top 3 inches (7.6) open and unstitched for the armholes. Turn a ¼-inch (0.6) wide hem to the inside around each armhole opening and topstitch the hems.

4. To form the neckline facing, cut a strip of argyle sock 12 inches (30.5) long and 1½ (3.8) inches wide (if necessary, it can be pieced at the center point). Pin the strip to the neckline of the vest, placing right sides together. Begin and end at the center front (Figure L). Stitch the strip to the neckline, sewing a ¼-inch (0.6) seam.

5. Turn under a ¼-inch (0.6) hem along the remaining long raw edge of the strip, and fold the strip wrong sides together so that the hemmed edge is even with the sewn seamline. Whipstitch the hemmed edge to the inside of the sweater.

6. Cut away any excess at the center front of the strip, turn the raw edges to the inside, and whipstitch the folded edges together to form the center front of the V.

Finishing Details

Dress Brentwood in his shirt and trousers. Wrap the grosgrain ribbon around his neck under the collar and tie a windsor knot at the center front. Pull the V-neck sweater over his head.

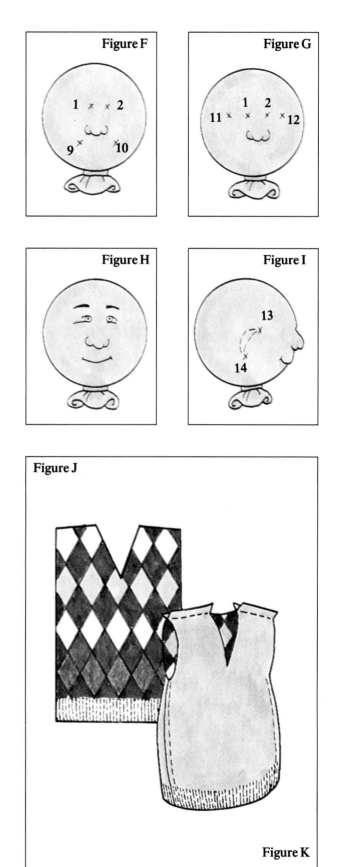

Figure F

Figure G

Figure H

Figure I

Figure J

Figure K

Gertrude Hortense (Amanda) Collingwood Weepeeple

Born: February 14, 1903

"Don't call me that!" were the first words little Gertrude Hortense Collingwood ever uttered. (She was, of course, referring to her given names.) Her mother was somewhat abashed (not to mention amazed that her daughter had learned to speak), because Gertrude Hortense had been named after the two kind and generous maiden aunts who had raised Mrs. Collingwood. By the time Amanda was five years old Mrs. Collingwood had capitulated, due to Amanda's frequent tirades which had resulted in a correspondingly frequent change of nurses. And so, when the thirty-second nurse arrived, Mrs. Collingwood introduced her daughter as Amanda.

The Collingwoods were an almost-socially-prominent family in Sedalia, Missouri. Mr. Collingwood was the proprietor of the Collingwood General Store & Seed Supply and did a brisk business. He was a good man and well-respected in the community, and could be counted on to extend credit in lean farming years. And so his business prospered.

The growth of the business did not pass Mrs. Collingwood by. With the birth of Amanda she immediately started planning for the day when Amanda would marry into the Beauchamps family, who owned everything that was anything in Sedalia (except, of course, for the Collingwood General Store & Seed Supply). But Mrs. Collingwood's plans fell apart immediately after Amanda's first date with Eldred Beauchamps. In response to her mother's inquiry about the eligible bachelor, Amanda replied, "That's what happens when cousins marry cousins."

As Amanda approached the end of her high school days, she expressed a desire to continue her education at the University of Missouri. Appalled, Mrs. Collingwood finally agreed to allow Amanda to enroll at Stephens College in Columbia, which she considered a more suitable atmosphere for a refined young lady. And so she filled Amanda's suitcases with demure full-length, high-necked, long-sleeved dresses, several pairs of white gloves, and a long list of do's and don't's—mostly don't's.

Upon her arrival at Stephens College, Amanda immediately set about putting things right. She discovered that if she removed the sleeves, yoke, and lower three feet from each dress, she was able to fashion matching headbands and hip sashes for the now low-necked, sleeveless garments. The one dress she was unable to convert remained in her closet in readiness for her occasional visits home.

The era of the twenties struck a harmonious chord in Amanda Collingwood, and so did Brentwood Weepeeple when she met him at a campus bonfire in the fall of 1921. Brentwood was singing a popular song while accompanying himself on the ukulele. Spellbound by his performance, Amanda inadvertently ignited her headband in the bonfire. Brentwood gallantly put the flames out with his ukulele, and thereby kindled the fires of love.

Materials and Tools

Metric equivalents in centimeters are indicated in parentheses

1 yard (0.92 m) of striped cotton fabric, preferably containing metallic threads
¼ yard (0.23 m) of black satin or similar fabric
½ yard (0.46 m) of white cotton fabric
½ yard (0.46 m) of flesh-colored cotton knit fabric
One leg cut from a pair of regular weave flesh-tone pantyhose (or one nylon stocking)
Small brown wiglet (or substitute brown yarn)
Pair of dark brown or black false eyelashes
½ yard (0.46 m) of 1-inch (2.5) wide white eyelet or lace trim
White, black, and red acrylic paint and a fine-tipped artist's paint brush
1 yard (0.92 m) of ¾-inch (1.9) wide metallic ribbon and lace trim
Regular and heavy duty flesh-colored sewing thread
White and black sewing thread, and thread to match the striped cotton fabric
½ pound (227 g) of polyester fiberfill
String of pearls, pale pink powdered cheek blusher, and white glue
Long sharp needle, scissors, straight pins, and a sewing machine (optional)

Turn to page 154 and make a body for Amanda, following the instructions for Making the Torso and Making the Arms. Use the scale drawings for adult-sized arm, leg, boot, and torso (Figure A, page 155) to make the full-size patterns. Like Brentwood, Amanda wears low-cut shoes rather than high-top boots. Turn to page 93 and follow the directions for recutting the leg and boot pattern to sew a low-cut shoe, substituting the black satin fabric for the white broadcloth and omitting any references to the flaps or saddles.

Bear in mind as you are sewing Amanda's body, that it is the era of Clara Bow and that Amanda has a lot of "It" too—which means that the bustline must be nonexistent, and that certain additions are required, particularly in the critical area of the knees.

Sculpturing the Knees

1. Working with the finished leg, pinch up a generous ridge approximately ½ inch (1.3) high and 2 inches (5) below the leg/body seam. Stitch back and forth underneath the ridge at the center only. Lock the stitch to secure the ridge, and cut the thread. Repeat the procedure to form a knee on the other leg.

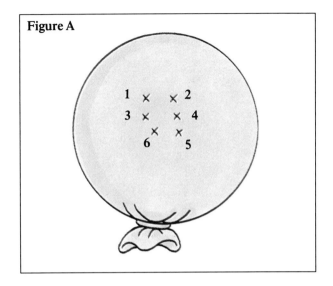

Figure A

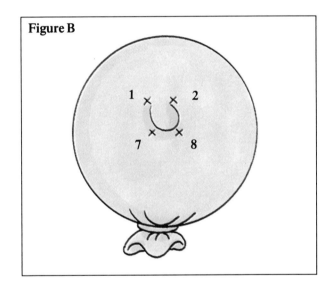

Figure B

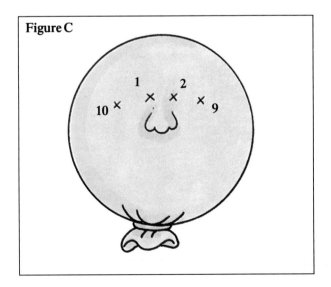

Figure C

2. Brush a generous amount of powdered blusher on each of Amanda's knees. She would absolutely not be caught without knee rouge any more than she would leave the dormitory without her headband. (Amanda knows how to assign priorities and always puts first things first. One morning, to her horror, she discovered that her roommate had purloined the last bit of her knee rouge! This was doubly unfortunate, since Amanda was forced to miss her chemistry mid-term in an effort to replace it. Wrapping herself in a full-length coat so as not to expose her naked knees, she ran to the local drugstore, only to find that the shelves were empty. Amanda was not amused. Undaunted, her next stop was the vegetable market, where she purchased a large beet. Borrowing a knife from the grocer, she sliced the beet and rubbed it vigorously over both knees, producing a brilliant shade of deep fuchsia. The good news was that the color lasted until the drugstore was restocked.)

Making the Head

1. Tie the pantyhose leg or stocking into a tight knot near the open end, and cut the hose 6 inches (15) below the knot. Turn, so that the knot is on the inside.

2. Stuff a generous amount of fiberfill inside the hose, manipulating the shape until a head is formed. (Detailed instructions for stuffing and forming a head are given in the Soft Sculpturing Tips section of this book.) Amanda's head should be at least 12 inches (31) in circumference, measuring around the nose and ear line. It should be approximately 4½ inches (11) in diameter from top to bottom. Tie the stuffed hose in a knot at the open (neck) end.

3. Use a long sharp needle and a 36-inch (90) length of heavy duty flesh-colored thread to sculpture the facial features. Amanda's nose is quite small and has an extremely stylish tilt to it, so stitch very carefully, in order not to detract from "It." Follow the entry and exit points illustrated in Figure A.

   a. Enter where the hose is tied at the neck, pass through the center of the head, and exit at point 1. Pinch up a vertical ridge, approximately ⅜ inch (1) high, between points 1 and 2. (This will be the bridge of the nose.)

   b. Reenter at 1 and exit at 2. Reenter at 2 and exit at 1, pulling the thread tightly. Keep the thread pulled tightly as you take an additional stitch underneath the surface between points 1 and 2 to secure the ridge. Exit at 1.

   c. Pinch up the nose ridge between points 3 and 4. These points should be approximately ¼ inch (0.6) directly below points 1 and 2. Pull the thread across the surface, enter at 3 and exit at 4. Pull the thread across the surface, enter at 2 and exit at 1.

   d. Hold the thread with one hand near point 1 to maintain the tension, reenter at 1 and exit at 5. (Points 5 and 6 should be about ⅜ inch [1] below and slightly wider apart than points 3 and 4). Pull

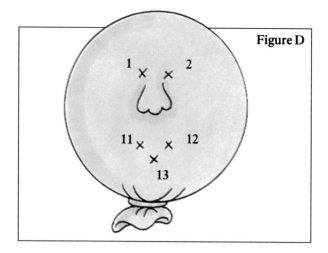

Figure D

the thread across the surface, enter at 6 and exit at 2. Pull the thread until the end of the nose appears (between points 5 and 6).

   e. Holding the threat taut, reenter at 2 and exit at 3. Hold the thread tension near point 3, pull the thread across the surface, enter at 6 and exit at 4. Pull the thread across the surface, enter at 5 and exit at 1.

   f. Tighten and hold the thread as you take one or two stitches back and forth under the surface between points 1 and 2 to secure the nose form. Exit at 2.

4. Continue working with the same thread to form the nostrils. Follow the entry and exit points in Figure B.

   a. Reenter at 2 and exit at 8. Reenter slightly above 8 and exit at 2. Pull the thread until a nostril forms, and lock the stitch.

   b. Reenter at 2 and exit at 1. Reenter at 1 and exit at 7. Reenter slightly above 7 and exit at 1. Pull the thread until a second nostril appears, and lock the stitch.

   c. Reenter at 1 and exit at 7. Pull the thread around the tip of the nose, enter at 6 and exit at 8. Pull the thread gently around the other side of the nose, enter at 5 and exit at 7. Pull the thread gently across the bottom of the nose, enter at 8 and exit at 2. Lock the stitch, exiting at 2.

5. Amanda's eye lines are stitched and then her open eyes are painted on. To stitch the eye lines, use the same length of thread and follow the entry and exit points indicated in Figure C.

   a. Pull the thread across the surface, enter at 9 and exit at 1.

   b. Pull the thread across the surface, enter at 10 and exit at 2. Pull the thread to form the eye lines, maintain the tension and lock the stitch, exiting at 2.

6. Amanda's mouth is beautifully heart-shaped, and she uses a generous amount of lip rouge. To form Amanda's mouth, follow the entry and exit points illustrated in Figure D.

Figure E

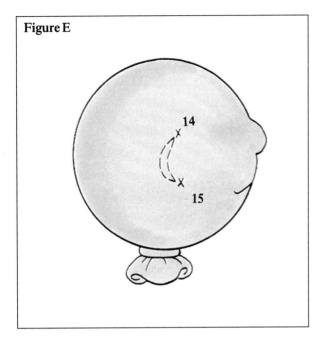

Figure F

a. Reenter at 2 and exit at 11. Pull the thread across the surface, enter at 12 and exit at 1. Pull the thread firmly until the mouth line appears, and lock the stitch, exiting at 1.

b. Amanda's bottom lip is formed by taking one additional stitch just below the mouth line. Reenter at 1 and exit at 13. Enter just barely to the left of point 13, and exit at 1. Pull the thread firmly, and lock the stitch.

c. Reenter at 1 and exit at the bottom of the neck near the tied knot. Lock the stitch and cut the thread.

7. Follow the entry and exit points illustrated in Figure E to sculpture Amanda's ears.

a. Enter at the neck knot and exit at 14. (Point 14, which will be the top of the ear, should be even with the lower portion of the nose.) Pinch up a small curved ridge at an angle, as shown, just below point 14.

b. Stitch back and forth under the ridge, moving toward point 15 with each stitch, and pulling the thread gently until an ear forms. Exit at point 15.

c. Lock the stitch behind the ear, reenter at that point, and exit at the neck knot.

d. Lock the stitch and cut the thread.

e. Repeat steps a through d on the opposite side of the head.

8. Trim the brown wiglet to fit Amanda's head and glue it in place. Her hair is stylishly bobbed, so don't make it too long or she will suffer a great deal of humiliation and her headband won't look right.

9. Follow the illustration in Figure F to paint Amanda's eyes and mouth. Paint a small circle of white on the upper edge of each eyeline. Add a small black circle in the center of the white. Draw a short, straight, solid black line over the top of the circle. The better to vamp with, Amanda has long black eyelashes which she has learned to flutter with amazing dexterity. Trim the lashes to fit her eyes, and glue them in place. Paint small, arched, black eyebrows over the eyes. Finish her makeup by carefully painting a small heart-shaped mouth using red paint.

Attaching the Head to the Body

1. Turn a narrow seam allowance to the inside on the neck opening of the body. Gather the neckline ¼ inch (0.6) from the folded edge, using heavy-duty flesh-colored thread. Pull the gathering threads until the opening measures approximately 1 inch (2.5) across.

2. Center the head over the opening, inserting the tied neck portion inside the body. Whipstitch completely around the neck several times to secure the head to the body, because dancing the Charleston as often as Amanda does puts quite a strain on it.

Making the Flapper Dress

1. A scale drawing for Amanda's flapper dress, head band, and dress sash are given in Figure G. Enlarge the pieces to full-size paper patterns and cut the following pieces from striped cotton: two dresses, one sash, and one headband.

2. Pin the two dress pieces right sides together and stitch the shoulder and side seams, as shown in Figure H.

3. To finish the neckline and armholes, turn under a ¼-inch (0.6) hem on each edge and topstitch.

4. Turn under a ¼-inch (0.6) hem along the bottom edge of the dress and stitch.

5. To make the sash to complete Amanda's flapper dress, fold the striped sash piece lengthwise, right sides together, and stitch the seams along the raw edges, leaving one narrow end open and unstitched.

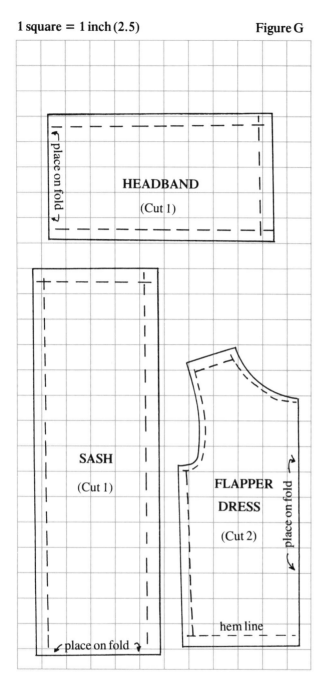

HEADBAND

(Cut 1)

place on fold

SASH

(Cut 1)

place on fold

FLAPPER

DRESS

(Cut 2)

place on fold

hem line

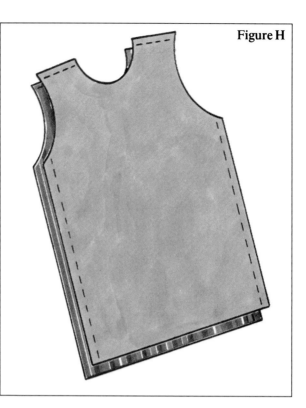

Figure H

6. Turn the sash right side out and press. Turn the remaining raw edges to the inside and whipstitch the opening together.

7. Repeat the procedures in steps 5 and 6 to sew the head band.

Making the Tap Pants

Amanda's tap pants are sewn from the same pattern as Maude's bloomers, except that they are cut very much shorter. Turn to page 34 and follow the instructions for making the bloomers, but trim the pattern so that Amanda's tap pants won't show below her flapper dress.

Finishing Details

Dress Amanda in her tap pants and flapper dress. Tie the sash around her hips, ending with a soft bow at the side. Tie the headband around Amanda's bobbed hair, ending with a double knot at the side. Tuck the ends of the headband under the knot. Double the strand of pearls around Amanda's neck, leaving one loop choker length and the other opera length. Tie a knot in the longer loop.

Finish by adding the shoe ties. Cut a 18-inch (46) length of gold and lace trim for each shoe. Place the center of the trim under Amanda's instep, pull it up over the top of her foot, cross the trim and pull it to the back of her ankle. Cross the trim behind the ankle and tie it in a bow at the front of her ankle.

Make certain that Amanda's shoes are tied securely in place. After their marriage she and Brentwood enter several dance marathons. They win most of them because Amanda reads an article on the "pickling procedure." It seems that one Mary Hercules Promitis, a frequent marathoner from Pittsburg, learned that some of the barefisted prizefighters had successfully tried pickling their hands for several days before a big fight, and Miss Promitis postulated (also successfully) that the same principle could be applied to feet.

After Amanda and Brentwood soak their feet in brine for three weeks prior to entering the marathon, they emerge victorious with their feet unscathed. Amanda and Brentwood are richer by a thousand dollars. Victoria is aghast. Casey is in Albuquerque.

Edward Barnyard (Leroy) Weepeeple

Born: November 27, 1930

Conflict over Edward's names has been rampant ever since he was born. While Amanda was still convalescing in the hospital, the proud father and both sets of grandparents regularly visited, bringing ever larger bouquets of flowers and increasingly adamant arguments for or against the currently proposed name. Thoroughly disgusted, Amanda named their son after her doctor, Edward Fullerton, who, she said, "is the only nice person left in the world."

Edward was also named after his grandfather Casey Weepeeple, a fact which is difficult to mistake. Brentwood wanted to name his son for his own father, but Victoria's decrepit mother got into the act, threatening to disinherit both Amanda and Brentwood if they dared put her through the agony a second time of dealing with the name Casanova on formal announcements. Far from having the effect she desired, this simply raised Amanda's dander and she chose Casey's middle name. Much to everyone's surprise, old Mrs. Mortimer decided she "admired that young 'un's spirit," and increased their share in her will.

To compound the confusion Edward later acquired a nickname. Grandmother Victoria was partly to blame; on Edward's eighth birthday she presented him with a blue satin suit in a style she considered proper for a young gentleman. Edward was beside himself with glee. His parents were appalled. Victoria was proud. Casey was in Detroit.

Following Victoria's departure and Amanda's subsequent fit of hysterical relief, Brentwood convinced her that in deference to Victoria they should have Edward's picture taken in the suit. The picture could then be sent to Victoria and the suit disposed of. But Edward had inherited his mother's stubborn streak, and once in the suit he refused to come out.

Edward's schoolmates immediately dubbed him Little Lord Fauntleroy, which over the course of the school term was shortened to Leroy. Upon hearing the latest outrage, Victoria was hospitalized. Amanda and Brentwood were amused. Casey had retired.

Materials and Tools

Metric equivalents in centimeters are indicated in parentheses.

1 yard (0.9 m) of blue satin or equivalent, at least 36 inches (90) wide

½ yard (0.46 m) of white cotton fabric

6-inch (15) length of 1-inch (2.5) wide single-fold white seam binding

½ yard (0.46 m) of flesh-colored cotton knit fabric

1 yard (0.9 m) of royal blue ½-inch (1.3) wide satin ribbon

Small amount of white embroidery floss

1 yard (0.9 m) of ¼-inch (0.6) wide elastic

12-inch (31) square of 12-count needlepoint canvas (or other open weave material)

¼ yard (0.23 m) of black cotton or vinyl fabric

White and royal blue sewing thread

Heavy-duty and regular flesh-colored thread

½ pound (227 g) of polyester fiberfill

One leg cut from a pair of regular weave flesh-tone pantyhose (or one nylon stocking)

Small brown wiglet (or substitute brown yarn)

One small metal snap

White and black acrylic paint and a fine-tipped artist's paint brush

Pale pink powdered cheek blusher and white glue

Long sharp needle, scissors, straight pins, and a sewing machine (optional)

Turn to page 154 and make a body for Edward, following the instructions for Making the Arms, Making Legs with Boots, and Making the Torso. (Since Edward wears fashionably laced boots with his blue satin suit, be sure to skip over the sections on Adding the Boot Flaps and Making Legs with Feet.) Use the scale drawings for child-size arm, leg, boot, and torso (Figure B, page 156) to make the full-size patterns. Cut the legs from white cotton fabric instead of flesh-colored knit, because Edward wears white leggings under his boots and knickers so his bare skin won't show. He's quite adamant about this (much to Amanda's dismay), and you're bound to have a temper tantrum on your hands if you omit the white legs.

Making the Head

1. Tie the pantyhose leg or stocking into a tight knot near the open end, and cut the hose 6 inches (15) below the knot. Turn, so that the knot is on the inside.

2. Stuff a generous amount of fiberfill inside the hose, manipulating the shape until a head is formed. (Detailed instructions for stuffing and forming a head are given in the Soft Sculpturing Tips section of this book.) Edward's head should be approximately 12 inches (31)in circumference (but no smaller), measuring around the nose and ear line. It should be at least 4½ inches (11.5) in diameter from top to bottom. Tie the stuffed hose in a tight knot at the open (neck) end.

3. Use a long sharp needle and a 36-inch (90) length of heavy-duty flesh-colored thread to sculpture the facial features. Edward's nose is very similar to his father's, but is somewhat smaller and runs more. (So as not to leave a lasting impression on his satin suit, Edward always carries a freshly ironed hanky in his knickers.) Follow the entry and exit points illustrated in Figure A.

   a. Enter where the hose is tied at the neck, pass through the center of the head, and exit at point 1. Pinch up a vertical ridge, approximately ½ inch (1.3) high, between points 1 and 2. (This will be the bridge of the nose.)

   b. Reenter at 1 and exit at 2. Reenter at 2 and exit at 1, pulling the thread tightly. Keep the thread pulled tightly as you take an additional stitch underneath the surface between points 1 and 2 to secure the ridge. Exit at 1.

   c. Pinch up the nose ridge between points 3 and 4. These points should be approximately ⅜-inch (1) directly below points 1 and 2. Pull the thread across the surface, enter at 3 and exit at 4. Pull the thread across the surface, enter at 2 and exit at 1.

   d. Hold the thread with one hand near point 1 to maintain the tension, reenter at 1 and exit at 5. (Points 5 and 6 should be about ½ inch [1.3] below and slightly wider apart than points 3 and 4). Pull the thread across the surface, enter at 6 and exit at 2. Pull the thread until the end of the nose appears (between points 5 and 6).

   e. Holding the threat taut, reenter at 2 and exit at 3. Hold the thread tension near point 3, pull the thread across the surface, enter at 6 and exit at 4. Pull the thread across the surface, enter at 5 and exit at 1.

   f. Tighten and hold the thread as you take one or two stitches back and forth under the surface between points 1 and 2 to secure the nose form. Exit at 2.

4. Continue working with the same thread to form the nostrils. Follow the entry and exit points illustrated in Figure B.

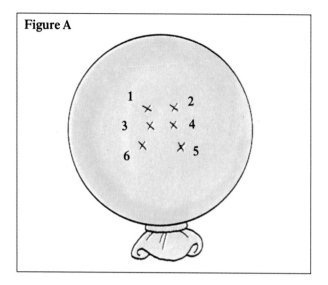

Figure A

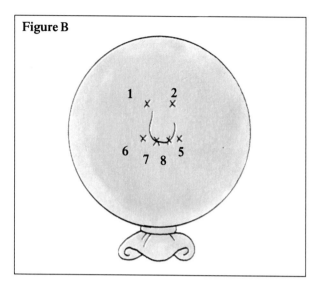

Figure B

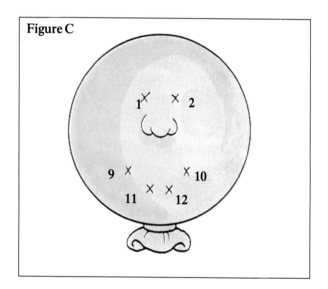

Figure C

a. Reenter at 2 and exit at 8. Reenter slightly above 8 and exit at 2. Pull the thread until a nostril forms and lock the stitch.

b. Reenter at 2 and exit at 1. Reenter at 1 and exit at 7. Reenter slightly above 7 and exit at 1. Pull the thread until a nostril appears. Lock the stitch.

c. Reenter at 1 and exit at 7. Pull the thread around the tip of the nose, enter at 6 and exit at 8. Pull the thread gently around the other side of the nose, enter at 5 and exit at 7. Pull the thread gently across the bottom of the nose, enter at 8 and exit at 2. Lock the stitch.

5. Continue working with the same thread to create Edward's smile, following the entry and exit points illustrated in Figure C.

a. Reenter at 2 and exit at 9.

b. Pull the thread across the surface, enter at 10 and exit at 1.

c. Pull the thread until a smile appears. With one hand, hold tension on the thread near point 1. With the other hand use the tip of the needle to gently lift the fiberfill above the smile and across the cheeks. Lift a small amount of fiberfill into the lower chin area.

d. Edward's bottom lip is formed by taking one additional stitch just below the mouth line. Reenter at 1 and exit at 11. Enter at 12 and exit at 2. Pull the thread firmly, and lock the stitch.

e. Reenter at 2 and exit at the neck knot. Lock the stitch and cut the thread.

6. Edward's eye lines are first stitched, and then his eyes are painted on. Stitch and paint the eyes carefully, because Edward has taken to reading the dictionary each night as a hobby, in hopes of finding out what all those words are that his parents spell in his presence.

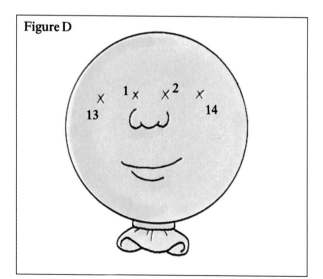

Figure D

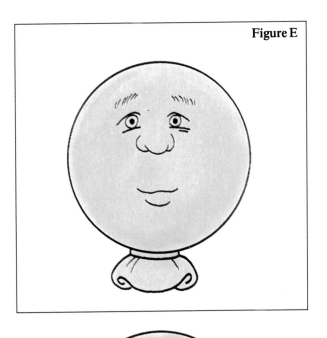

Figure E

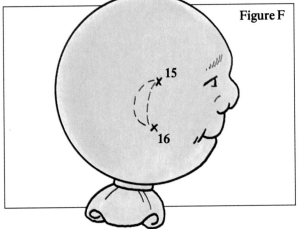

Figure F

7. Follow the illustrations given in Figure E to paint Edward's eyes and eyebrows. Paint a flat white oval above the eye line on each side of the nose. Paint a black circle in the center of each white oval. Paint a black line above each white oval at an angle, extending from the top of the inner eye to the outer corner. Paint a wide, short eyebrow above each eye as shown.

8. Follow the entry and exit points illustrated in Figure F to sculpture Edward's ears.

   a. Enter at the neck and exit at 15. (Point 15, which will be the top of the ear, should be even with the lower end of the nose.) Pinch up a small curved ridge, as shown, just below point 15.

   b. Stitch back and forth under the ridge, moving toward point 16 with each stitch. Pull the thread gently until an ear forms. Exit at 16.

   c. Lock the stitch behind the ear, reenter at that point, and exit at the neck.

   d. Lock the stitch and cut the thread.

   e. Repeat steps a through d on the opposite side of the head.

9. Brush a small amount of powdered cheek blusher over Edward's cheeks and across his bottom lip. Trim the wiglet to fit his head and glue it in place. Cut the hair in a Buster Brown style, with bangs in front.

Attaching the Head to the Body

1. Turn a narrow seam allowance to the inside on the neck opening of the body. Gather the neckline ¼ inch (0.6) from the folded edge using heavy-duty, flesh-colored thread. Pull the gathering threads until the opening measures approximately 1 inch (2.5) across.

2. Center the head over the opening, inserting the tied neck portion of the head inside the neck opening. Whipstitch completely around the neck several times to secure the head to the body.

Making the Knickers

As you are aware, for some perverse reason known only to the young man himself, Edward thinks his suit is "the bee's knees" (a phrase he picked up from his parents). While most other boys his age would rather be taken behind the woodshed than made to wear such an outfit, Edward remains steadfast in his love of what Amanda calls "the blue abomination." The only time that Edward was known to exhibit aggressive behavior, in fact, was on the occasion when his closest friend inadvertently insulted the suit. They were discussing the meaning of the word "vulgar," which Edward had heard his father use. His friend explained that the word was used to describe something in very bad taste, and then innocently gave an example of its use by posing the hypothetical question, "Why do you wear that vulgar suit?" Edward lost his temper and let fly with a right hook to his friend's nose. Receiving as good as he gave, Edward sustained a small rip to the jacket of his suit and was never known to fight again.

His main stumbling block so far is that he has not caught on to the fact that the book is arranged alphabetically. So it may be some time before he figures out what his parents are planning for him when they say, "W-A-S-H." To form the eye lines, follow the entry and exit points illustrated in Figure D. Point 13 will be the outside corner of the right eye line. It should be approximately 1 inch (2.5) directly to the left of point 1. Point 14, the corner of the left eye line, should be 1 inch (2.5) directly to the right of 2.

   a. Pull the thread across the surface, enter at 13 and exit at 2.

   b. Pull the thread across the surface, enter at 14 and exit at 1.

   c. Pull the thread gently until the eye lines appear. Hold the thread taut, and stitch one or two times under the surface between points 1 and 2 to secure the eyes, exiting at 1. Reenter at 1, exit at the neck knot, lock the stitch, and cut the thread.

1 square = 1 inch (2.5)   **Figure G**

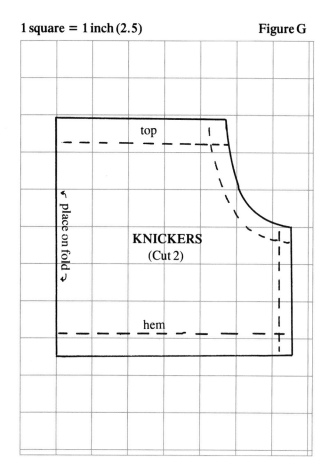

top

← place on fold ↲

KNICKERS
(Cut 2)

hem

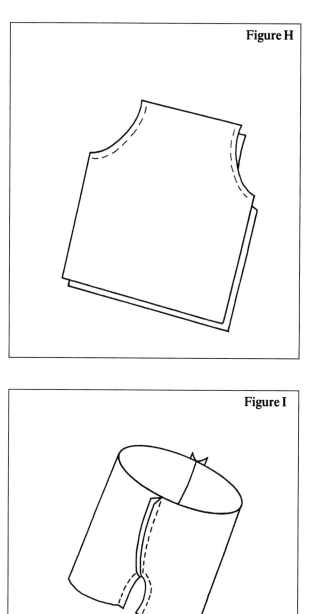

Figure H

Figure I

1. Enlarge the knicker pattern given in Figure G. Cut two knicker pieces from royal blue satin.

2. Pin the two knicker pieces right sides together, and stitch the center front and back seams (Figure H).

3. Refold the knickers right sides together, matching the center front and back seams. Stitch the inner leg seam (Figure I).

4. To make casings for the elastic, turn over a 3/8-inch (1) seam around the waistline and the bottom of each leg. Topstitch the seam, leaving an opening for the elastic. Measure Edward's waist and leg and cut three lengths of elastic 1 inch (2.5) longer than each of the measurements. Thread the elastic through the casings and stitch the ends securely together. Pull the elastic back inside the casing and whipstitch the opening in the casing together.

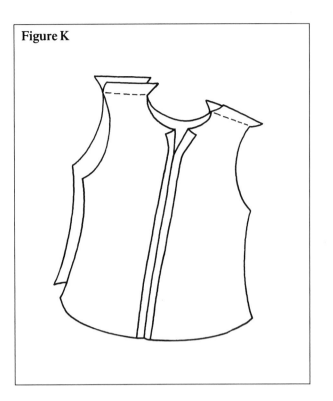

Figure K

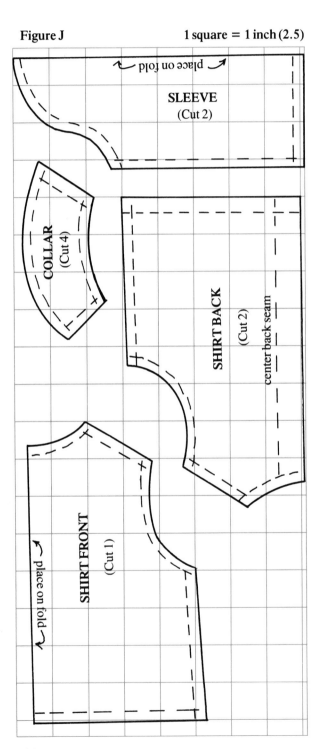

Figure J

1 square = 1 inch (2.5)

place on fold

SLEEVE
(Cut 2)

COLLAR
(Cut 4)

SHIRT BACK
(Cut 2)

center back seam

SHIRT FRONT
(Cut 1)

place on fold

Making the Shirt

1. Scale drawings for the shirt back, shirt front, sleeve, and collar patterns are given in Figure J. Enlarge the drawings to full-size paper patterns.

2. Cut the following pieces, paying particular attention to the "place on fold" notations: two shirt backs, one shirt front, two sleeves, and four collars.

3. Place the two shirt backs right sides together. Stitch the center back seam from the bottom to the small circle, leaving the back neckline open and unstitched. Turn over a ¼-inch (0.6) hem on the remaining raw edges of the center back seam, and whipstitch.

4. Place the shirt back and shirt fronts right sides together. Stitch the shoulder seams (Figure K).

5. Sew a ¼-inch (0.6) hem along the straight edge of each sleeve. Sew the curved edges of the sleeves to the armhole edges of the shirt with right sides together (Figure L), easing the sleeves to fit.

6. Fold the shirt right sides together and stitch the side and underarm seams (Figure M).

7. Place two collars right sides together and stitch a continuous seam around three edges (Figure N), leaving the short curved edge open and unstitched. Clip the corners and curves, turn the collar right side out, and press. Repeat the procedure using the remaining two collars.

8. Pin the collars to the shirt neckline on the right side of the fabric, so that they meet at the center front (Figure O). Topstitch the collars in place, and stitch seam binding over the lower raw edges of the collars.

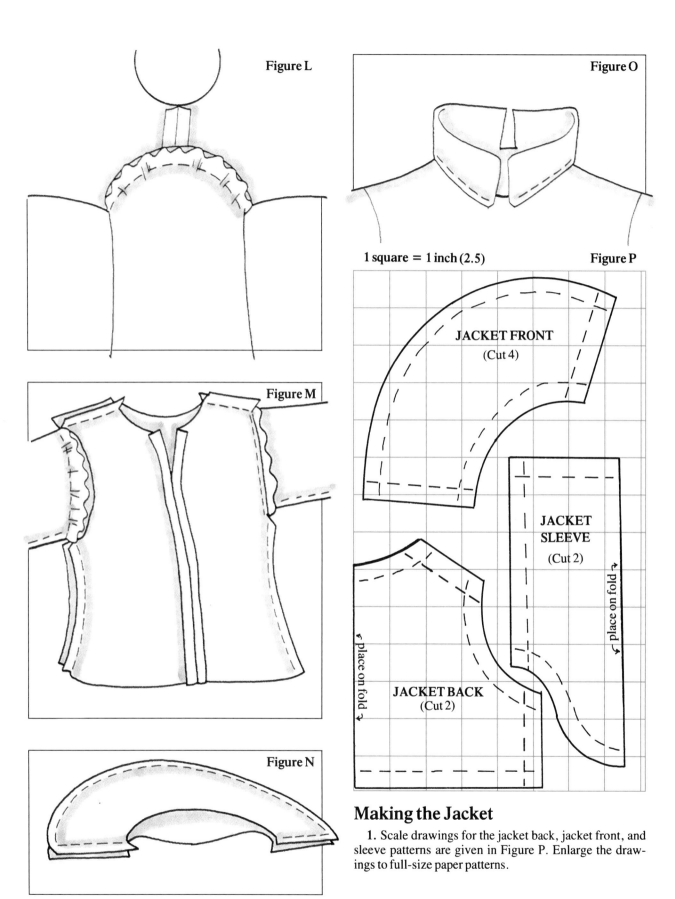

Figure L

Figure O

1 square = 1 inch (2.5)

Figure P

JACKET FRONT
(Cut 4)

JACKET
SLEEVE
(Cut 2)

place on fold

Figure M

JACKET BACK
(Cut 2)

place on fold

Figure N

Making the Jacket

1. Scale drawings for the jacket back, jacket front, and sleeve patterns are given in Figure P. Enlarge the drawings to full-size paper patterns.

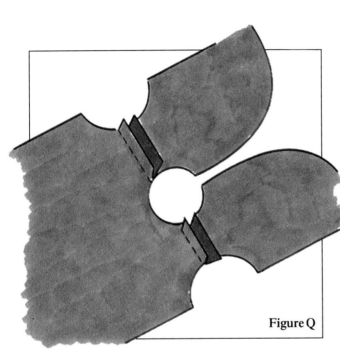

Figure Q

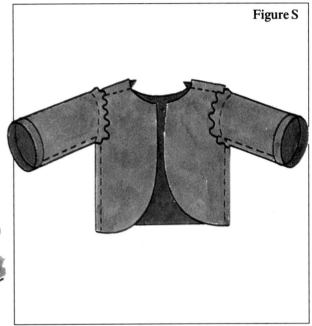

Figure S

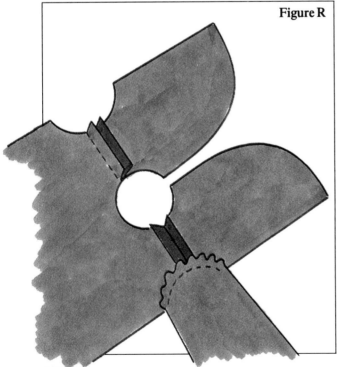

Figure R

2. Cut the following pieces from the blue satin, paying particular attention to the "place on fold" notations: two jacket backs, four jacket fronts, and two sleeves. The extra pieces (one back and two fronts) will serve as the lining for the jacket.

3. Place one jacket back and two jacket fronts right sides together. Stitch the shoulder seams (Figure Q). Repeat the procedure to form the lining, using the remaining back and front pieces. Set the lining aside.

4. Hem the straight edge of one sleeve, turning a ½-inch (1.3) allowance to the wrong side of the fabric. Sew the curved edge of the sleeve to the armhole edge on one side of the jacket with right sides together (Figure R), easing the sleeve to fit. Repeat the procedure to hem and attach the remaining sleeve.

5. Fold the jacket right sides together and stitch the side and underarm seam on each side (Figure S). Sew the side seams only on the lining.

6. Place the assembled jacket and lining right sides together and join them by stitching a ½-inch (1.3) seam around the entire outer edge (Figure T). Turn the assembly right side out by pulling the jacket through the armhole in the lining.

7. Clip the seam allowance around the raw edges of the armhole on both the jacket and the lining. Turn the seam allowances to the inside, and whipstitch the folded edge of the lining to the sleeve seam of the jacket. All seam allowances should be hidden by the folded edge.

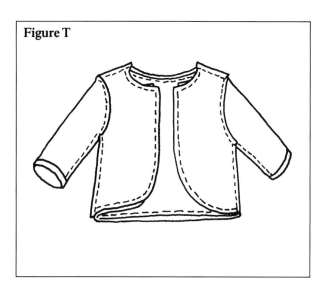

Figure T

Making the Hat

1. Cut two circles from the needlepoint canvas; one 6 inches (15) in diameter for the brim, and one 4 inches (10) in diameter for the crown.

2. Clip the smaller crown piece ½ inch (1.3) deep at ½-inch (1.3) intervals, around the entire circumference. Fold the clipped edge down and glue it in place (Figure U). Use straight pins to hold it together until the glue dries completely.

3. Whipstitch the crown to the center of the larger brim. Cut a 16-inch (41) length of royal blue satin ribbon, and tie it around the crown, ending with a knot at the back.

Finishing Details

Dress Edward in his shirt, jacket, and knickers. Wrap an 18-inch (46) length of blue satin ribbon around his neck and tie it in a bow in the front. Thread a large needle with a length of white embroidery floss. To create the laces, start at the top of one boot and take long stitches back and forth across the front until you reach the bottom. Stitch back up, crossing each previous stitch. Tie the ends in a bow at the top. When finished, the stitches should look like a normal pattern of boot laces (Figure V). We gave Edward an embroidery hoop to play with, but he'll probably be happier if you supply him with a dictionary.

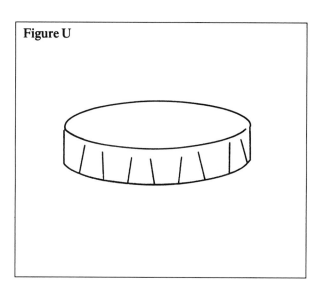

Figure U

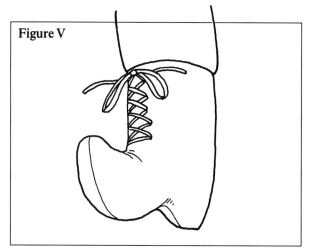

Figure V

Hugo Weepeeple

Born: October 1, 1860

Bertha Sloane had been in residence at the Weepeeple farm for five full months when Hugo finally arrived. Ma and Pa had had no means of reaching Bertha to let her know that the schedule was running late that year so she appeared, as usual, on May 1. Bertha did not wish to make the arduous trek home and then back again, so she simply took up residence on the daybed for the duration.

Bertha was given the task of deciding on a suitable name for the soon-to-be-born Weeperson. By October she had divined a first and middle name for a girl, but only a first name for a boy. Try as they might, Ma and Pa could come up with no ideas either. As Pa put it, "Hugo's the twelfth we've had and we're plumb named out."

Fortunately, Hugo turned out to be good-natured about everything, and the lack of a middle name never bothered him in the least. He actually considered it a blessing of sorts since Ma was in the habit of calling the children by their full given names when she was fit to be tied over something they'd done. Hugo reasoned that with no middle name, he'd never get in trouble. And as it turned out he never did, leading his brothers and sisters to believe that his theory was correct.

Hugo always did his chores, washed his neck and behind his ears, never participated in horseplay inside the house, and never opened the outhouse door without knocking first. Most importantly, he always wiped his feet before going inside the house after he'd been working in the hog pen. Had Hugo not been such a likable sort, his older brothers and sisters probably would have severely maimed him before his seventh birthday.

But Hugo never really excelled at anything either (though his performance was always satisfactory) and nothing seemed to take his fancy, as hogs and the railroad had for his brother Barney, or as public speaking had for his brother Calvin, or as sewing fancy dresses had for his sister Clementine. And so instead of seeking his fortune elsewhere, as his brothers and sisters had done, he stayed on the farm. Being such a hard worker, most odd jobs in the county came his way.

This, in a round about way, led to his permanent employment as caretaker of the Pleasant Hill Cemetery. It seems that Mr. Frumpus, who owned the land adjoining the Weepeeple farm, needed some extra help with his newfangled threshing machine and naturally called on Hugo. Not being acquainted with this modern equipment, Hugo approached it from the wrong direction and was soundly threshed for the entire length of an acre of wheat. Although Mr. Frumpus extricated Hugo from the machine as soon as he realized what was causing the strange thumping sound, Hugo never quite got over the shock. He took to brooding and couldn't even look at a piece of bread.

Hugo finally found his niche when the caretaker at the cemetery became a caretakee, and the job was immediately open. He tended the graves with care and devotion, and was always helpful in locating loved ones for visitors. As Hugo often said, "It's gotten so I know more people here than I do in town."

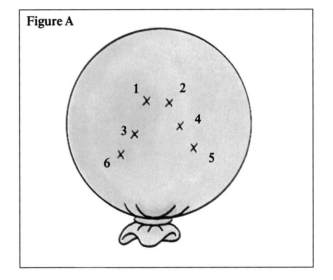

Figure A

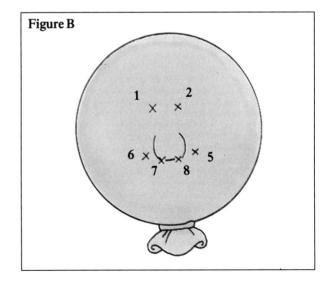

Figure B

Materials and Tools

Metric equivalents in centimeters are indicated in parentheses.

½ yard (0.46 m) of light blue denim fabric, at least 36 inches (90) wide

¼ yard (0.23 m) of rust and beige striped cotton fabric, at least 36 inches (90) wide

6-inch (15) length of single-fold red seam binding, 1 inch (2.5) wide

½ yard (0.46 m) of flesh-colored cotton knit fabric

¼ yard (0.23 m) of black vinyl or cotton fabric

Rust, light blue and white sewing thread

Heavy duty and regular flesh-colored thread

Six small white buttons

Two 1-inch (2.5) wide buckle fixtures for the overall straps, and two metal buttons for the overall sides

½ pound (227 g) of polyester fiberfill

One leg cut from a pair of regular weave flesh-tone pantyhose (or one nylon stocking)

Small amount of red-brown fiber (or substitute red-brown yarn)

Small amount of white and black acrylic paint and a fine-tipped paint brush

Pale pink powdered cheek blusher and white glue

Long sharp needle, scissor, straight pins, and a sewing machine (optional)

Turn to page 154 and make a body for Hugo, following the instruction for Making the Arms, Making Legs with Boots, and Making the Torso. Since Hugo still has a problem looking at or eating wheat products due to his unfortunate encounter with the thresher, he is somewhat thinner than his brother. His wife Susie mourns the fact that she was not the one who had the experience, since she has no problem whatsoever looking at or eating wheat products — especially biscuits and bread and pancakes and cookies and more bread and shortcake and doughnuts and pies and more bread and cakes.

Use the scale drawings for the adult-size arm, leg, boot, and torso (Figure A, page 155) to make the full-size patterns for Hugo's body. To make certain that he remains thin and trim, sew the seams ¼-inch wider on all of the body parts than you have for the other adults. Since Hugo does not wear flaps on his boots (he considers it in bad taste to be flashy in the cemetery), skip over the section on Adding the Boot Flaps.

Making the Head

1. Cut a 6-inch (15) length from the upper portion of the pantyhose leg or stocking, and slit it lengthwise so that you have a flat rectangle.

2. Wrap the rectangle around a large handful of fiberfill. Gather the edges of the hose together and twist, to create a head form. The twisted ends will be at the back of the head, just above the neck. (Detailed instructions for stuffing and forming a head are given in the Soft Sculpturing Tips section of this book.) Hugo's head should be approximately 12 inches (31) in circumference, measuring around the nose and ear line. It should be at least 4½ inches (11.4) in diameter from top to bottom. Add or remove fiberfill until the head is the correct size, and then wrap the twisted hose tightly with heavy-duty thread.

3. Use a long sharp needle and a 36-inch (91) length of heavy-duty flesh-colored thread to sculpture the facial features. To form Hugo's nose, follow the entry and exit points illustrated in Figure A. (Hugo's nose is somewhat fuller than his brother's, and is slightly off-kilter, due in part to his accident and in part to a hereditary resemblance to his great-great uncle Ignatius. As Ma Weepeeple recalls, "Uncle Ignatius' nose was always out of joint." Fortunately, Hugo's resemblance to Iggie is only physical. Hugo has a good and considerate nature, which Uncle Iggie never possessed. It was said of Iggie, rest his soul, that he was mean right from birth, and as a child spent more time behind the woodshed than in school. His teacher remarked many years later that "most kids outgrow their stubborn meanness, but even at age eighty-six, Iggie would still benefit from a trip to the woodshed.")

a. Enter where the hose is tied at the neck, pass through the center of the head, and exit at point 1. Pinch up a vertical ridge, approximately ½ inch (1.3) high, between points 1 and 2. (This will be the bridge of the nose.)

b. Reenter at 1 and exit at 2. Reenter at 2 and exit at 1, pulling the thread tightly. Keep the thread pulled tightly as you take an additional stitch underneath the surface between points 1 and 2 to secure the ridge. Exit at 1.

c. Pinch up the nose ridge between points 3 and 4. (These points should be approximately ½ inch [1.3] directly below points 1 and 2.) Pull the thread across the surface, enter at 3 and exit at 4. Pull the thread across the surface, enter at 2 and exit at 1.

d. Hold the thread with one hand near point 1 to maintain the tension, reenter at 1 and exit at 5. (Points 5 and 6 should be about ½ inch [1.3] below and slightly wider apart than points 3 and 4, but not any lower than the center line of the head.) Pull the thread across the surface, enter at 6 and exit at 2. Pull the thread until the end of the nose appears (between points 5 and 6).

e. Holding the thread taut, reenter at 2 and exit at 3. Hold the thread tension near point 3, pull the thread across the surface, enter at 6 and exit at 4. Pull the thread across the surface, enter at 5 and exit at 1.

f. Tighten and hold the thread as you take one or two stitches back and forth under the surface between points 1 and 2 to secure the nose form. Exit at 2.

4. Continue working with the same thread to form the nostrils. Follow the entry and exit points shown in Figure B.

a. Reenter at 2 and exit at 7. Reenter slightly above 7 and exit at 2. Pull the thread until a nostril forms, and lock the stitch.

b. Reenter at 2 and exit at 1. Reenter at 1 and exit at 8. Reenter slightly above 8 and exit at 1. Pull the thread until a second nostril appears and lock the stitch.

c. Reenter at 1 and exit at 7. Pull the thread around the side of the nose, enter at 6 and exit at 8. Pull the thread gently around the other side of the nose, enter at 5 and exit at 7. Pull the thread gently across the bottom of the nose, enter at 8 and exit at 2. Lock the stitch.

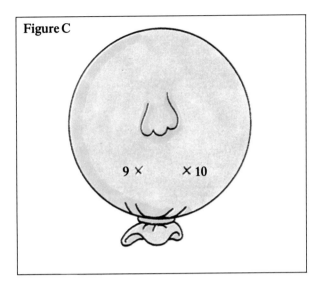

Figure C

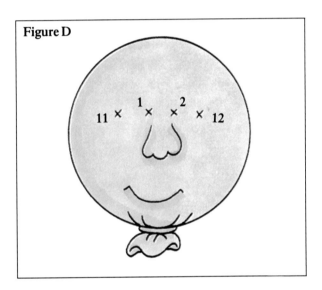

Figure D

Figure E

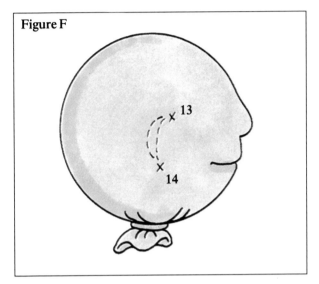

Figure F

5. Continue working with the same thread to create Hugo's engaging smile, which comes from within and spills out all over his face. (Hugo feels that an engaging smile is essential for cemetery work since the visitors are already somewhat down-at-the-mouth. As he so aptly puts it, "If I was frownin', they'd most likely be concerned 'bout me, and I figure they got enough to worry about what with loved ones who've just bought the farm or the worrisome job of finding ones who've been long gone.") Follow the entry and exit points illustrated in Figure C. Points 9 and 10 will be the corners of the mouth. They should be 1¾ inches (4.5) apart, on a line approximately 1 inch (2.5) below the end of the nose.

   a. Reenter at 2 and exit at 9.

   b. Pull the thread across the surface, enter at 10 and exit at 1.

   c. Pull the thread until a wide smile appears. With one hand, hold tension on the thread near point 1, and with the other hand use the tip of the needle to lift a small amount of additional fiberfill into the upper lip and into the chin area, forming the chin shape.

   d. Reenter at 1 and take one or two stitches under the surface between points 1 and 2 to secure the stitches. Exit at 1.

6. To form the eyes, follow the entry and exit points illustrated in Figure D. Hugo's eye lines are stitched first and then his open eyes are painted on. Point 11 will be the outside corner of the closed right eye. It should be approximately 1 inch (2.5) directly to the left of point 1. Point 12, the outside corner of the left eye, should be 1 inch (2.5) directly to the right of point 2.

a. Pull the thread across the surface, enter at 11 and exit at 2.

b. Pull the thread across the surface, enter at 12 and exit at 1.

c. Pull the thread gently until eye lines appear. Hold the thread taut, and stitch one or two times under the surface between points 1 and 2 to secure the eyes. Exit at 1. Reenter at 1, exit at the neck knot, lock the stitch, and cut the thread.

7. Paint a small white circle, about ⅜-inch (1) in diameter, slightly off center on the eye line, closer to the nose than to the outside of the line. Let the paint dry, then add a smaller black circle in the center of the white one. Paint a black line across the eye at the top of the black circle, as shown in Figure E.

8. Brush powdered blusher on the cheeks. Paint prominent front teeth, centered just below the stitched mouth line, using white paint. (Hugo's teeth also suffered from the threshing incident. Suzie has begged him to go to the dentist to get them fixed, but he considers that unnecessary since there's only a couple of days every winter when they cause trouble. Even then, his teeth don't hurt. Hugo says it's "just the whistlin' sound the wind makes when it blows acrost 'em" that bothers him some.

9. Follow the entry and exit points illustrated in Figure F to sculpture the ears.

a. Enter at the neck and exit at 13. (Point 13, which will be the top of the ear, should be even with the lower end of the nose.) Pinch up a small curved ridge, as shown, just below point 13.

b. Stitch back and forth under the ridge, moving toward point 14 with each stitch. Pull the thread gently until an ear forms. Exit at 14.

c. Lock the stitch behind the ear, reenter at that point, and exit at the neck.

d. Lock the stitch and cut the thread.

e. Repeat steps a through d on the opposite side of the head.

10. Arrange the brown fiber over Hugo's head, leaving a bald spot on the top. (Hugo's hair is somewhat unmanageable, but has settled down considerably in the last few years. Right after his accident, he was forced to wear a hat to bed each night. Without the hat, his hair stuck out so much all over his head that it was well-nigh impossible to keep his head put on the pillow.)

Attaching the Head to the Body

1. Turn a narrow seam allowance to the inside on the neck opening of the body. Gather the neckline ¼ inch (0.6) from the folded edge using heavy duty, flesh-tone thread. Pull the gathering threads until the opening measures approximately 1 inch (2.5) across.

2. Center the head over the opening, inserting the tied neck portion of the head under the back edge of the neck opening. Whipstitch completely around the neck several times to secure the head to the body.

Making the Overalls

Hugo wears overalls sewn from the same patterns as Barney's. (At first, Hugo wore his Sunday suit to work so he'd blend in better with the folks who came to bury loved ones or pay their respects. But he found that a mud-splattered Sunday suit wasn't very conducive to blending after all, so he took to wearing his everyday overalls. Besides, he says, "they got a lot of bend in all the right spots.") Turn to page 20 and follow the instructions for making the overalls, substituting light blue denim for the blue and white striped fabric.

Making the Shirt

Hugo's shirt is made exactly like Barney's, although it is cut from rust and beige cotton fabric. Turn to page 23 and follow the instructions for Making the Shirt, substituting red and beige cotton fabric for the plaid flannel that is specified for Barney's shirt.

Finishing Details

Dress Hugo in his shirt and overalls. Be sure to roll the shirt sleeves up above his elbows, since he likes them that way for work. Pull the overall straps to the front and tack the ends over the upper edge of the bib. Sew a buckle to each strap.

The waist edge of the overalls will be considerably larger than Hugo's waist. Fold the excess fabric into a pleat at each side of the waist, making the pleats as even as possible. Tack the pleats in place, and sew a metal button over each at the waist edge.

Hem the lower edge of each overall leg. Hugo wears them rather short, since it's handier for digging. "If you leave 'em long," he says, "you just have to roll 'em up, and then you wind up takin' half the graveyard home every night."

Suzanne (Susie) Biggers Weepeeple

Born: April 15, 1867

The lovely Miss Biggers was born on a date which at that time in history did not strike fear into the hearts of American breadwinners. It did, however, cause a considerable amount of distress for her mother, due to Susie's hefty birth weight of close to thirteen pounds.

Folks always commented that Susie was large for her age, but the young lady managed to expand dramatically upon her already generous proportions when she was only eight. She had been trying to reproduce her mother's delicious baking powder biscuits, and on the fourth attempt decided that the biscuits needed, "a whole passle more bakin' powder." The resulting biscuits were so thoroughly leavened that they all merged together and became one enormous oven-shaped (but very yummy) biscuit, which Susie promptly ate.

The effect was, as Doc Bigsby later described it in technical terms, "one of them things you don't see any too often." Susie had inflated, adding a full eighteen inches to her waistline. Doc Bigsby said that short of popping her, he didn't know what could be done besides wait for a natural deflationary trend. That never did occur although, proportionally speaking, things appeared to even out as Susie grew taller.

Susie had a heart that was even bigger than her waistline, so it was no surprise to her parents when she brought Hugo home from the 1882 spring hoedown. Although Susie was only fifteen when she and Hugo were married, she worked hard to overcome her inexperience and learn the skills that would make her "the best wife Hugo ever had."

When they were first married, Hugo was only too pleased to devour the numerous baked goods that Susie produced. After Hugo's threshing encounter, however, Suzy noticed that her breads and biscuits were standing untouched. This presented a serious problem, since her most outstanding domestic skill was "baking a mean biscuit." Hugo, being a kind-hearted soul himself, recognized Susie's quandary and began surreptitiously feeding the bread and biscuits to the dog. Susie was indescribably relieved, and increased her baking output just to please her husband. The poor dog (along with several cats and eventually a few assorted barnyard animals) began to inflate much like Susie had earlier in her baking career.

It was not until several months later, when the output of baked goods and the number and size of the under-the-table animal population had reached alarming proportions, that Susie began to realize something was amiss. Being advised by the vet that, "Short of popping them animals, there's nothing to do but wait," the light dawned on Susie and she began distributing her wheat products to the poor folks in the community, instead of to "that kind but mostly misguided husband of mine."

Materials and Tools

Metric equivalents in centimeters are indicated in parentheses.

1½ yards (1.4 m) of 36-inch (90) wide blue and white gingham fabric

1 yard (0.9 m) of white cotton fabric

1½ yards (1.4 m) of white eyelet trim

2½ yards (2.3 m) of 1-inch (2.5) wide pale blue satin or grosgrain ribbon

½ yard (0.46 m) of light blue cotton fabric

½ yard (0.46 m) of flesh-colored cotton knit fabric

¼ yard (0.23 m) of black vinyl or cotton fabric

Regular and heavy-duty flesh-colored sewing thread

One leg cut from a pair of regular weave flesh-tone pantyhose (or one nylon stocking)

White and light blue sewing thread

Small blond wiglet (or substitute yellow yarn)

Brown, light blue, white, and red acrylic paint and a fine-tipped artist's paint brush

½ pound (227 g) of polyester fiberfill

Pale pink powdered cheek blusher and white glue

1 yard (0.9 m) of ¼-inch (0.6) wide elastic

One hook and eye closure

One small white pearl button

Long sharp needle, scissors, straight pins, and a sewing machine (optional)

Turn to page 154 and make a body for Susie, following instructions for Making the Arms, Making Legs with Boots, and Making the Torso. As a result of Susie's love of biscuits, she is (as Hugo puts it) "plump all over." So sew the seams on the body parts just a bit more narrow to faithfully recreate Susie's ample size. Although Susie would like to have some boots with flaps on them for Christmas, she doesn't have them yet, so skip the section on Adding the Flaps. Hugo is working on this, but finds it most difficult to provide the frills for his wife on a care-taker's salary. Of course, use the scale drawings for adult-sized arm, leg, boot, and torso (Figure A, page 155) to make the full-size patterns.

Making the Head

1. Tie the pantyhose leg or stocking into a tight knot near the open end, and cut the hose 6 inches (15) below the knot. Turn, so that the knot is on the inside.

2. Stuff a generous amount of fiberfill inside the hose, manipulating the shape until a head is formed. (Detailed instructions for stuffing and forming a head are given in the Soft Sculpturing Tips section of this book). Susie's head should be at least 12 inches (31) in circumference, measuring around the nose and ear line. It should be approximately 4½ inches (11) in diameter from top to bottom. Tie the hose in a tight knot at the open (neck) end.

3. Use a long sharp needle and a 36-inch (90) length of heavy-duty flesh-colored thread to sculpture the facial features. To form Susie's nose, follow the entry and exit points illustrated in Figure A.

   a. Enter where the hose is knotted at the neck, pass through the center of the head, and exit at point 1. Sew a clockwise circle of deep basting stitches approximately 1 inch (2.5) in diameter, and exit at point 2.

   b. Use the tip of your needle to carefully lift fiberfill within the circle just enough to make a small bulge. Gently pull the thread until a round nose appears inside the circle.

   c. Hold the thread with one hand and take another stitch, entering at 2 and exiting at 1.

   d. To form the nostrils, reenter at 1 and exit at 3. Reenter ¼ inch (0.6) above 3 and exit at 2.

   e. Pull the thread gently and maintain the tension while you reenter at 2 and exit at 4. Reenter ¼ inch (0.6) above 4 and exit at 1.

   f. Pull the thread gently and maintain the tension while you take another small stitch at point 1.

4. Continue working with the same thread to form the mouth. Susie's mouth is generously sized, and she has deep dimples on each side of her face. (Susie was not born with dimples. They appeared as a side effect, as it were, of her inflationary episode. The fact was that well-meaning friends and family members continually took Susie's face in their hands, lovingly pinched her cheeks, and said such comforting things as, "My my, girl, you sure are swole up!" After several weeks of pinching, Susie sustained permanent dimples.)

   a. Enter at 1 and exit at 5. Pull the thread across the surface, enter at 6 and exit at 1. Pull the thread until a smile appears.

   b. Reenter at 1 and exit at 2. Reenter at 2 and exit at 7. Pull the thread across the surface, enter at 8 and exit at 2. Pull the thread gently to form Susie's lower lip.

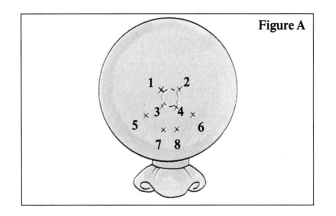

Figure A

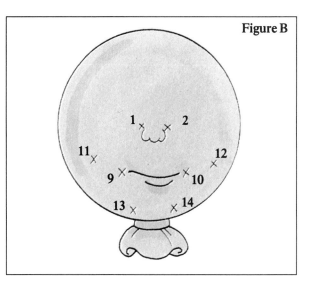

Figure B

c. To dimple the corners of Susie's mouth, follow the entry and exit points illustrated in Figure B. Reenter at 2 and exit at 9. Reenter at 9 and exit at 2. Reenter at 2 and exit at 1. Reenter at 1 and exit at 10. Reenter at 10 and exit at 1. Pull the thread to form the corners of the mouth, and lock the stitch.

d. To create the dimples in Susie's cheeks, reenter at 1 and exit at 12. Reenter at 12 and exit at 1. Enter at 1 and exit at 2. Reenter at 2 and exit at 11. Reenter at 11 and exit at 2. Pull the thread and lock the stitch.

5. To create Susie's double chin, reenter at 2 and exit at 13. Pull the thread across the surface, enter at 14 and exit at 1. Pull the thread and lock the stitch, exiting at 1.

6. Susie's eye lines are stitched, and then her open eyes are painted on. To form the eyes, follow the entry and exit points illustrated in Figure C.

a. Pull the thread across the surface, enter at 15 and exit at 2. Pull the thread across the surface, enter at 16 and exit at 1.

b. Gently pull the thread until the eye lines appear. Lock the stitch, exiting at 1.

c. Reenter at 1, guide the needle through the interior of the head to the knot at the top. Exit near the knot, pull the thread taut, lock the stitch, and cut the thread.

7. Follow the entry and exit points illustrated in Figure D to sculpture the ears.

a. Enter at the neck knot and exit at 17. (Point 17, which will be the top of the ear, should be even with the lower portion of the nose.) Pinch up a small curved ridge at an angle, as shown, just below point 17.

b. Stitch back and forth under the ridge, moving toward point 18 with each stitch, and pulling the thread gently until an ear forms. Exit at point 18.

c. Lock the stitch behind the ear, reenter at that point, and exit at the neck knot.

d. Lock the stitch and cut the thread.

e. Repeat steps a through d on the opposite side of the head.

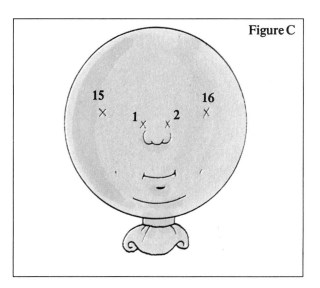

Figure C

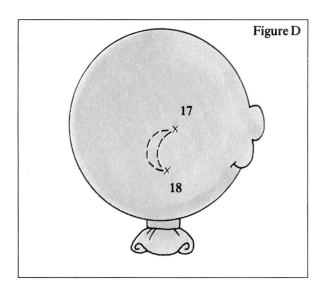

Figure D

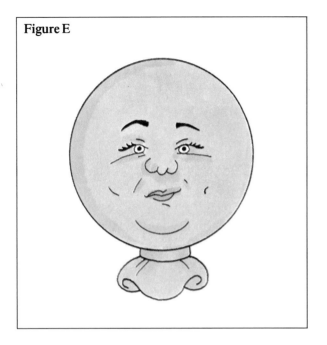

Figure E

8. Follow the illustration in Figure E to paint Susie's eyes and mouth. Paint a white oval above each eye line. Paint a large blue circle in the center of the oval. Paint a soft black dot in the center of the blue. Add just a hint of blue eye shadow above the eyes. Paint feathered eyelashes over the eyes, widening them at the outer corners. Paint soft eyebrows above Susie's eyes. Paint a generous red mouth to finish her toilette.

9. Trim the blond wiglet to fit Susie's head and glue it in place. Cut soft bangs across her forehead, and trim the sides shorter around her face. (Susie mostly wears her hair pulled back in a bun at the nape of her neck, but she wears it down on special occasions. She had the sides trimmed shorter around her face on the advice of Ottumwa's foremost hair stylist, Mrs. Violet Hardy. Violet had heard tales of the "fancy city women" who had taken to this new style, but she had had no luck convincing any of the local ladies to give it a try. Susie, however, was ready and willing the first time Violet made the suggestion, she being such an unfearful and philosophic soul. As she said when Violet went to get the hair-cutting scissors, "It'll always grow out again if I don't like it, God willin' and the creek don't rise.")

Attaching the Head to the Body

1. Turn a narrow seam allowance to the inside on the neck opening of the body. Gather the neckline ¼ inch (0.6) from the folded edge, using heavy-duty flesh-tone thread. Pull the gathering threads until the opening measures approximately 1 inch (2.5) across.

2. Center the head over the opening, inserting the tied neck portion inside the body. Whipstitch completely around the neck several times to secure the head.

Making the Apron

Susie wears an apron over her blue and white checked dress to protect it when she's cooking. Susie's cooking and other homemaking skills, in addition to pleasing Hugo, have proved to be an invaluable asset to the Mt. Zion Ladies' Auxiliary. The first time that Susie attended their regularly scheduled, every-other-Thursday-except-during-harvest meeting in Bertha Smock's parlor, she was elected chairman of the Bake Sale Committee. Because Susie was a new member, the chairmanship was largely honorary, as the auxiliary had not held a bake sale in several years. But Susie took the assignment to heart. She scrubbed the church meeting hall until it shined, borrowed gingham tablecloths from members of the congregation, assigned baking duties to each member of the committee, and hand lettered notices which read "COME TO MT. ZION BAKE SALE THIS WEDNESDAY." Hitching up the buggy, she proceeded to post the signs on trees all over the county, and returned home to do her baking, hurriedly.

Wednesday came, and the bake sale was a huge success. Susie was thrilled and Hugo was proud. She returned home victorious, and prepared to rest on her laurels, which were quite exhausted.

The following Tuesday night Hugo was to utter the words which changed the course of Susie's history. Returning home from the cemetery he put down his shovel and remarked, "Did you remember to take down all those signs?" Horrified (since she hadn't) Susie fired up the stove and began baking. Thus, with very little preparation time, the second bake sale took place and was a tremendous success due to the Herculean effort Susie put forth to make it so. Recognizing great talent and motivation when they saw it, the Ladies' Auxiliary asked Susie if she would consider becoming the proprietress of the Mt. Zion Bakery and Tea Room, which was not in existence, but had been a gleam in the eyes of the auxiliary ladies for several years. Thrilled and flattered, Susie accepted, and ran a successful business for many years.

1. The skirt and sash portions of Susie's apron are cut from the same patterns as Maude's. However, Susie's apron was a special gift from her mother, so it has a front bib and eyelet trim. Turn to page 30 and follow the instructions for Making the Apron.

2. For the bib, cut a 7½ x 5-inch (19 x 13) piece of white cotton fabric. Fold it in half widthwise to form a double-layered 3¾ x 5-inch (9.5 x 13) rectangle. Stitch the seam along each shorter edge, and turn the bib right side out. Turn the remaining raw edges to the inside, and press. Center and whipstitch the open edges to the wrong side of the sash.

3. Cut two 10-inch (25) lengths of eyelet trim. Whipstitch one end of one length under an upper corner of the bib. Attach one end of the remaining length to the opposite upper corner. The free ends will be attached to the back of the sash when Susie is dressed.

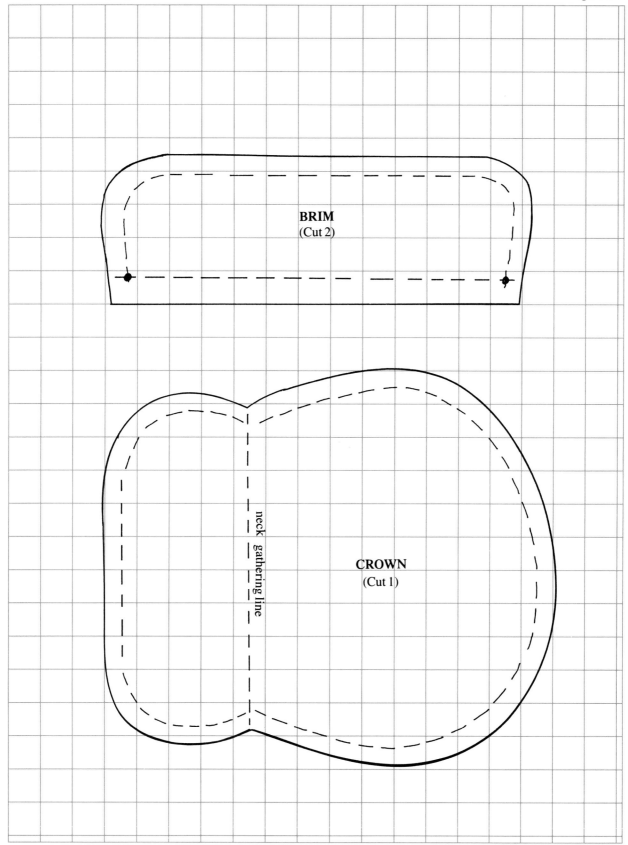

BRIM
(Cut 2)

neck gathering line

CROWN
(Cut 1)

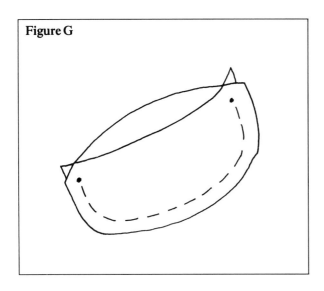

Figure G

Making the Dress

Susie's dress is also the same as Maude's. Turn to page 33 and follow the instructions for Making the Dress, substituting blue gingham fabric for Maude's calico. Instead of lace trim, use eyelet at the ends of Susie's sleeves. Do not add eyelet around the yoke.

Making the Bloomers

Susie's bloomers are the same as Maude's too. Turn to page 34 and follow the directions in the section entitled Making the Bloomers.

Making the Bonnet

1. Scale drawings for the bonnet pieces are given in Figure F. Enlarge the patterns to full size and transfer the small circles and gathering lines. Cut two brims and one crown from light blue cotton.

2. Place the two brims right sides together and stitch the seam along the curved edges between the placement circles (Figure G). Clip the curves and turn the brim right side out. Press the seam allowances to the inside along the remaining raw edges.

3. Sew a ¼-inch (0.6) wide hem along the square lower portion of the crown, easing the hem where necessary so that it lies flat (Figure H).

4. To form a casing for the elastic at the back of the bonnet, pin a length of seam binding along the gathering line on the wrong side of the fabric. Topstitch along both edges of the seam binding. Cut a 3-inch (8) length of elastic and thread it through the casing, tacking the ends securely at the side edges.

5. Sew a double line of gathering stitches within the seam allowance around the circular top portion of the crown (Figure I). Pull the threads to form even gathers and insert the gathered edge of the crown between the pressed open edges of the brim. Adjust the gathers evenly across the length of the brim, and pin them in place (Figure J). Topstitch along the open edge of the brim, stitching through all three layers.

6. Cut a 1-yard (0.9 m) length of pale blue satin ribbon and run a line of basting stitches close to one edge. Pull up even gathers. Pin the gathered edge just underneath the outer edge of the bonnet, working all the way around, beginning and ending at an inside corner of the brim. Adjust the gathers evenly, and topstitch the ribbon in place.

7. Cut two 12-inch (31) lengths of ribbon and stitch them to the brim for ties.

8. To make the roses for the bonnet, use an 18-inch (46) length of blue ribbon. Fold the ribbon in half lengthwise (do not press). Starting at one end, roll the ribbon tightly several times around, and stitch the lower (unfolded) edges together to secure the rolls. Continue rolling the ribbon, more loosely, tacking each subsequent roll at the lower edge until you have a ¾-inch (2) diameter rosebud. Make a second smaller bud in the same manner. Tie the remaining length of ribbon in a bow, and tack the rose buds and the bow to the bonnet brim.

Finishing Details

Dress Susie in her bloomers, dress, apron, and bonnet. Pull the eyelet apron straps to the back, and tack the ends underneath the apron sash. Tie the bonnet ribbons in a bow under Susie's chin.

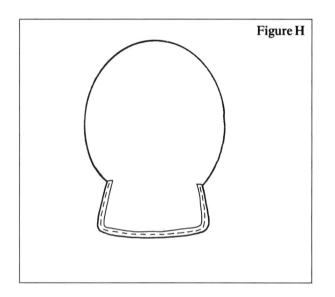

Figure H

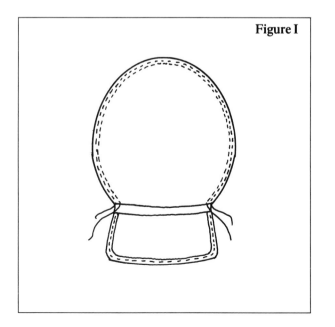

Figure I

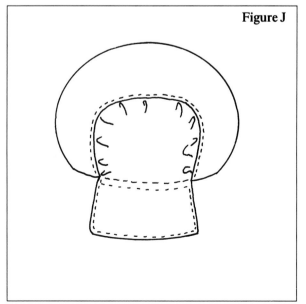

Figure J

Titus Thurston (Hugger Dog)

Born: September 12, 1900

Although Hugger is technically JayJay's dog, he is quite an independent fellow, and has a closer spiritual kinship with Gal (as do most of the other farm animals). JayJay has always been very kind and generous to Hugger, so Hugger takes time out from his busy schedule to do his duty. Since JayJay is currently working on his first aid merit badge, Hugger makes himself available for practice sessions; thus, the ever-present white bandage.

Hugger does not consider himself to be a hound (although he takes his dogly duties seriously), but visualizes himself as resembling an Arabian stallion. He is not at all a snob, but simply prefers acting to squirrel chasing and contemplating the metaphysical properties of existence to rooting through the garbage. As a result, the neighboring dogs have stopped asking him along on coon hunts and digging forays, although Hugger still gets quite miffed if they neglect to inform him where spring courting activities are going on.

Hugger's idol is Teddy Roosevelt, who he attempts to emulate in every way that a dog can. Hugger was first impressed by Mr. Roosevelt when the president supported the Elkins Law in 1903 forbidding rebates to favored corporations, on which subject Hugger had very strong feelings even as a pup. Hugger did object to Mr. Roosevelt's choice of Philander C. Knox as attorney general. (Hugger differs with Mr. Knox on several legal questions.) This objection was removed, however, when William H. Moody assumed the post in 1904.

To keep himself abreast of political developments, Hugger voraciously reads all the newspapers that he can get his paws on.

Marmalade Cat

Born: October 4, 1903

The only explanation that Birdie has ever given for naming an all-white cat Marmalade is that, "She reminds me of that wonderful orange jelly you put on your toast in the morning."

Due to an unfortunate set of circumstances, Marmalade was separated from her natural mother at quite an early age. Casting about for a warm, soft, parent figure, as any creature would, Marmalade fastened on Hugger. Over the years she has developed a real admiration for his intellect and cunning, and has worked very hard to become his valued assistant. Hugger finds it especially helpful to have such an astute partner who is willing to read and summarize the political reports in the overwhelming number of newspapers and magazines which he collects.

It's really quite a treat to see the two of them hunkered down over several erudite journals, their concentration interrupted only by an occasional "rurrf" or "meow."

Hugger—Materials and Tools

Metric equivalents in centimeters are indicated in parentheses.

1½ yards (1.4 m) of tan fake fur, at least 36 inches (90) wide

¼ pound (113 g) of polyester fiberfill

Small scraps of white, brown, and pink felt

1 x 8-inch piece of medium-weight white fabric

Black pompon, about 1½ inches (4) in diameter

Heavy-duty tan sewing thread, long sharp needle, pins, scissors, sewing machine (optional), black felt-tip marker, white glue

Cutting the Pieces

1. Enlarge the scale drawings for the patterns given in Figure A, and cut the following pieces from fake fur: two bodies, four forelegs, four hind legs, two ears, two heads, and one tail. Pay attention to the "place on fold" notations, and transfer the small circles and x-shaped placement marks to the fabric pieces.

2. Full-size drawings for the remaining patterns are given in Figure B. Trace the drawings to make paper patterns. Cut the following pieces from fake fur: two eyelids and two lower lips. Cut two eyes from white felt, two pupils from brown felt, and one tongue from pink felt.

Making the Body and Head

Note: All seams are ⅜ inch (1) unless otherwise specified in the instructions.

1. Pin the two body pieces right sides together and stitch the seam around the edges, leaving the neck edge open and unstitched (Figure C). Clip the curves and turn the stitched body right side out. Stuff the body lightly with fiberfill, and press the seam allowance to the inside around the neck opening. (Although Hugger consumes a large amount of table scraps courtesy of Maude, dog food courtesy of JayJay, dog biscuits courtesy of Gal, and an inordinate number of baking powder biscuits courtesy of Hugo whenever he visits, Hugger remains fairly lean due to the abundant exercise he gets working on the farm. His mornings are spent in surveillance duty on the front porch. At ten o'clock he makes the rounds of the barnyard and then retires to the porch for a mid-morning nap. At midday he surveys the kitchen door for lunch scraps, and most of the afternoon is spent guarding the back porch against would-be attackers with time out only for a short mid-afternoon nap. Late afternoon is set aside for daily lessons with Gal, who has taught Hugger the fine arts of sitting up, begging, shaking hands, rolling over, playing dead [this is Hugger's favorite], and pointing butterflies. Following that, they work on Hugger's budding career as a canine thespian. The current project is a recreation of Teddy Roosevelt's charge up San Juan Hill. Hugger, of course, plays the title role. Lily Langtry [the calf] plays Teddy's horse. Advanced for his time, Hugger is a method actor and requires an appropriate atmosphere in order to faithfully portray Mr. Roosevelt at war, so JayJay and Baby Gladys have assented to provide sound effects and smoke. Hugger's evening hours are set aside for magazine and newspaper reading.)

1 square = 1 inch (2.5)

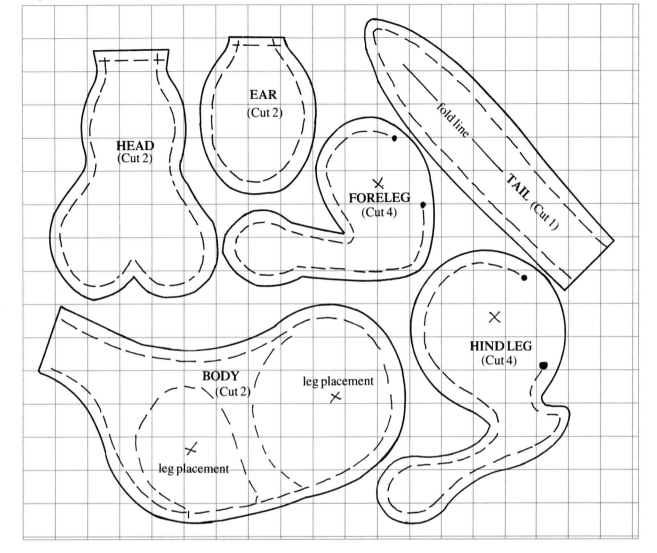

HEAD
(Cut 2)

EAR
(Cut 2)

fold line

TAIL (Cut 1)

FORELEG
(Cut 4)

HIND LEG
(Cut 4)

BODY
(Cut 2)

leg placement

leg placement

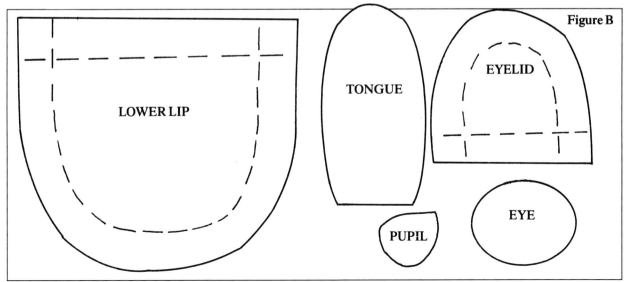

LOWER LIP

TONGUE

EYELID

PUPIL

EYE

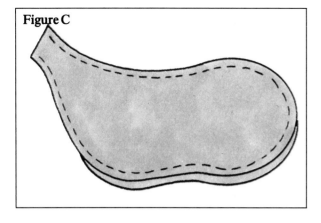

Figure C

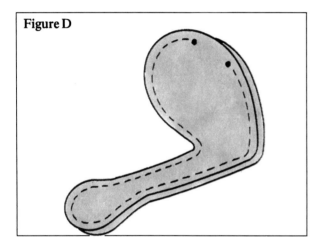

Figure D

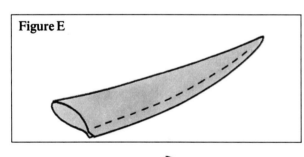

Figure E

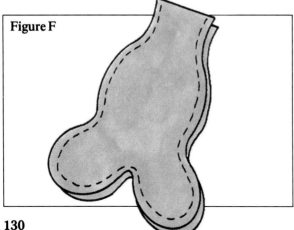

Figure F

2. Pin two forelegs right sides together and stitch the seam around the edges, leaving it open and unstitched between the small circles (Figure D). Clip the curves, turn the stitched foreleg right side out, and press the seam allowances to the inside on the remaining raw edges. The forelegs are not stuffed—simply whipstitch the pressed edges together. Repeat these procedures to make another foreleg, using the remaining two foreleg pieces.

3. Follow the procedures described in step 2 to make two hind legs, using two fur hind leg pieces at a time. The hind legs are not stuffed.

4. Fold the tail piece in half lengthwise, placing right sides together, and stitch the seam along the long edges, leaving the short straight edge open and unstitched (Figure E). Turn the stitched tail right side out, using a pencil or other similar object to turn the point. Press the raw edge to the inside around the open edge. Do not stuff the tail, and leave the open edge unstitched.

5. Pin the two head pieces right sides together and stitch the seam around the contoured edges, leaving the straight edge at the top open and unstitched (Figure F). Clip the curves, turn the stitched head right side out, and stuff fairly full with fiberfill.

6. Insert the unstitched straight edges at the top of the head inside the neck opening of the body, and whipstitch around the neck several times to secure the head.

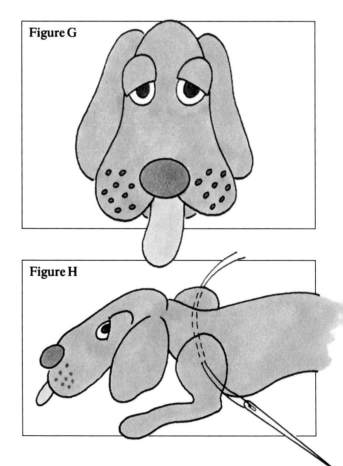

Figure G

Figure H

Adding the Ears and Facial Features

1. On each ear, turn the seam allowance to the wrong side of the fabric all the way around the edge. Whipstitch the seam allowances in place.

2. Whipstitch an ear to each side of the head as shown in Figure G. (Refer to Figure G for placement of all remaining facial features as you work.)

3. On each eyelid, turn the seam allowance to the wrong side of the fabric all the way around the edge, and whipstitch. Whipstitch the eyelids to the head.

4. Glue the white eyes in place, just under the eyelids, and then glue the brown pupils on top of the eyes.

5. Pin the two lower lips right sides together and stitch the seam around the edges, leaving it open and unstitched between the small circles. Clip the curves, turn the lip right side out, and press the seam allowances to the inside on the remaining raw edges. Do not stuff the lip—simply whipstitch the opening edges together. Whipstitch the lower lip underneath the head as shown.

6. Glue the black pompon nose to the center front of the head, and the pink felt tongue just underneath the nose. Make nine or ten small dots on each of Hugger's jowls, using the black felt-tip marker.

Finishing

1. Place the two assembled forelegs on opposite sides of the body, matching placement marks. Use a long sharp needle and heavy-duty thread to stitch back and forth through the body and both legs several times, at the placement marks (Figure H).

2. Repeat the procedures described in step 1 to attach the hind legs to the back of the body.

3. Place the open end of the tail against the center back of the body, and whipstitch around the tail several times.

4. Fold the white fabric in half lengthwise, wrap it around the tail one or two times, and tie the ends in a knot. (Don't tie the bandage too tight, as Hugger is quite fond of chasing his tail and would be greatly disturbed if his circulation were cut off.)

Marmalade—Materials and Tools

Metric equivalents in centimeters are indicated in parentheses.

1 yard (0.9 m) of white fake fur, at least 36 inches (90) wide
Small scraps of pink and white felt and blue satin
12-inch (31) length of pink yarn
Small amount of polyester fiberfill
Short piece of six-strand pink embroidery floss
Heavy-duty white thread, regular and long sharp needles, white craft pipe cleaner, white glue, scissors, pins, sewing machine (optional)

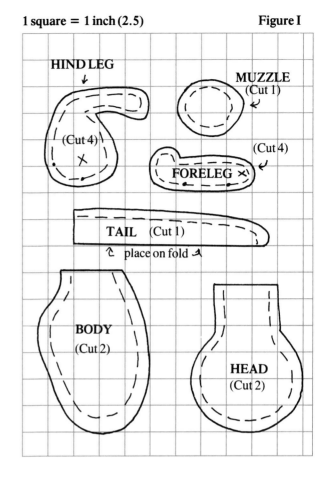

1 square = 1 inch (2.5)   Figure I

HIND LEG
MUZZLE (Cut 1)
(Cut 4)
(Cut 4)
FORELEG
TAIL (Cut 1)
place on fold
BODY (Cut 2)
HEAD (Cut 2)

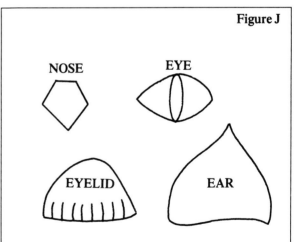

Figure J

NOSE   EYE
EYELID   EAR

Cutting the Pieces

1. Enlarge the scale drawings for the pattern pieces given in Figure I to full-size patterns. Cut the following pieces from white fur: one muzzle, four forelegs, four hind legs, two bodies, two heads, and one tail. Transfer the small circles and the x-shaped placement marks to the fabric pieces.

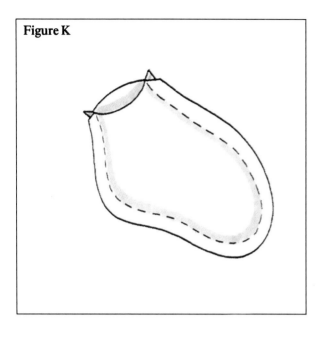

Figure K

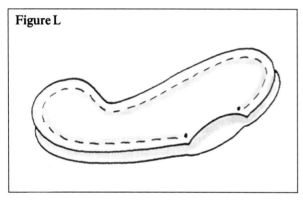

Figure L

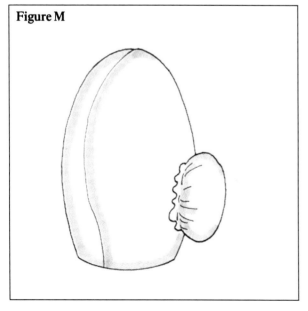

Figure M

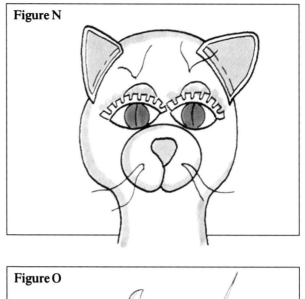

Figure N

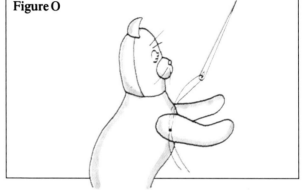

Figure O

2. Full-size drawings for the remaining patterns are given in Figure J. Trace the drawings to make paper patterns. Cut two ears from white fur. Cut two eyelids from white felt and slit each one along the cutting lines to form the eyelashes. Cut two additional ears and one nose from pink felt, and cut two eyes from blue satin.

Making the Body and Head

Note: All seam allowances are ⅜ inch (1) unless otherwise specified in the instructions.

1. Pin the two body pieces right sides together and stitch the seam around the edges, leaving the neck edge open and unstitched (Figure K). Clip the curves, turn the stitched body right side out, and press the seam allowances to the inside around the open neck edge. Stuff the body firmly with fiberfill.

2. Pin two foreleg pieces right sides together and stitch the seam around the edges, leaving it open and unstitched between the small placement circles (Figure L). Clip the curves, turn the stitched foreleg right side out, and press the seam allowances to the inside on the opening edges. Stuff the foreleg firmly with fiberfill. Repeat these procedures to create another foreleg, using the remaining two fur foreleg pieces.

3. Follow the procedures described in step 2 to make two hind legs, using two fur hind leg pieces at a time. Stuff the toe portion firmly, and the haunch portion not so firmly. (Marmalade is somewhat vain about her appearance, and takes great pride in the condition of her forelegs. She follows a regular exercise schedule which she read in a recent issue of *Feline Fitness Quarterly*.)

4. Fold the tail piece in half lengthwise, placing right sides together, and stitch the seam along the long edges, leaving the straight short edge open and unstitched. Clip the seam allowances, turn the tail right side out, and press the raw edges to the inside around the opening. Insert the pipe cleaner all the way into the tail and trim off any excess that extends past the pressed edges.

5. Pin the two head pieces right sides together and stitch the seam around the long curved edges, leaving the straight neck edge open and unstitched. Clip the curve, turn the stitched head right side out, and stuff it firmly with fiberfill. Leave the neck edge open—do not turn the raw edges to the inside.

6. Run a line of basting stitches close to the edge of the fur muzzle piece. Wrap the muzzle piece around a small tuft of fiberfill (approximately 1 inch [2.5] in diameter), and pull up the basting threads to gather the fabric edge together around the fiberfill. Tie off the basting threads to secure the gathers.

Assembly

1. Insert the open neck edges of Marmalade's head inside the neck opening of her body. Whipstitch several times around the neck.

2. Center the muzzle on the front of the head ¾ inch (2) above the neckline, placing the gathered edge of the muzzle against the head (Figure M). Whipstitch the muzzle in place.

3. Refer to Figure N as you complete the facial features. Thread a needle with all six strands of the pink embroidery floss. Anchor the thread at the bottom center of the muzzle and take one stitch over the surface along the vertical center line of the muzzle. Glue the pink felt nose just above the floss. (Marmalade's nose is such a bright pink because she has an unnatural fondness for strawberries and will root through the patch at the first sign of berries. When the family discovered who was to blame for the missing berries, they erected barriers and took a number of other more drastic measures to keep Marmalade out. Alas, nothing seemed to work. It was Maude who finally suggested a practical solution based on her simple rhetorical question, "How many strawberries can a cat eat, anyway?" The solution was to plant extra berries and let the cat eat to her heart's content.)

4. Draw a straight vertical line across the center of each blue eye using the black felt-tip marker, to create the pupils. Glue the eyes to the head above the nose. Glue the eyelids over the eyes.

5. To form the whiskers on each side of the muzzle and above each eyelid, use heavy-duty thread. Take a single stitch at each location, pull the thread through, and cut two equal ends about 2 inches (5) long. Tie the ends in a knot to secure the stitch, and leave them long to form the whiskers.

6. Glue a pink felt ear to the wrong side of each fur ear. Glue or whipstitch the ears to the head where indicated in Figure N. Wrap the length of pink yarn around Marmalade's neck and tie it in a bow.

7. Place the two forelegs on opposite sides of the body, matching placement crosses. Use heavy-duty thread and take several stitches back and forth through the body and forelegs to secure the joints (Figure O).

8. Repeat the procedures described in step 7 to attach the hind legs to the body, matching placement marks.

9. Place the open end of the tail against the center back of the body and whipstitch around it several times.

Superstitious (Sue Pig)

Born: April 15, 1899

Sue Pig was actually named after Susie, because they share the same birthday. The Superstitious part came later, after Sue Pig developed ursidaephobia. At first, the family referred to Sue Pig's malady as simply "fear of bears." But Gal, who was fast becoming her school's star Latin pupil, discovered the proper name for the illness and insisted that everyone call it that. Bowing to Gal's mastery of book learnin', everyone took a few lessons in pronouncing this new word and thereafter used it. All except JayJay, that is, who continued to describe the little porker as, "flat scared of bears."

Not that there are any bears in Iowa. But Sue Pig heard one described when Gal narrated the tale of Goldilocks, and has lived in fear of them ever since. Sue Pig enlisted Gal's aid in developing and setting out "bear scarers" around the pig sty, so the family members have learned to be beary careful when slopping. Sue Pig, of course, insists that her bear scarers work perfectly, pointing out that narry a bear has been seen in the entire county. She suspects, however, that someone has been sleeping in her bed.

Rutabaga (Turnip)

Born: August 12, 1902

Little Turnip was originally named Rutabaga because at birth he immediately displayed his innate talent for rooting. But Gal never did like the name, and since a rutabaga is the same thing as a turnip she figured it would be all the same to call him that. Turnip himself heartily agrees.

Turnip showed great enjoyment of his role as Gal's theatrical barnyard assistant right from the start, and in fact has admitted to entertaining aspirations of becoming a professional stage manager when he grows up. He has, of course, heard horror stories of the discrimination that exists against pigs in certain New York theatrical circles, but is undaunted in his desire to give it a try.

Gal at first thought that he would make a better actor than manager. She encouraged him to learn the classic leading roles of the great plays, such as Hamlet, and to study the great essayists, particularly Sir Francis Bacon. But Turnip has remained staunchly devoted to his behind-the-scenes career.

Sue Pig—Materials and Tools

Metric equivalents in centimeters are indicated in parentheses.

⅜ yard (0.4 m) of pale pink cotton knit fabric

⅝ yard (0.6 m) of ½-inch (1.3) or ¾-inch (2) wide purple satin ribbon

Small scraps of brown felt

6-inch (15) length of white craft pipe cleaner

Pale pink powdered cheek blusher

Large handful of polyester fiberfill

Heavy-duty and regular white thread, needle, pins, sewing machine (optional), scissors

Cutting the Pieces

1. Enlarge the scale drawings for the body, nose, and head patterns provided in Figure A. Cut one of each piece from the pink knit fabric.

2. Trace the full-size drawings provided in Figure B to make paper patterns for the ear, leg, and eyelashes. Cut two ears and four legs from pink knit fabric, paying attention to the "place on fold" notation for the legs. Cut two eyelashes from brown felt.

Making the Head

1. Run a line of basting stitches ½ inch (1.3) from the raw edge of the fabric head. Pull the threads to gather the edge slightly, forming a cup. Stuff a small amount of fiberfill into the cup and pull the gathering threads tightly. Adjust the amount of fiberfill inside if necessary and tie off the gathering threads securely.

2. Follow the procedures described in step 1 to gather and stuff the nose. To attach the nose to the head, place the gathered edge of the nose against the stuffed head, directly opposite the gathered edge of the head (Figure C). Press the two stuffed balls together and whipstitch several times around the nose so that the gathered edge is pressed flat against the head.

3. To sculpture the facial features, use a long sharp needle and a length of heavy-duty thread and follow the entry and exit points illustrated in Figure D. Begin with the closed eye lines.

   a. Enter at the gathered neck edge and exit at point 1. Pull the thread across the surface, enter at 2 and exit at 3.

   b. Pull the thread across the surface, enter at 4 and exit at 1. Pull the thread gently until the closed eye lines appear. Take one or two stitches under the surface between points 1 and 3 to secure the eye lines, exiting at point 1.

Figure A   1 square = 1 inch (2.5)

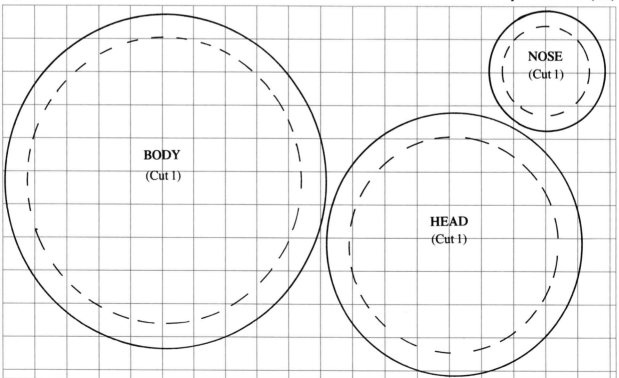

BODY (Cut 1)

NOSE (Cut 1)

HEAD (Cut 1)

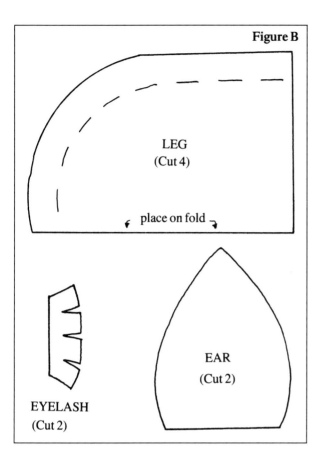

Figure B

LEG
(Cut 4)

place on fold

EYELASH
(Cut 2)

EAR
(Cut 2)

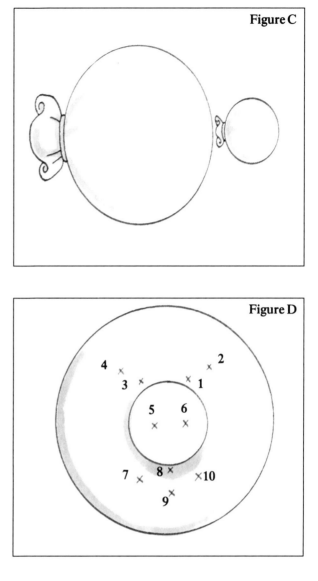

Figure C

Figure D

4
2
3
1
5   6
7
8
10
9

c. To create the nostrils, reenter at 1 and exit at 5. Enter about ⅛ inch (0.3) just below point 5 and exit at 3. Pull the thread gently until a nostril appears and take one or two stitches under the surface at point 3 to secure the nostril, exiting at 3.

d. Reenter at 3 and exit at 6. Enter about ⅛ inch (0.3) just below point 6 and exit at 1. Pull the thread gently until a nostril appears and take one or two stitches under the surface at point 1 to secure the nostril, exiting at 1.

e. To form the mouth, reenter at 1 and exit at 7. Pull the thread across the surface, enter at 8 and exit at 3. Pull the thread until a mouth appears.

f. Reenter at 3 and exit at 9. Pull the thread across the surface, enter at 10 and exit at 1. Pull the thread until a lower mouth line appears.

g. Take one or two stitches under the surface between points 1 and 3 to secure the mouth lines. Exit at the gathered neck edge, lock the stitch, and cut the thread.

4. Glue or whipstitch an eyelash over the closed eye line on each side of the head.

5. Gather the straight lower edge of each ear slightly. Whipstitch the ears to the top of the head, approximately 1½ inches (3.8) above the eye lines. The side edge of each ear should be bent slightly forward (Figure E).

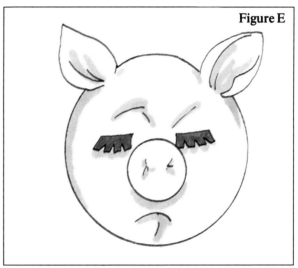

Figure E

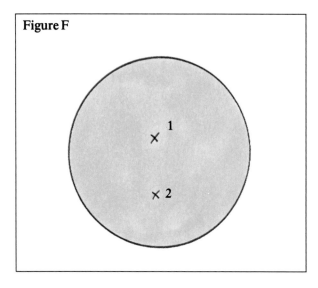

Figure F

Figure G

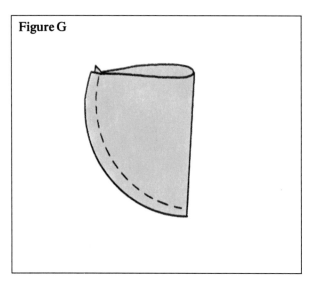

Figure H

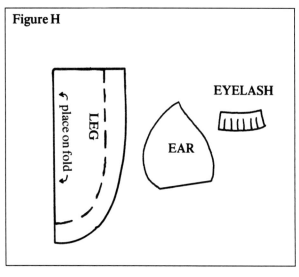

LEG

place on fold

EYELASH

EAR

Assembling the Body

1. Follow the procedures described in step 1 under Making the Head to gather and stuff the body. To sculpture the "anatomical feature," use a long sharp needle and a length of heavy-duty thread. Refer to the entry and exit points illustrated in Figure F, which shows the stuffed body from the back. If you could see straight through it, you would see the gathered neck edge at the opposite side.

    a. Enter at the gathered neck edge and exit at point 1 on the opposite side.

    b. Pull the thread straight downward across the surface and enter at point 2. Push the needle straight through the stuffed body and exit at the gathered neck edge.

    c. Pull the thread gently until the "anatomical feature" appears. Lock the stitch and cut the thread.

2. To make each leg, leave the fabric leg folded in half and stitch a ½-inch (1.3) wide seam along the long curved edge, leaving the straight short edge open and unstitched (Figure G). Clip the curve, turn the stitched leg right side out and press the seam allowance to the inside on the open upper edge. Stuff the leg tightly with fiberfill. Make all four legs in this manner.

3. Place the stuffed head and body together, matching gathered edges. Press them together and whipstitch around the neck several times, placing your stitches well outside of the gathered edges so that they are hidden.

4. Pin two assembled legs to the bottom of the body just behind the neck seam, approximately 1½ inches (3.8) apart. The pointed bottom corner of each leg should face forward. Whipstitch around the upper edge of each leg several times to attach it to the body.

5. Pin the remaining two legs to the bottom of the body, approximately 1½ inches (3.8) behind the front legs and the same distance apart (pointed corners facing forward). Whipstitch each back leg to the body.

Finishing Details

Twist the length of pipe cleaner into a spiral tail. Glue or whipstitch it to the body between the hams at the top of the "anatomical feature."

Brush powdered blusher across the cheeks (front and back), on the nose, above the eyes, inside the ears, across the mouth, and across the front of each forefoot.

Wrap the purple ribbon around Sue Pig's neck, and tie it in a bow on top.

Turnip—Materials and Tools

Metric equivalents in centimeters are indicated in parentheses.

¼ yard (0.23 m) of pink cotton knit fabric
12-inch (31) length of deep pink yarn
Small scraps of deep pink felt
Two doll eye beads, each ¼ inch (0.6) in diameter
    with a deep pink center
2-inch (5) length of white craft pipe cleaner
Small handful of polyester fiberfill
Heavy-duty and regular pink thread, pale pink
    powdered cheek blusher, white glue, scissors, pins,
    needle, sewing machine (optional)

Cutting and Assembly

Turnip is put together very much like Sue Pig, with a few exceptions noted here.

1. Cut three circular pieces of pink cotton knit fabric; a body 6 inches (15) in diameter, a head 5 inches (13) in diameter, and a nose 2½ inches (6) in diameter.

2. Full-size drawings of the leg, ear, and eyelash patterns are provided in Figure H. Trace the drawings to make paper patterns. Cut two ears and four legs from pink cotton knit fabric, and cut two eyelashes from pink felt.

3. Gather and stuff the body, head, and nose, and whipstitch the nose to the head as you did Sue Pig's. Sculpture the nostrils in the same manner. To create the eye sockets and mouth, use a needle and heavy-duty pink thread. Follow the entry and exit points in Figure I.

    a. To create the eye sockets, enter at the gathered neck edge and exit at point 1. Reenter at 1 and exit at point 2.

    b. Reenter at 2 and exit at 1. Pull the thread gently to create a slight indention at each point, and take another stitch back and forth under the surface between 1 and 2 to secure the sockets, exiting at 1.

    c. To create the mouth, reenter at 1 and exit at 3. Pull the thread across the surface, enter at 4 and exit at 5. Pull the thread across the surface, enter at 4 and exit at the gathered neck edge.

    d. Pull the thread gently until the mouth appears, lock the stitch and cut the thread.

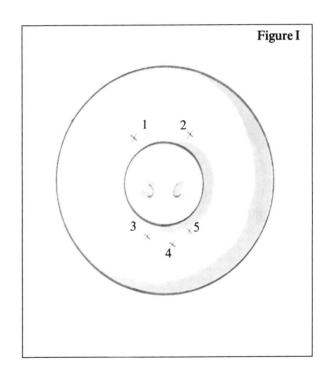

Figure I

4. Glue the eye beads over the eye sockets. Glue an eyelash over each eye, but not directly on top. The eyelashes should be placed slightly to the sides. Glue or whipstitch the ears to the head as you did for Sue Pig.

5. Sculpture the "anatomical feature" and attach the head to the body as you did for Sue Pig.

6. Stitch, turn, and stuff the legs as you did for Sue Pig. Attach the legs to the body in the same manner.

7. Twist the pipe cleaner into a spiral tail and glue it in place. Tie the pink yarn around Turnip's neck.

Millard Fillmore (Shutup Rooster)

Hatched: June 1, 1904

Shutup was originally named after the nation's thirteenth president. Former vice-president Fillmore, who served as president for only two years when Zachary Taylor died in office, was renominated in 1856 by the American (Know Nothing) party, but lost the election to Buchanan. Birdie named the new rooster Millard Fillmore because she felt the two had so much in common. After all, the little rooster obviously knew nothing, and would almost certainly never be elected president.

The family informally changed the rooster's name when it became apparent that his internal clock was unalterably set on Greenwich Mean Time. The result of this unnatural characteristic is that Shutup regularly crows the dawn at midnight, which is, of course, upsetting to a farm family who hold to a routine of early to bed and early to rise. So they really cannot be faulted for yelling, "Shut-up, Rooster!" each night when the crowing begins.

Sue Pig secretly appreciates Shutup's nocturnal ruckuses, since they help keep the bears away.

Jane Chicken

Hatched: March 3, 1905

Jane has some extremely unusual characteristics for a chicken. Some of them, such as her prowess as a jacks player, were noticed by the family soon after her hatching. Others are less obvious, and were recognized only after certain events unfolded.

Gal was the first to realize that Jane is a psychic hen. The rest of the family was not convinced until Casey returned with the news of his ill-fated trip to San Francisco during the great quake and fire of 1906. On the day he was to leave, Gal noticed that Jane had been nervous all morning. When Casey picked up his bag and prepared to mount the wagon, Jane began clucking wildly and then threw herself at his legs in an apparent effort to block his exit. Jane worked herself into a frenzy and stayed that way until Casey's return, whereupon she fainted with relief at the sight of him.

Jane's name has no special significance, but it would be best if she remains ignorant of that fact. She was named quickly on one of Birdie's very busy days. Since the circumstances of her naming are unknown to Jane, she has made the assumption that she is named after the famous, much-heralded Jane Doe, and continually pumps Hugger and Marmalade for more information about this great lady.

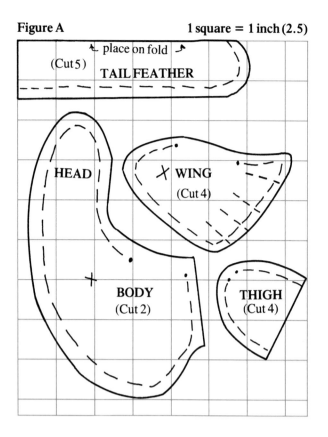

Shutup Rooster—Materials and Tools

Metric equivalents in centimeters are indicated in parentheses.

½ yard (0.45 m) of light-weight white terry cloth
Five white craft pipe cleaners
One orange craft pipe cleaner
4 yards (3.6 m) of red yarn
Scraps of yellow and white felt
Handful of polyester fiberfill
White glue, scissors, pins, white and red heavy-duty
     thread, black felt-tip marker

Making the Body

1. Enlarge the scale drawings given in Figure A to full-size patterns. Cut the following pieces from white terry cloth: two bodies, four thighs, four wings, and five tail feathers. Transfer the small circles, the x-shaped placement markings, and the broken topstitching lines to the fabric pieces.

2. Pin the two body pieces right sides together and stitch the seam around the edges, leaving it open and unstitched between the small circles (Figure B). Clip the curves, turn the stitched body right side out, and press the seam allowances to the inside along the opening edges. Stuff the rooster firmly with fiberfill.

3. Fold one tail feather piece in half lengthwise, placing right sides together, and stitch the seam along the long

edges, leaving the short straight edge open and unstitched. Turn the tail feather right side out, and press the seam allowances to the inside on the open edge. Insert a white pipe cleaner all the way into the tail feather and trim off the excess. Repeat these procedures to create the remaining four tail feathers.

4. Hold all five tail feathers together with open ends even, and tie a length of heavy-duty thread tightly around them to hold them together. Insert the tied ends of the tail feathers inside the opening on the body, positioning them as shown in Figure C. Whipstitch the opening edges together, stitching the feathers securely inside. Bend the feathers so that they curve gracefully toward the back. (Shutup's tail feathers are a source of great pride, as is the case with most roosters worth their salt. During an unusually cold winter, however, Shutup fell prey to the dreaded Terminal Tail Droop disease which was ravaging roosters for miles around. Although the disease caused no lasting physical damage, the psychological effects were devastating. Birdie tried everything she could think of to perk up her rooster's tail feathers and spirits, all to no avail. Fortunately, Gal finally hit on a temporary solution which improved Shutup's psychological malaise until the disease had run its course. What she did was to whip up a batch of heavy-duty starch which she applied directly to the drooping feathers, and tied them around a tomato stake which held them erect until the starch hardened. This did the trick, and by the next morning, Shutup was once again strutting his [stiff] stuff.)

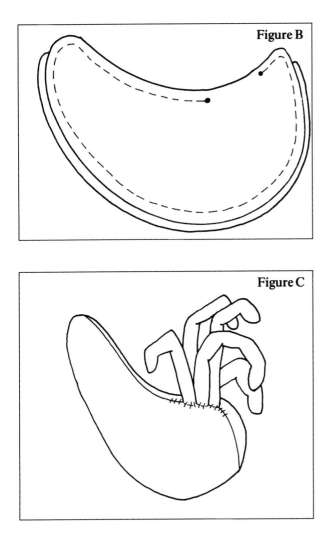

Figure B

Figure C

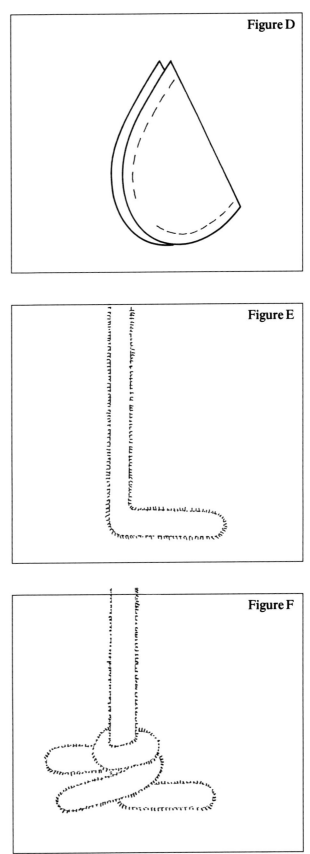

Figure D

Figure E

Figure F

5. Pin two thigh pieces right sides together and stitch the seam along the long curved edge, leaving a ¼-inch (0.6) opening at the bottom and leaving the straight upper edge open and unstitched (Figure D). Clip the curves, turn the thigh right side out, and press the seam allowance to the inside around the upper edge. Stuff firmly with fiber-fill. Repeat these procedures to create another thigh, using the remaining thigh pieces.

6. To make a lower leg and foot, cut two pieces of orange pipe cleaner; one 3½ inches (9) long, and one 1½ inches (4) long. Bend a ¾-inch (2) portion of the longer piece at a right angle (Figure E). Fold the shorter piece in half and twist it around the bend in the longer piece to form the foot. Bend the tips of the two front claws downward, as shown in Figure F. Insert the straight end of the pipe cleaner assembly into the small opening at the bottom of one thigh and push it up until the end of the pipe cleaner is even with the open upper edge of the thigh. Put a dab of glue at the small opening to secure the pipe cleaner. Repeat these procedures to create and attach a second foot.

143

7. Whipstitch the thighs to the bottom of the body, on either side of the body seam where indicated in Figure G.

8. Pin two wing pieces right sides together and stitch the seam around the edges, leaving it open and unstitched between the small circles. Clip the curves, turn the wing right side out, and press the seam allowances to the inside on the opening edges. Stuff the wing very lightly with fiberfill, and whipstitch the opening edges together. Repeat these procedures to create another wing.

9. To sculpture the feathers, topstitch through each wing along the broken lines shown on the scale drawing.

10. Place the wings on opposite sides of the body, matching placement crosses. To secure the wings, take several stitches through the body and both wings using a long sharp needle and heavy-duty thread.

Adding the Features

1. To make Shutup's comb and wattle, you will be working with a continuous length of red yarn and a needle threaded with heavy-duty red thread. Begin by stitching one end of the yarn to the top of the head. Don't cut the thread—just leave the needle where you can easily find it again.

2. Wrap the yarn ten or twelve times around a pencil. Insert the needle between the yarn and pencil, and pull it out through the opposite end (Figure H). Pull the pencil out and take another stitch into the head to secure the curl. Continue making curls in this manner, working down the center front of the head. End with two large loops below the last curl, to form the wattle (Figure I).

3. A full-size pattern for the beak is provided in Figure J. Cut one beak from yellow felt and fold it at the widest point to form the upper and lower lips, as it were. Glue the beak to the red yarn face.

4. Cut two ⅜-inch (1) diameter circles of white felt for the eyes. To form the pupils, draw a black circle in the center of each eye, using the felt-tip marker. Glue the eyes to the red yarn on either side of the head.

Jane Chicken—Materials and Tools

Metric equivalents in centimeters are indicated in parentheses.

¼ yard (0.23 m) of thin white terry cloth
One orange craft pipe cleaner
1 yard (0.9 m) of red yarn
Small scraps of yellow and white felt
Small amount of polyester fiberfill
Black felt-tip marker, white and red heavy-duty thread, scissors, pins, needle, sewing machine, white glue

Cutting and Assembly

1. Enlarge the scale drawings for the patterns provided in Figure K. Cut two bodies, four wings, and four thighs from terry cloth.

2. Assemble Jane Chicken in the same manner you did Shutup Rooster, disregarding the references to the tail feathers. Make Jane's comb slightly shorter as befits her size, and do not make a wattle as that would be quite inappropriate for a feminine young thing like Jane. When cutting the pipe cleaner to make the lower legs and feet, cut one 2½-inch (6.5) length and one 1¼-inch (3) length for each side. (Jane is somewhat bowlegged, which accounts for her rather strange walk. She wasn't that way at birth, but acquired it as a result of one of Birdie's experiments. Trying to encourage her hens to lay, Birdie placed porcelain doorknobs in the nests. Jane sat on her doorknob for nearly a month straight, concentrating all her efforts on hatching it, before Birdie realized something was amiss. It took Birdie another month of cajoling and special feedings to assuage Jane's wounded pride and get her back to a normal routine of scratching, picking, laying, and setting. Her legs, however, remained permanently doorknob-shaped.)

3. A full-size pattern for Jane's beak is provided in Figure J. Cut one from yellow felt, and proceed as you did for Shutup. Jane's eyes are just slightly smaller than Shutup's.

4. To sculpture Jane's tail feathers, use a long sharp needle and heavy-duty white thread. Take a stitch through the body ¾ inch (2) from the upper point of the scalloped tail edge (Figure L). Pull the thread across the surface, wrapping it around the back of the tail at the point of the scallop, and take another stitch through the body over the original stitch (Figure M). Pull the thread gently and lock the stitch. Make an identical sculpturing stitch at the lower point of the scalloped tail edge.

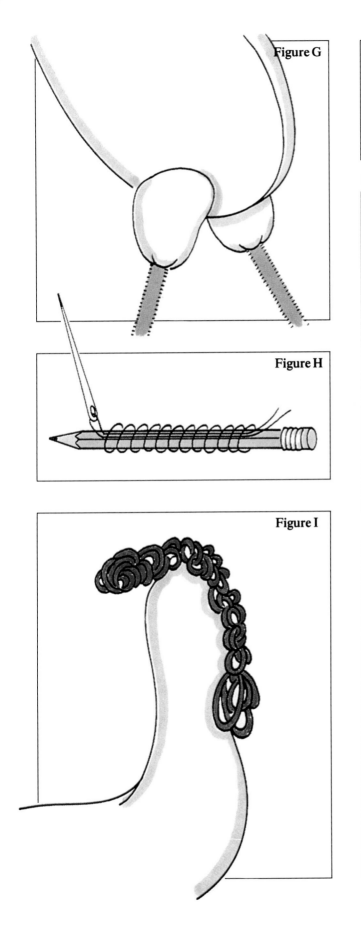

Figure G

Figure H

Figure I

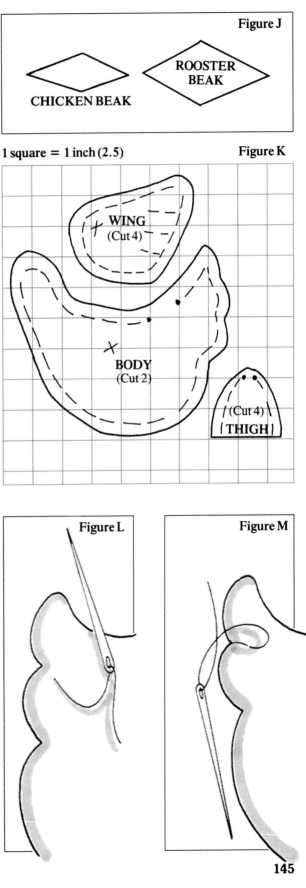

Figure J

CHICKEN BEAK

ROOSTER BEAK

1 square = 1 inch (2.5)

Figure K

WING
(Cut 4)

BODY
(Cut 2)

(Cut 4)
THIGH

Figure L

Figure M

145

Homer Cow

Born: April 17, 1894

Homer had no name at all until Gal became involved in a barnyard production of *The Odyssey*, by the famed ancient Greek poet. In that performance, Gal played a double role as Penelope (of course), the wife of Odysseus, and as one of the irresistable sirens who lured sailors to their deaths on the rocks of the Ionian Sea.

Homer's soulful cow eyes inspired Gal in her performance, and so she began calling the bovine by the poet's name. Homer (the cow) apparently took the name to heart, because it was noted thereafter that her moos had a poetic lilt.

Someone did mention to Gal that Homer is a female, but Gal quite precisely pointed out that she has a brother named Gladys, and if that is acceptable, then a cow named Homer is certainly not too out of line.

Homer is a peace-loving docile animal whose formidable anger is aroused by only one thing; the alleged cause of the Chicago fire in 1871. Homer feels very strongly that one of her own has been continually maligned in this regard, and insists that Ma O'Leary's lantern was more likely tipped over by some drunk than by a cud-chewing bovine who was probably sleeping at that time of night. (We don't mean to tell tales, but you should be aware of this since you will be having Homer in your household.)

Lily Langtry

Born: May 22, 1903

Lily was the firstborn of Homer and a particularly handsome bull named Jethro, who took advantage of a broken fence and made an unscheduled visit to the Weepeeple farm one Sunday evening while the family was at vespers. Homer was taken unaware. Maude was thrilled with the prospect of a new calf. Barney set about mending the fence. Casey was in Chicago.

Lily, of course, was named by Gal. Like her mother, she takes her name seriously, and is constantly singing. This works out well, since her mother's mooing provides the background for most of her songs. She has become so accomplished in her performances that she is known now by her stage name, The Jersey Lily.

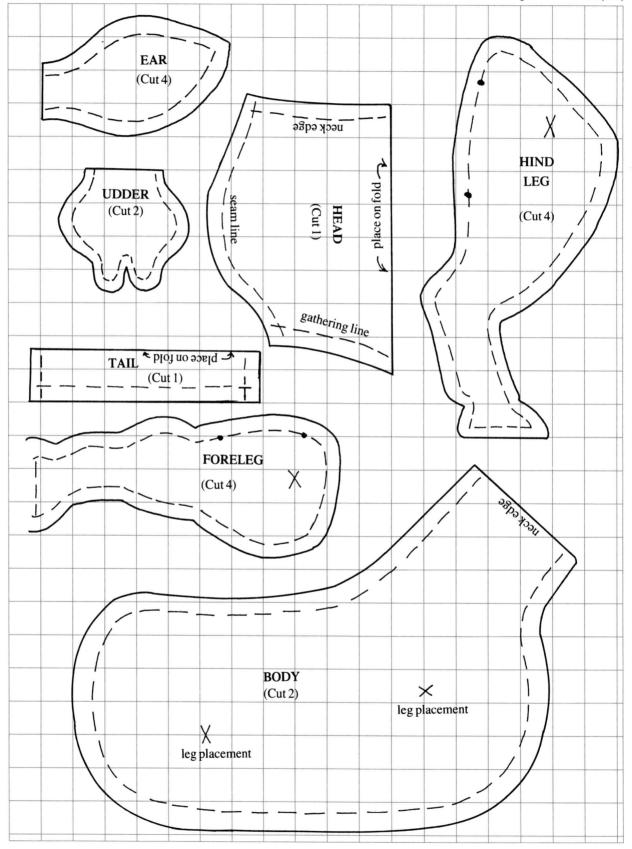

Homer Cow—Materials and Tools

Metric equivalents in centimeters are indicated in parentheses.

1 yard (0.9 m) of narrow-wale brown corduroy
5 x 10-inch (13 x 25) piece of pink cotton knit fabric
12-inch (31) square of brown felt
Small scrap of white felt
1 yard (0.9 m) of brown yarn
Small amount of brown fiber
½ pound (227 g) of polyester fiberfill
Black felt-tip marker, heavy-duty and regular brown thread, white glue, regular and long sharp needles, pins, scissors, sewing machine (optional)

Cutting the Pieces

1. Enlarge the scale drawings for the pattern pieces given in Figure A. Cut the following pieces from brown corduroy: two bodies, four forelegs, four hind legs, one tail, four ears, and one head. Cut two udders from pink cotton knit fabric. Cut four hooves from brown felt. Pay attention to the "place on fold" notations, and transfer the small circles and other placement markings to the fabric pieces.

2. Full-size drawings of the remaining patterns are provided in Figure B. Trace the drawings to make paper patterns. Cut two eyelashes and two pupils from brown felt. Cut two eyes from white felt.

Making the Body

1. Pin the two body pieces right sides together and stitch the seam around the contoured edges, leaving the straight neck edge open and unstitched. Clip the curves, turn the stitched body right side out, and press the seam allowance to the inside around the neck edge. Stuff the body tightly with fiberfill.

2. Pin two foreleg pieces right sides together and stitch the seam around the long contoured edges, leaving it open and unstitched between the small circles. Clip the corners and curves, turn the leg right side out, and press the seam allowances to the inside along the opening edges. Stuff the leg tightly with fiberfill and whipstitch the opening edges together. Repeat these procedures to make another foreleg, using the remaining two corduroy foreleg pieces.

3. Follow the same procedures described in step 2 to make the two hind legs, using two corduroy hind leg pieces at a time. (Be sure to stitch the hind legs securely, since they will be under an unusual amount of strain. Homer, you see, has been an incorrigible leaper ever since she heard Gal's recital of "Hey Diddle Diddle," the famous Mother Goose rhyme in which a cow jumps over the moon. Gal was aparently quite convincing on the occasion of that barnyard performance, and Homer always had been motivated by a good challenge. So, believing that such a lunar leap can in fact be accomplished by a bovine high-jumper, Homer has been in training ever since the recital. Consider yourself forewarned, then, that once you have assembled Homer Cow, you'd best put the irreplacable breakables out of harm's way.)

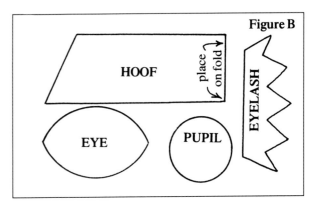

Figure B

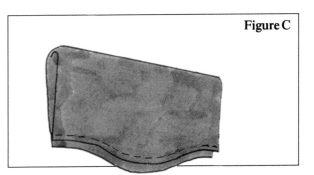

Figure C

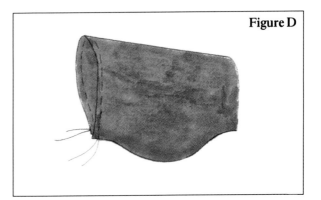

Figure D

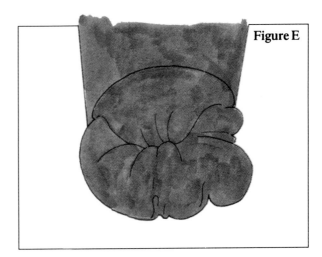

Figure E

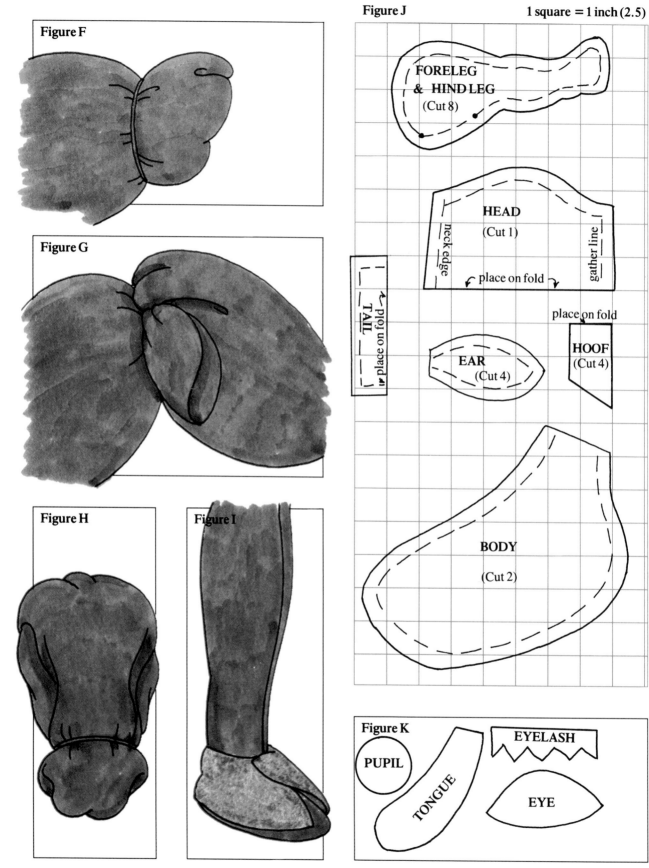

Figure F

Figure G

Figure H

Figure I

Figure J

1 square = 1 inch (2.5)

FORELEG & HIND LEG (Cut 8)

HEAD (Cut 1)

neck edge

gather line

place on fold

TAIL place on fold

EAR (Cut 4)

place on fold

HOOF (Cut 4)

BODY (Cut 2)

Figure K

PUPIL

TONGUE

EYELASH

EYE

4. Fold the tail in half lengthwise, right sides together, and stitch the seam along the long edges only. Turn the stitched tail right side out, and press the seam allowances to the inside on both short ends.

5. Cut several 6-inch (15) lengths of brown yarn and tie them together at the center. Fold the yarn lengths in half and insert the tied center portions inside one open end of the tail. Whipstitch over the yarn to secure it in place.

6. Pin the two udders right sides together and stitch the seam around the contoured edges, leaving the straight upper edge open. Clip the curves, turn right side out, and press the seam allowances to the inside along the open upper edges. Stuff with fiberfill.

7. Pin two ears right sides together, and stitch the seams along the two curved edges, leaving the short lower edge open. Clip the curves and turn the stitched ear right side out. Repeat these procedures to create a second ear.

8. Leave the head piece folded right sides together, and stitch the seam along the lower curved edge (Figure C). Clip the curve and turn the head right side out. Run a line of basting stitches (by hand) around the neck edge (Figure D).

9. Stuff fiberfill loosely inside the head. Run a line of hand basting stitches around the nose end, approximately ½ inch (1.3) from the edge. Do not cut the thread. Pull the thread to gather the opening, turning the raw edge to the inside. Manipulate the gathered nose to form two nostrils as shown in Figure E. Insert the needle through the center of the gathered opening, and exit at the bottom of the head at the seam line, approximately 2 inches (5) from the gathered opening measuring along the seam line. Wrap the thread completely around the nose, pulling it tightly to form the muzzle as shown in Figure F. Lock the stitch at the seam line and cut the thread.

Assembly

1. Pull the basting thread at the neck edge of the head to form even gathers. Pin the neck edge inside the neck opening of the body. Adjust the gathers to create a pleat on each side to accommodate an ear.

2. Fold one ear in half lengthwise and insert it between the head and neck opening at the pleat on one side, so that the folded edge of the ear faces the back (Figure G). Pin the ear in place. Pin the remaining ear in place, and whipstitch around the neck several times to secure the head and ears.

3. Pinch up a vertical ridge between the eye positions on the head, approximately 1 inch (2.5) above the muzzle thread (Figure H). Take one or two stitches back and forth underneath the ridge between the eye points to secure the ridge. Glue the white felt eyes over the stitches, and glue the brown felt pupils on top of the eyes. Glue the felt eyelashes just above the eyes, with outer edges even.

4. Use the black marker to draw a circle in the center of each brown pupil, and to darken the gathered end of the nose. Glue a small tuft of brown fiber to the top of the head and comb it forward.

5. Place the two forelegs on opposite sides of the body, matching placement crosses, and take several stitches back and forth through the body and both legs at the marks to secure the joints. Attach the hind legs in the same manner.

6. Pin the open edge of the udder to the body, just in front of the hind legs, and whipstitch in place. (It's a good idea to warm your hands before you attach the udder because Homer is quite sensitive. T.J., one cold winter's morning, forgot to warm his hands before milking time and when the dust settled he found himself in the next county.) Pin the open edge of the tail to the body at the center back and whipstitch.

7. Wrap one felt hoof around the bottom of one leg, so that the ends meet in a v-shape at the front (Figure I). Glue the hoof in place. Glue a felt hoof to each leg.

Lily Langtry Calf—Materials and Tools

Metric equivalents in centimeters are indicated in parentheses.

¾ yard (0.7 m) of narrow-wale brown corduroy
10-inch (25) square of brown felt
Small scraps of pink and white felt
12-inch (31) length of pink satin ribbon, ¾ inch (2) or
    1 inch (2.5) wide
1 yard (0.9 m) of brown yarn
¼ pound (113 g) of polyester fiberfill
Black felt-tip marker
Heavy-duty and regular brown thread, regular and
    long sharp needles, pins, scissors, white glue,
    sewing machine (optional)

Cutting and Assembly

1. Enlarge the scale drawings for the patterns provided in Figure J. Full-size patterns for the remaining pieces are provided in Figure K.

2. To make Lily Calf, follow the cutting and sewing directions given for Homer Cow. Do not make an udder for Lily and do not glue fiber to her head. Cut one tongue from pink felt, using the full-size pattern provided in Figure P, and glue the straight short end inside the gathered nose end of the head. When making the tail, cut 4-inch (10) lengths of yarn instead of the 6-inch (15) lengths specified for Homer. Tie the satin ribbon around Lily's neck.

Tips & Techniques

Choosing Materials

Pantyhose are available in many colors, weights, and weaves. While the heavier weights and weaves are sturdier, they are too firm to allow for easy sculpturing, and support-type hose should never be used.

For best results, we suggest you use regular-weave pantyhose in a medium skin tone. When stuffed properly, this material will be pliable enough to sculpture easily.

For body fabric, we have specified flesh-colored cotton knit. This should be a double-knit; one that stretches both horizontally and vertically. When selecting the knit fabric choose a cotton-polyester blend, not a fabric that is 100 percent polyester. The latter will not only be more difficult to work with, but it will tend to run just like hose. A blend of cotton and polyester won't do that. It is also more pliable and nicer to the touch.

For the boot fabric, choose a very thin vinyl that is cotton backed. If you wish, substitute thin leather or black cotton.

Be sure that all clothing fabrics are colorfast, washable, and preshrunk. If you're not sure, wash the fabric before cutting the patterns.

We have specified heavy-duty thread for all sculpturing and for sewing that will be taking an unusual amount of stress. The best thread for this purpose is 100 percent nylon with a bonded finish, usually sold for drapery making. It will take the strain without breaking and is not apt to hurt your hands.

You have a choice of several different materials for the hair. We used wiglets (available in wig shops or department stores) for most of the dolls because they look so realistic, but you may use weaver's fiber or yarn. Mohair yarn is preferred because its fuzzy texture resembles real hair.

If you are working with yarn or fiber, follow these suggestions. After the yarn or fiber has been placed across the head and backstitched to create a center part, untwist each strand. Use a hair pick or brush to gently comb out the yarn or fiber. Arrange or cut the hair in the desired style and glue it to the head all the way around the natural hairline.

Tools You Will Need

A long sharp needle is specified for sculpturing. A "sharp" is a type of needle commonly available in fabric stores. Unfortunately, these needles do not have specific sizes, so we can't recommend a particular size for a particular job. Select a needle that is long enough to push through a stuffed pantyhose head without getting lost, but which is not so large that the eye of the needle makes holes

(and resulting runs) in the hose. The needle should be fairly sturdy; not too flimsy or flexible.

When making the body, we suggest you use straight pins with a rounded point (called "ball point" pins). These pins are recommended for use with knit fabrics because they will not pierce the fibers, which regular pins will do. We usually use ball-headed pins (those with large, spherical colored-plastic heads) because they are much easier to find in the fabric (and on the floor).

Although ordinary white can be used whenever glue in specified in the book, hot-melt adhesive is a real timesaver. Suprisingly enough, the hot glue will not melt the hose and holds much better than white glue.

Hot-melt adhesive comes in solid sticks which are inserted in a special glue gun. The gun heats the glue sticks and dispenses melted glue when you pull the trigger. It is a very quick process, and will eliminate the clamping time required for white glue. It can also be used as a substitute for hand stitching.

Use extreme care when working with a glue gun. The glue is very hot when it is ejected from the gun and will blister your fingers if you touch it before it cools.

Sewing Tips

Stitching may be done by hand or machine. Although a sewing machine will be faster, all of the dolls can be created using only hand stitches.

Whipstitching joins two fabric pieces together, catching an equal amount of fabric on each edge (Figure A). Insert the needle up through the bottom fabric. Bring the needle diagonally forward and insert it down through the top fabric. Guide the needle straight across underneath both edges, and then up through the bottom fabric. Each stitch is worked straight across, perpendicular to the fabric edges, resulting in a diagonal stitch pattern on the visible side of the fabric.

Blindstitching (also called slipstitching) is used to invisibly sew one edge to another (Figure B). Insert the needle inside the folded edge of the fabric. Keep the needle inside the fold for the length of one stitch. Bring the needle out and take an invisible stitch in the other fabric side.

Basting stitches (Figure C) are used to hold fabric in place temporarily before the final stitching is done by hand or machine. They are removed after the project is complete. To baste, simply make a line of long running stitches through the fabric layers. Hand basting stitches are usually about ½ inch (1.3) long. To make machine basting stitches, use the longest stitch setting. To facilitate removal, use a thread color that will be easy to see.

Topstitching is a final stitch on the visible side of the assembly. The stitching line should be very straight, and a uniform distance from the edge of the fabric.

Clipping seam allowances is necessary on curves and corners so the assembly wil lie flat when turned right side out and pressed. To eliminate excess fabric on an outward curve or corner, cut v-shaped notches in the seam allowance. An inside curve or corner must be clipped or there will not be enough slack to turn the assembly right side out. Make straight cuts as close as possible to the stitching line without cutting through the stitches.

To **enlarge a scale drawing**, first draw a grid of 1-inch (2.5) squares on a large piece of paper. (Or, use dressmaker's pattern paper which has a grid already drawn on it.) Copy the scale drawing to the larger grid, working square by square (Figure D). You can either cut out the full-size pattern or transfer the outline to fabric using carbon paper and a pencil.

Fitting is very important. The exact size of your finished doll bodies will depend on your accuracy in several procedures; enlarging the scale drawings, cutting the fabric, and sewing the seams. A slight variation in each of these steps will add up to a significant difference in the size of the dolls. For this reason, we suggest that after you have made full-size paper patterns for the clothing, you fit the patterns to the doll before cutting the fabric. Then you can make necessary **adjustments** before any damage is done. If you want to be doubly sure, fit the paper patterns and then cut the fabric pieces for the clothing with extra-wide seam allowances.

You may baste the seams before the final assembly. Basting stitches are much easier to remove than smaller finishing stitches. If you are at all unsure of an assembly procedure, we suggest that you baste first.

Soft Sculpturing Tips

The main thing to remember when sculpturing pantyhose is that you do not have to settle for what you get the first time. Stuffed hose are remarkably pliable and moldable—almost like working with clay.

Even after a length of hose has been stuffed and tied off, you can manipulate the shape to an amazing degree. If you wish to enlarge a small area you can use the tip of your needle to pull the fiberfill out. For larger areas you can pull the fiberfill out using your hands. By working with the stuffed hose you can manipulate it to assume many characteristics.

It is easier to work with a shape that has not been overstuffed. You want just enough fiberfill to fill out the desired shape, but not so much that you cut down on your working ability. If a shape is very tightly stuffed, there will be no room for the fiberfill to give when you wish to manipulate a specific shape.

When stuffing the head, use your fingers to mold the fiberfill inside the pantyhose in the same way a sculptor would mold the clay in making a bust. You want to mold a head shape, not simply a round sphere.

Again, remember not to stuff the head too tightly. Leave a cavity in the core of the stuffing; you want to have plenty of give when you stitch the facial features.

When attaching the head to the body begin stitching at the center back and then continue around the neck. We've found that starting at any other point causes the head to swivel into a strange position.

In the instructions, "Reenter at same point" means to insert the needle as near as possible to the last exit point. Do not try to find the precise exit point.

Where the instructions indicate to pull the thread tension "tightly," do so in a gentle manner, being careful not to rip the hose.

To secure the sculpturing stitches temporarily as you are working on a section, take one or two stitches under the surface. To lock the stitches permanently at the end of a section, take several stitches at the designated point and knot the thread with each stitch.

Apply a thin coat of clear acrylic spray to your finished work. It will help prevent runs and maintain the molded shape. If you see a run about to develop, touch it with a small amount of clear nail polish and allow the polish to dry before you continue working.

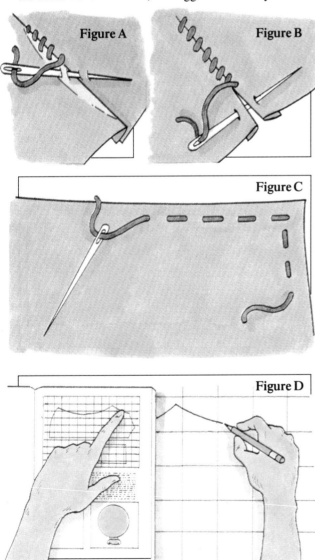

Figure A

Figure B

Figure C

Figure D

Making the Dolls' Bodies

The Weepeeple are a very closely knit family, as evidenced by the fabric from which their bodies are made. You'll be following the same basic procedures to make a body (arms, legs, and torso) for each doll; size and details vary, so that each family member is a unique personality. The supplies you will use to make each body are included in the Materials and Tools lists for the individual dolls, in the front section of this book.

In addition to the listing, we suggest that you include certain other materials when making the Weepeeple. We find that they turn out much better if you add some things that you probably have around your house—generous amounts of love, a pinch of kindness, and as many scraps of humor as you can find.

Scale drawings for the body patterns are given in Figures A and B on the two pages following. Note that there are adult and child sizes, so be sure to use the appropriate size for each doll. Instructions for making the bodies are divided into five sections: Making the Arms, Making Legs with Boots, Adding Boot Flaps, Making Legs with Feet, and Making the Torso. The instructions for the individual family members in the front of this book indicate which sections to use for each doll.

1 square = 1 inch (2.5)

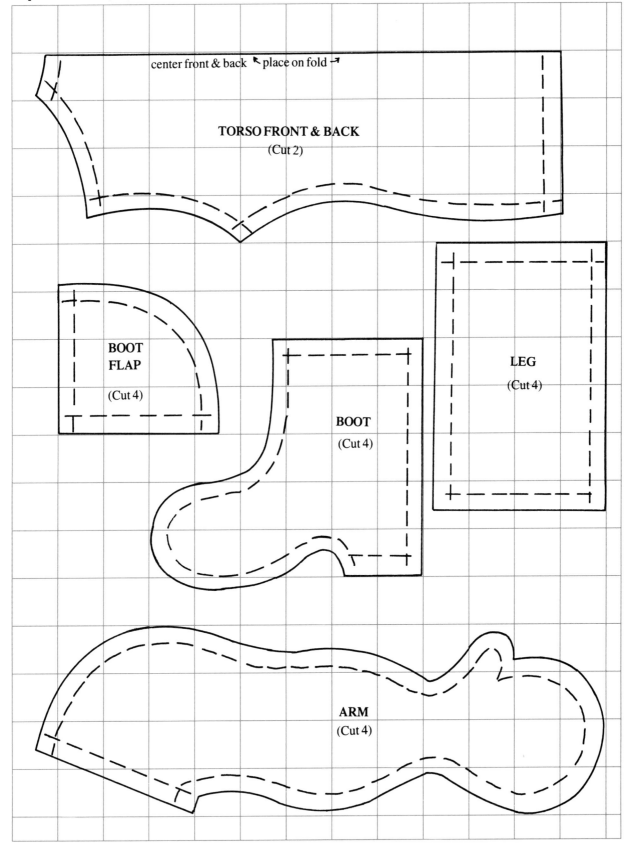

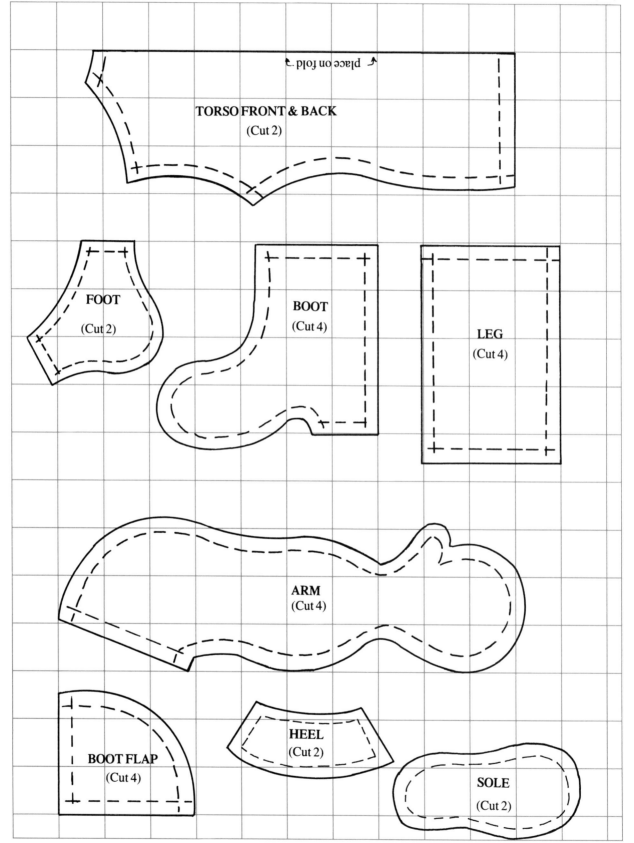

TORSO FRONT & BACK
(Cut 2)

place on fold

FOOT
(Cut 2)

BOOT
(Cut 4)

LEG
(Cut 4)

ARM
(Cut 4)

BOOT FLAP
(Cut 4)

HEEL
(Cut 2)

SOLE
(Cut 2)

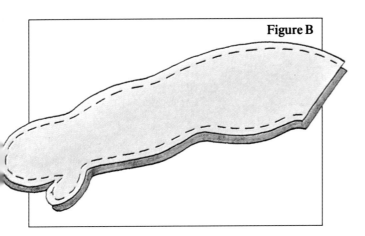

Figure B

Making the Arms

1. Make a full-size paper arm pattern by enlarging the appropriate scale drawing given in Figure A or B. Cut four arms from the flesh-colored knit fabric.

2. Place two fabric arms right sides together and stitch along the seam line, leaving the straight shoulder edge open and unstitched (Figure B). Repeat using the remaining two arms.

3. Clip the curves, turn the stitched arms right side out, and press gently with a steam iron. Stuff the arms lightly with fiberfill, leaving the upper ½ inch (1.3) unstuffed at the open shoulder edge.

4. To sculpture the fingers on each hand, thread a needle with heavy-duty flesh-colored thread and follow the entry and exit points illustrated in Figure C.

    a. Insert the needle at point 1 on the palm of the hand, and exit directly opposite 1 on the back of the hand. This will be the base of the first finger.

    b. Wrap the thread around the end of the hand as shown, reenter at 1 on the palm, and exit at 1 on the back. Pull the thread tightly to form the first finger, and lock the thread by taking another very small stitch at 1.

    c. Reenter at 1 (where you just exited) and exit at 2 on the back of the hand. This is the base of the second finger.

    d. Repeat steps b and c at point 2 and then at point 3 to form the remaining fingers. When you have completed the steps at point 3, lock the stitch securely and cut the thread.

Making Legs with Boots

1. Make full-size paper patterns for the leg and boot by enlarging the appropriate scale drawings given in Figure A or B. Cut four legs from the flesh-colored knit fabric, and four boots from black vinyl.

2. Place one leg and one boot right sides together and stitch the seam as shown in Figure D. Press the seam open. Repeat this step three more times, using the remaining boot and leg pieces.

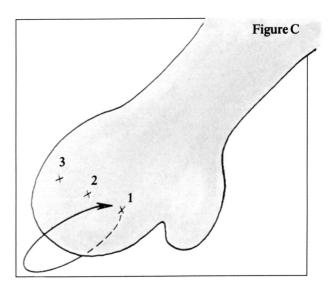

Figure C

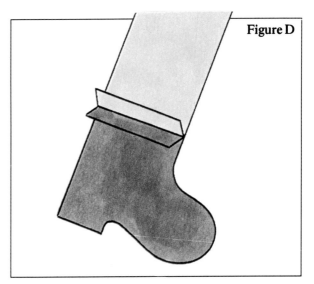

Figure D

157

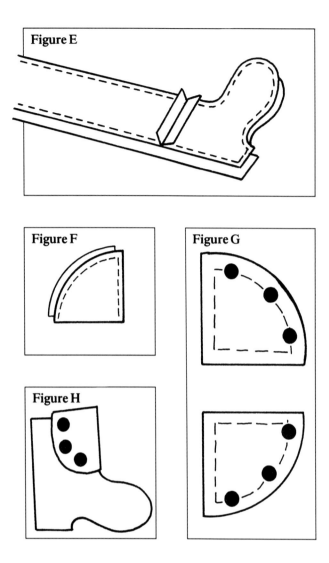

Figure E

Figure F

Figure G

Figure H

3. Place two of the assembled legs right sides together (Figure E), and stitch along the seam line, leaving the straight top edge open and unstitched. Repeat this step using the remaining two assembled legs.

4. Clip the corners and curves, and turn the legs right sides out. Stuff the boot portions tightly. Stuff and manipulate the leg portions until they are round, leaving the top ½ inch (1.3) unstuffed.

Adding Boot Flaps

1. Make a full-size paper boot flap pattern by enlarging the appropriate scale drawing given in Figure A or B. Cut four boot flaps from black vinyl

2. Place two vinyl flaps right sides together and stitch along the seam line, leaving the top edge open and unstitched (Figure F).

3. Turn the stitched flap right side out. Turn the top raw edges to the inside along the seam line and topstitch close

to each edge. Repeat steps 2 and 3 using the remaining two vinyl flaps.

4. Glue or sew three small black beads along the curved edge on one side of each flap, spacing them evenly along the curve. The flaps should be mirror images of each other as shown in Figure G .

5. Glue or whipstitch a completed flap to the front of each boot, as shown in Figure H. The curved edge of the flap should be on the outer side of the boot.

Making Legs with Feet

1. Make full-size paper patterns by enlarging the scale drawings given in Figure B for the leg, foot top, heel, and sole. Cut four legs and two each of the foot patterns from flesh-colored knit fabric.

2. Pin the short lower curved edge of one foot to one short edge of one leg and stitch the seam (Figure I). Clip the curve and press the seam open.

3. Pin the shorter curved edge of one heel to one short edge of a second leg and stitch the seam (Figure J). Clip the curve and press the seam open.

4. Pin the front and back leg/foot assemblies right sides together and stitch the side seams from the top of the leg to the bottom of the foot pieces (Figure K). Press the seams open.

5. Pin the sole to the foot top and heel, placing right sides together (Figure L). Stitch along the seam line.

6. Turn the assembled leg right side out and stuff, manipulating the leg until it is round, and leaving the upper ½ inch (1.3) unstuffed at the open upper edge. Pinch up a small ridge on the front of the leg, about halfway between the open top edge and the foot. Use a needle and heavy-duty flesh-colored thread to take one or two stitches through the ridge, to create a knee. Repeat steps 2 through 6 to make a second leg.

7. Follow the entry and exit points illustrated in Figure M as you sculpture the toes on each foot. Use heavy-duty flesh-colored thread and a long sharp needle to stitch through and around the end of each foot as you did to create the fingers.

   a. Insert the needle on the bottom of the foot and exit at point 1 on the top of the foot. This will be the base of the big toe.

   b. Wrap the thread around the end of the foot as shown, reenter directly opposite 1 on the bottom, and exit at 1 on the top. Pull the thread tightly to form the big toe. Lock the stitch by taking another tight stitch back and forth through the foot at 1.

   c. Reenter at 1 (where you just exited) and exit at 2 on the top of the foot. This is the base of the second toe.

   d. Repeat steps b and c at point 2, then at points 3 and 4 to form the remaining toes. When you have completed the steps at point 4, lock the stitch securely and cut the thread.

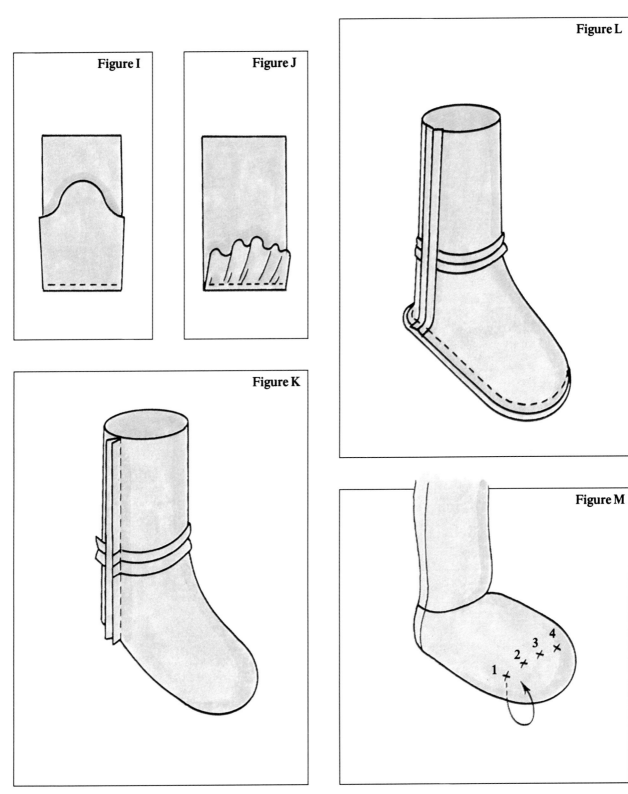

Figure I

Figure J

Figure K

Figure L

Figure M

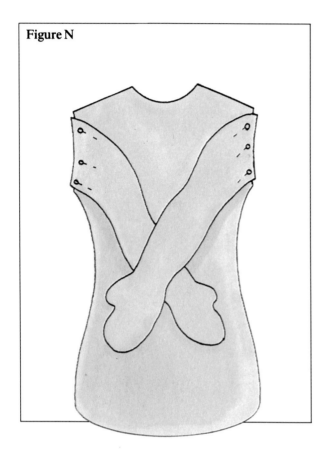

Figure N

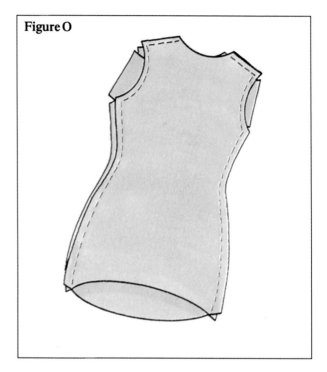

Figure O

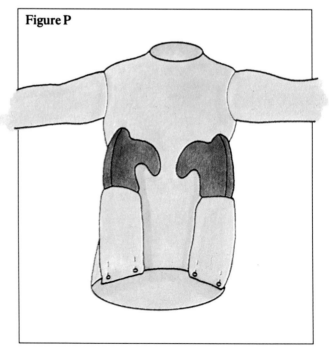

Figure P

Making the Torso

1. Make a full-size paper pattern for the torso by enlarging the appropriate scale drawing given in Figure A or B. Cut two torsos from flesh-colored knit fabric.

2. Pin the open unstitched shoulder edges of the arms to the armhole edges of one torso, so that the thumbs are pointing upward (Figure N). Pin the two torsos right sides together (the arms will be sandwiched between them), and stitch along the seam lines, leaving the neckline and lower edges open and unstitched (Figure O).

3. Turn the stitched torso right side out and stuff gently, leaving a ½-inch (1.3) allowance unstuffed at the lower edge, and a ¼-inch (0.6) allowance unstuffed at the neckline opening.

4. Pin the tops of the legs to the lower edge of the front torso, with the toes pointing toward the body (Figure P). Stitch ¼ inch (0.6) from the edge.

5. Turn the legs down, and turn a ¼-inch (0.6) seam allowance to the inside around the remaining portion of the lower edge. Whipstitch the folded front and back lower edges together.

160